Europe's Economic Dilemma

John Mills

Managing Director
John Mills Ltd

First published in Great Britain 1998 by
MACMILLAN PRESS LTD
Houndmills, Basingstoke, Hampshire RG21 6XS and London
Companies and representatives throughout the world

A catalogue record for this book is available from the British Library.

ISBN 0–333–71837–2 hardcover
ISBN 0–333–72821–1 paperback

First published in the United States of America 1998 by
ST. MARTIN'S PRESS, INC.,
Scholarly and Reference Division,
175 Fifth Avenue, New York, N.Y. 10010

ISBN 0–312–21114–7

Library of Congress Cataloging-in-Publication Data
Mills, John.
Europe's economic dilemma / John Mills.
p.   cm.
Includes bibliographical references and index.
ISBN 0–312–21114–7 (cloth)
1. Monetary unions—European Union countries.   2. European
currency unit.   3. European Union countries—Economic conditions.
I. Title.
HG925.M53 1998
332.4'566'094—dc21   97–37277
                                                       CIP

This book is printed on paper suitable for recycling and made from fully managed and
sustained forest sources.

10   9   8   7   6   5   4   3   2   1
07   06   05   04   03   02   01   00   99   98

Printed in Great Britain by
The Ipswich Book Company Ltd
Ipswich, Suffolk

Contents

Preface

My mother's father was killed by a sniper's bullet in a trench in Flanders in 1915, when my mother was less than a year old. My father joined the army in 1940, when I was two. He emerged from wartime military service unscathed, but I hardly knew him until I was nine, when our family was reunited. My uncle was badly wounded, fighting in Italy in 1944, and spent months in hospital. He never really completely recovered. During World War II, my family lived south of London, and most of my early memories are of bombs and evacuations. Many families in Europe unquestionably suffered worse experiences during the first half of this century. Ours were bad enough to impress on me the importance of avoiding more European wars.

Since 1947, I have travelled constantly all over Europe both on holiday and on business. Over the years, I have visited almost every region in Europe. Since leaving university, I have always been involved in buying and selling consumer products, much of this trading being with European customers and suppliers. I can speak French, German and Spanish, in addition to English, at least well enough to negotiate commercial agreements. I have business and personal friends all over Europe. I am not, therefore, either by temperament or by experience a Little Englander.

Those who criticise the way in which efforts to achieve greater unity in Europe over the last half century have developed are, sometimes justifiably, written off as lacking any perspective about how important good relations are between the nations making up the European tradition. They are thought to be unaware of how vital it is that Europe should be at peace with itself, and that international friendship and co-operation should prevail in place of previous enmities. Critics are frequently accused of being covert, or even open nationalists, unable to appreciate a wider international canvas, and disinterested in what is happening outside their immediate environment. I do not think these criticisms can reasonably be applied to me.

For many years, I have been interested in the political and economic developments which have taken place in Europe, not least because of the way they have affected Great Britain. Like everyone else who was there at the time, I watched those who run Britain move from disdain at the initial efforts to establish the European Coal and Steel Community and then the Common Market to a near desperate wish to join the emerging institutions, almost regardless of the cost. When Britain did become a member, following the 1972 Treaty of Accession, it seemed to me that we had done so on very poor terms. No doubt this had much to do with the fact that Britain was not one of the original participants in the establishment of the Common Market, but this did not make the terms on which Britain joined any better.

Since the 1975 referendum on whether Britain, having already joined the Common Market, should reaffirm its decision to do so, I have been involved in working with others to analyse the impact of membership on Britain, and to formulate policies to deal with the disadvantages which I believe have been entailed. This has been a difficult rearguard action, though I do not regret my scepticism. I think it has been well justified by events. It has, however, in some ways been a dispiriting experience. Inevitably, much of the criticism of EU policies and developments has been negative and unconstructive.

This book is an attempt to redress the balance, at least by looking at developments from a wider perspective. Instead of focusing on the difficulties that membership of the Community has caused Britain, it is concerned with the problems of the European Union as a whole. Its remit is to analyse the reasons why for a quarter of a century the economies of the countries of the European Union have done so much worse than the world average. Its conclusions are that there was nothing inevitable about the slow growth and high unemployment which have increasingly characterised the EU. They occurred because of policies which were misconceived, and their results could have been avoided. Looking ahead, however, it seems all too likely that the same strategic mistakes are going to be made again. This book also, therefore, puts forward alternative policies, and sets out the arguments for believing that they would have a much better chance of success than those currently offered by nearly all the EU's current leaders.

The ideas it contains are, of course, not ones which have evolved solely from my own experiences. I have been very lucky to have worked for a long period with an exceptionally talented group of people who have shared my interests. Some are no longer with us. These include Douglas Jay who died in 1996 and Shaun Stewart in 1997. Bryan Gould returned to his native New Zealand in 1994, a great loss to British politics. Others are still actively involved, particularly Peter Shore, Austin Mitchell and Nigel Spearing. I am particularly indebted for their support over a long period to two close colleagues in organisations with which we have all been involved, Charles Starkey and Edward Barber. I have also had the good fortune to have been able to exchange ideas over many years with Brian Burkitt and his colleagues Mark Baimbridge and Philip Whyman, and more recently with Geoffrey Gardiner and Michael Moore. I owe all of them a great debt of gratitude.

While preparing this book, I have also drawn heavily on the work of many other people. Rather than breaking up the text with footnotes, or providing endnotes to each chapter, a bibliography will be found at the end, listing the

Preface

main books and articles which I have read over the last year or so. The bibliography is inevitably incomplete, however, and I need to thank not only the authors cited but all the others whose writings have influenced my opinions over the years on the way European history has developed. I hope, nevertheless, that the publications which are in the list will provide guidance as to where to find references which may be required to support the information given in the main text.

I am also addicted to statistics, and I have used, I hope to the full, the very wide range of excellent statistical material which is available. The arguments this book puts forward are quantitative as well as qualitative, and the figurework which underpins them is therefore an important component of the case presented. The International Monetary Fund, the World Trade Organisation, the United Nations Organisation, the European Commission and the Organisation for Economic Co-operation and Development all helped with their publications. No-one embarking on the kind of study which this book contains can fail to be grateful to all these bodies for the comprehensive way in which economic events are now documented. I have also relied extensively on figures in a publication compiled and written by Thelma Liesner for *The Economist* called *Economic Statistics 1900–1983*, which provides long and revealing runs of statistics for most of the world's major economies, going back to the beginning of the twentieth century. Again, references to all the figures cited in the text are not provided individually. I hope an acknowledgement of this important data source will be sufficient.

There are other people who need to be thanked too, especially among my extended family. My wife Barbara has not only tolerated with very little complaint all the time I have spent reading and writing while preparing this book, but has also read and corrected successive drafts. We share the view that books should read well, whatever their contents. Sentences should be short. Adverbs should be used sparingly. The text should be clear and concise. These worthy objectives are easy to list, but more difficult to achieve consistently, and her help, and that of Charles Starkey and Austin Mitchell, both hard taskmasters in similar vein, have been invaluable. My sister Eleanor and her husband Stephen have allowed me and my wife to use their house near Avignon in France as a retreat from distractions, to allow drafting to be done. My mother has provided another exceptionally pleasant environment for redrafting and revisions at her house near London. My office, and especially my secretary Jan and her colleague Janet, have been very tolerant of my use of all the facilities there, and have been exceptionally helpful. Ruth Weinberg has also played a strong supportive role in digging out missing information, checking facts and suggesting improvements to the text.

A matter which has caused some problems is to know what to call the organisation which has metamorphosed itself over a period of decades from being the Common Market to the European Economic Community, then the European Community and now the European Union. In the end, the best solution seemed to use these titles interchangeably, while trying to choose those most appropriate to the period concerned. I hope this causes no confusion.

I am also very grateful to Macmillan, and especially to Tim Farmiloe, for publishing another book written by me. The period in front of us is going to be crucially important in Europe's history. Decisions are going to be taken which are going to have a profound effect on all our futures. I have strong views about what should and should not be done, as this book makes clear. It is a great privilege to have a platform provided by such an excellent publisher from which to put them forward.

In the end, however, it is authors who have to take responsibility for what their books say, especially if they oppose the way in which events are developing, inevitably striking discordant notes in the process. I am only too well aware of the fact that the tide of history in Europe towards greater integration is still in flood, though not as strongly as it was. Recent events such as the stand-off in May 1997 between Helmut Kohl and the Bundesbank over revaluing the German gold reserves, and the result of the French elections on 1 June 1997 are clear signs that many people are becoming exasperated and disillusioned with key elements of the European project. This is especially the case with the Single Currency proposals which are due to be implemented over the next few years, with key decisions being taken less than a year from the date when this book is being completed, in May 1997. Like many other people who are sceptical of the way events are developing, I am wholeheartedly in favour of good relations between all the nations of Europe. I am all for co-operation in solving mutual international problems wherever this makes sense. I think that more is required, however, than just good will. Careful analysis and hard-headed judgement are also needed. It is these which this book argues have been lacking too often in Europe over the last forty years. The well meaning drive to build international institutions, and the 'ever closer union' set out as the long-term objective in the preamble to the Treaty of Rome, establishing the Common Market, has too often ignored the underlying economic realities. Blithe presuppositions have been made that what sounds good politics will work economically – a very dangerous assumption. The result has been a long series of decisions on integration, based on supposedly pressing political needs, which in total have made no economic sense.

The evidence lies in the historical and statistical records. The EU has done dismally badly over the last quarter of a century, compared to the rest of the world. Its growth rate has been barely half the average achieved elsewhere. One in eight of its registered workforce in unemployed, though this statistic, bad as it is, significantly underestimates the total number of people in the EU who would like to work but for whom there are no jobs. The EU's industries are increasingly uncompetitive. The power and influence of European countries in the world is being relentlessly undermined by their relatively poor economic performance.

This book argues that none of these unwelcome developments was inevitable. They are all the consequences of policies which could have been different, and which need to be changed. The problem is that time is running short. More major commitments, particularly on Monetary Union, are looming up, which are going to be just dangerous as those made earlier, but increasingly difficult and expensive to reverse. There is thus a pressing need for a reassessment before final decisions are made which Europe, if the analysis in the pages which follow is correct, will sooner or later come deeply to regret.

The tide towards integration may still be in flood, but there are signs that the flow may well be reversed before long, allowing less centralised and more flexible arrangements between EU Member States to emerge. The issue at stake is whether the changes in direction which need to be made to allow Europe to become more prosperous will be chosen by its leaders over the next year or two. If they are, the major current economic problems would be relatively easy to solve. If not, the risk is that, as Europe's economies continue to stagnate, the co-operation and good relations which almost everyone wants could be put at risk. The stakes are very high.

Foreword

Austin Mitchell MP

Economics is a practical art gone wrong. Before the War, Keynes and a generation of practical economists, gave sound advice directly relevant to the problems of the day. Which may be one reason why Britain suffered less from the Depression than most. Since the War the obsessive desire to turn an art into science has made economics highly specialised and far more academic so clear advice has degenerated into a babble of conflicting theories, pseudo-scientific econometrics, endless model building and paid posturing, usually serving the vested interests of wealth, class, financial institutions, or all three. As Economists and economic advisers have multiplied the economy has got worse with slow growth, rising unemployment, increasing poverty and declining profitability. In default of clear practical advice on all this from the economists the field has been left to moralists with theories ranging from monetarism to discipline, all adding to the damage they claim to correct.

John Mills is different. A skilled and unusually lucid economist, his work is eminently practical because illuminated by his business experience in trade, production and the tough world of exports and imports by which he lives. His are the economics of the real world, of production, jobs and growth. Having applied them to the British economy transforming views of its problems and performance in the process, he now turns his attention, and his skill, to Europe. Not before time either for in the European Union a group of politically motivated men committed to ever closer union have portrayed that political process as economic wisdom, promising substantial benefits in jobs and growth when they are really peddling an ever closer union built from the top down without the consent of electorates. John Mills provides an antidote to a lot of rubbish.

We in Britain joined what was then sold as a Common Market to hitch our slow wagon to faster European growth and to enjoy the benefits of the cold shower of competition, both arguments which demonstrate the puerility of 'economic' thinking among our political elite. We were told that the benefits of entry were mainly political. The economic arguments were said to be more balanced. In fact, because trade created by entry was far less than trade diverted, the effects were adverse. Britain lost out and our less powerful economy has had to carry heavy burdens from membership which has been an economic drain.

As soon as we joined Europe's growth slowed. The result has been resentment and a feeling of having been cheated. Explaining this is neither a pro nor an anti-European argument but a statement of cold economic sense. As John Mills demonstrates this growth has been checked by the obsessive desire to build political union by locking currencies together, first through the snake, then the ERM, and finally in a Single Currency. All other paths to union by democratic consent, by agreement between governments, by the growth of parliamentary power, seemed closed. The monetary path to union was the only one open and promised to build central institutions and impose a common economic and tax policy on the back of the Single Currency. Other nations built political union first then currency union. Europe's decision to do it the other way round was a matter of faith not economic rationality, a process rightly compared to jumping off the Eiffel Tower holding hands and hoping not only to be able to design the parachute on the way down but also to get agreement on whether it is to be a soft or a hard landing.

John Mills, with his keen eye for the practical and his sense of the economic consequences of political decisions, dispels the rhetoric to reveal the economic reality behind it. His practical economics has led him to place increasing emphasis on the role of the exchange rate. Our competitors grew rapidly because they started out from undervalued currencies making exporting industry profitable and powerful. The British economy was dragged down and priced out of markets by our penchant for an overvalued exchange rate. His insight into these processes now allows him to highlight the damage done by the Franc-fort and the economic consequences of using the currency as a political instrument of Europe building thereby distorting its economic role. All this has been compounded by pressures to reach wholly artificial Maastricht convergence criteria expressed in monetarist terms, rather than measures of real power, strength and productivity, all of which must converge if a Single Currency is to work without damage or massive redistribution.

So Europe has made itself the low growth, high unemployment blackspot of an expanding, growing world: a DIY disaster which is wholly unnecessary. The consequences of this rush to folly fall on electorates who are rejecting them or turning to extremist politics without necessarily realising the monetary cause of their very real discontents. Difficulties and confusions multiply. Both timetable and conditions look increasingly uncertain. Yet the elite presses on against the wishes of the European peoples and with damaging consequences for Britain. The argument has already split the Tory party. It would divide Labour, too, had the government decided not to join during this Parliament. Yet our growth will be less because they are deflationary and we must still adjust our economic management, hopefully to take advantage of their self inflicted folly by sustained competitiveness. John Mills' penetratingly practical book brings out the consequences and the dangers facing Europe. It will have a powerful effect in this country but really needs the attention and recognition in Europe, particularly among the policymakers and leaders driving this headlong rush to folly. The case is powerfully put. If they ignore it then folly becomes wilful and perverse. I can only hope they heed it. Only then can we all gain.

1 Introduction

'Every man prefers belief to the exercise of judgement.'
Seneca

This book has two interlocking objectives. The first is to explain why the economic performance of the European Union has been so poor during the last twenty-five years. The second is to put forward proposals which are feasible and practical, to enable the economies of Europe to operate much better than they have done recently, growing faster, with much less unemployment, and thus generating more social and political cohesion.

During the twenty-three-year period from 1950 to 1973, the average annual rate of growth in the six countries which came together in 1958 to make up the Common Market was 5.4%. The average level of unemployment over the whole of this period was less than 2%. The rate of inflation was about 4%. Germany did even better than the mean. The *Deutcheswirtschaftwunder* achieved a cumulative growth rate of 5.9%, with consumer price rises averaging only 2.7% per annum over the whole period. With a growth rate of 5.4%, the standard of living doubles in about thirteen years, even allowing for a modest increase in the population.

The countries experiencing these high rates of growth enjoyed an unprecedented increase in their prosperity and standard of living. Not only did private living standards rise dramatically, but there were also enormous advances in public provision. Much more effective and generous social security networks were put in place. Great strides forward were taken in improving the infrastructure. New public buildings were opened. Housing conditions improved radically. Educational standards rose by leaps and bounds, particularly in higher education, as a much larger proportion of young adults went on from school to university. Standards of medical care rose rapidly, reflected in lower infant mortality and longer life expectancy.

Conditions at work greatly improved. Not only did wages and salaries rise rapidly in real terms, reflecting the general increase in prosperity, but jobs were easy to obtain. Working conditions for most people were secure, and unemployment a distant and unreal threat for almost everyone. As output increased, skill levels rose rapidly, broadening the outlook of those involved, and enhancing their capacity to deal successfully with the next range of challenges as technology advanced. In most countries, although not so much in Italy, economic success generated a wage negotiation climate where moderation was seen to be a sensible approach, enabling wage rises to be

1

kept at least roughly in line with productivity increases. In consequence, inflation was not a major problem.

After a quarter of a century of rising prosperity, full employment and modest inflation, most people assumed that these apparently securely established trends would continue for the foreseeable future. The economic changes which hit Europe in the mid-1970s were therefore a major shock. Adjusting policies to meet the altered circumstances proved to be exceptionally difficult. Much of the history of Europe since then has been an unsuccessful attempt to return to the achievements of the 1950s and 1960s. This book is principally about why the policies adopted since the 1970s did not work nearly as well as their proponents hoped they would. It is also about what could and should have been done instead, and the lessons to be learnt for the future from the experience of the recent past.

The changes to the trends from the mid-1970s onwards have indeed been dramatic. The cumulative growth rate for the original six economies making up the Common Market, which between 1950 and 1973 had been 5.4% per annum, has been only 2.1% between 1973 and 1996, and barely 1.7% since 1979. For almost a quarter of a century, the rate of economic growth has been only just over a third of the amount achieved during the previous twenty-three years. Unemployment, scarcely an issue prior to 1973, has now become perhaps the largest and most intransigent problem facing the European Union. From less than 2% up to 1973, the raw average rate of unemployment among the Six since then has been about 7%, and it is now higher than ever, at 12%. In Germany alone, in March 1997, a total of 3.5m people were out of work, almost 10% of the civilian labour force. In France, registered unemployment was over 3m, with an even higher percentage out of work than in Germany. Nor has the record on the inflationary front been good, although price rises are now much lower than they were. Whereas the average increase in the retail price level among the Six from 1950 to 1973 was just under 4%, since 1973 it has risen to 7.8%. While recently the inflation rate has gone down, unfortunately the unemployment problems have become worse.

Looking beyond the six countries which came together to establish the Common Market to the widening group of fifteen countries which now comprise the European Union, the trends are the same. Across the whole of the EU, the rate of economic growth averaged only 1.7% between 1979 and 1993. Registered unemployment at the end of 1996 averaged 10.9%. Some countries, such as Britain, have done better than the mean, with 7.9% of the registered labour force out of work at the end of 1996, but others have done much worse. In Spain, 21.6% of the labour force was then jobless, at least outside the black economy. Unemployment among those under twenty-five was a horrifying 40.8%. Inflation is now at lower levels than it was in the 1970s and 1980s, but the average over the last two decades has still been very uncomfortably high, particularly in relation to the low rate of growth which has been achieved.

The figures for registered unemployment are bad enough, but throughout Europe they greatly underestimate the true extent to which the potential of the labour force is being underused. The figures for registered unemployment cited in the EU's Eurostat publications are based on the International Labour Organisation's definitions of claimants, standardised as far as possible for all the countries concerned. They do not include very large numbers of people who would like to work if it was worth their while to do so, but who for one reason or another have dropped out of the labour force, and who are not, therefore, counted as claimants. These categories include those who have been pushed involuntarily into early retirement, people who would lose more than they would gain from the social security system if they took on a job at relatively low pay, and those who, having given up hope of finding a job, have therefore dropped off the claimants' register.

The latest fully comparable figures available are from the European Labour Force Survey in 1995. Across the whole of the EU they show a very depressing picture of wasted economic resources and blighted lives. The Survey showed that in Greece only 1.4% of the economically inactive population would like to work, and 1.7% in France, but 13.1% in Denmark, 12.1% in Britain and 11.4% in the Netherlands. Even though the figures for some countries look very low, the Survey clearly indicates that nearly 17% of the total potential EU labour force was not working in 1995 – a total of almost 26m people. As EU unemployment has worsened over the last two years, the total number of people in the spring of 1997 in the EU who would like to work, but for whom there are no jobs, must be close to 30m.

If the whole world had experienced a sea change in economic conditions after 1973, with growth slowing down to about one third its previous annual rate of increase, unemployment rising inexorably and inflation being a major preoccupation, the problems in the EU might be easier to accept. Most of the rest of the world, however, does not share the EU's problems, at least not to anything like the same degree. Whereas the EU's growth rate has been less than 2% per annum for the last two decades, the rest of the world has achieved about 3.5% – not far short of twice the EU average. Large numbers of countries have done much better than this. The 'tiger' economies of the Far East, South Korea, Taiwan, Singapore and Hong Kong, have grown from low starting points to come close to, and sometimes exceed European standards of living by expanding cumulatively at 7% or 8% per annum. China has done even better, with a growth rate over the last twenty years averaging

more than 9% over the whole of its vast economy. Now Malaysia and
Thailand have joined the high growth league, and the huge Indian economy
is beginning to expand rapidly. In other parts of the world, Brazil has for
many years achieved annual growth rates of 6% or so. Many of the other
economies in South America, once a byword for sloth and poor economic
management, are now growing fast. So are several of the East European
economies.

Even closer to the EU in traditions and experience, as well as geography,
Norway, which opted not to join the EU in 1995 at the same time as Finland,
Sweden and Austria became members, is growing much faster than the EU
average. The Norwegians also have very low levels of unemployment – 2.5%
in March 1997 – as do most of the other parts of the world which are growing
fast. Mass unemployment is not a world problem, at least among developed
countries. It is largely confined to the EU. Even the United States, which
for long periods after World War II had much higher rates of unemployment
than those prevailing in Europe, now has a much lower rate – 5.2% at the
end of 1996 compared with 10.9% for the EU. In countries such as Taiwan,
there is almost no unemployment at all. Why should Europe, almost on its
own among developed countries, suffer from the scourge of having so many
people who want to work with no job? One of the major theses in this book
is that it is not inevitable that this problem should exist. Unemployment, right
across the EU, only exists because of avoidable policy errors. It is not true
that there is no solution. There are feasible and practical policies available
which will greatly reduce the number of people out of work. They ought to
be implemented.

Not only does the EU suffer from serious and damaging problems of low
growth and high unemployment, the consequences of its failure to manage
its economic affairs successfully in these central respects have spilled over
in numerous other directions. The government budgets of all EU countries
are under unprecedented pressures. Public expenditure is constantly
constrained. EU countries are spending relatively little nowadays on creating
the infrastructure needed for the future. Investment rates have fallen, and are
now much lower than in many other parts of the world. In Europe, about
20% of GDP is reinvested, compared to 35% and more in fast-growing
economies such as Korea, Malaysia, Indonesia and Singapore. Businesses
within the EU are less and less competitive with those in other areas of the
world economy, particularly those on the Pacific rim. EU countries are no
longer, on the whole, at the cutting edge of technology developments. The
buzz and excitement of the high growth era of the 1950s and 1960s has given
way to the less confident, more cautious and defensive business atmosphere
of the 1990s.

Reflecting this relatively poor economic performance, there is an increasingly marked disillusionment with some of the political developments within the EU. There is overwhelming support for the maintenance of friendship, good relations and strong links between the nations of the EU, but it is much less obvious that there is general enthusiasm for the ways in which these objectives are being pursued. There is a widespread feeling, reflected in the results of the referendums about the Maastricht Treaty in France and Denmark, that the political élites in the EU have lost touch with the people at large. The cuts in expenditure required by the Maastricht convergence criteria, to reduce government deficits to 3% or less of GDP at a time when the EU generally has large underused resources, particularly of labour, have generated opposition on an unprecedented scale. There have been massive swings in votes against governments pursuing deflationary policies to meet the Maastricht convergence criteria. Well supported strikes in the heartlands of France and Germany, as well as marches and demonstrations in many other Member States against the provisions of the Maastricht Treaty, have been a new and disturbing development. There is a lack of confidence that the Maastricht prescriptions for the EU economies are really going to work. At best, there is a passive acceptance that further moves to monetary union in Europe are inevitable, even if not particularly desirable, because no credible alternative set of policies is on offer.

The aim of this book is both to explain what has gone wrong, and to set out an alternative set of policies. The starting point is to reject decisively any idea that the EU economies need to continue to languish in their present condition of low growth, high unemployment, widening income differentials, and developing social strains. On the contrary, there are no good reasons why they should not do at least as well, if not better, than those in the rest of the world. This book sets out how this could be done, and offers a series of prescriptions for increasing the rate of economic growth in the EU to a much higher level. It argues that this should be at least 4% per annum, a little above the world average, although perhaps it would be wise to aim higher. It sets out why unemployment in the modern world is not inevitable, and how it can be overcome. There is no reason why almost everyone who wants to work should not be able to do so, while there are compelling social as well as economic reasons why low levels of unemployment should be attained if at all possible. It might be thought that the expansionist policies entailed by such changes would inevitably involve taking large risks with inflation. These risks are generally greatly exaggerated. In the EU, as elsewhere in many parts of the world where there is less social cohesion and therefore more difficulty in keeping inflation at bay, there is no good reason why high rates of economic growth cannot be combined with moderate and tolerable rises in the price level.

Policies to achieve these economic objectives would inevitably require changes to the way the EU is run, particularly an end to the current drive towards monetary union. They would certainly involve reassessment of where the EU is trying to go, and what kind of political entity it is trying to become. The case put forward is that the root cause of most of the EU's problems has been the attempts to lock currency values together in inappropriate circumstances. The Single Currency is therefore a high-risk strategy which will very probably turn out to be a disastrous mistake. Not proceeding with Monetary Union does not, however, mean abandoning everything else which the EU does. It would not therefore involve a major restructuring of EU institutions. The major change would be for the EU to decide not to implement the current plans for the Single Currency, which are due to come into effect, at least in their first phase, at the beginning of 1999. This would involve a big alteration in course for the EU, but not one which it is impossible to achieve. Indeed, it looks as if it would be more and more in line with the way public opinion generally is developing in Europe.

Subsidiary decisions about how to proceed with the Single Currency project are being taken all the time, as the date when it is due to start approaches. The critical decision as to whether it is to go ahead on schedule in January 1999, and who the participants might then be, will have to be taken not later than the first half of 1998, probably in March. The major message in this book is that Monetary Union is wrong for the EU. The primary reason for this is that a decision to proceed with it, at least in anything like the form proposed at the moment, would lock the EU into being unable to make the changes required to revitalise its constituent economies. The Single Currency is thus wrong for the European Union, wrong for the EU Member States, and wrong for the people living in them. It will hold down their living standards, and perpetuate their problems of unemployment. In the end, it will even fail to deliver the most prominent target in the Maastricht Treaty convergence criteria, which is a low level of inflation.

The following pages are critical of many of the policies pursued by the EU over the last quarter of a century, yet arguments against present policies on their own are not sufficient. If the EU is not to proceed with the Single Currency, a new framework of ideas for running the EU economies is required. If the policy anchors which Monetary Union is designed to provide are to be abandoned, alternatives will have to be adopted. If one vision of how to proceed with developing the future of Europe is to be put on one side, another will have to be found to take its place. This book therefore is not just about why the EU should not go ahead with the Single Currency. It is about a different way of developing the European Union's policies, and an alternative vision for the future of Europe, which is less grandiose and more practical, less centralised and more flexible, less federalist and more devolved, less deflationary and more orientated to growth and full employment.

WHY ECONOMIC SUCCESS IS IMPORTANT

Does it really matter that the performance of the EU economies has been relatively poor over the last quarter of a century? Some argue that it does not. They point to the problems of sustaining high and rising levels of industrial output, reflecting the concerns expressed by the Club of Rome in the early 1970s. Others express doubt whether higher living standards make everyone happier, arguing that a less complicated and stressful life would be better than the pressures of consumer driven societies. Another form of scepticism challenges whether economic growth statistics really measure anything meaningful at all, because of the difficulties of comparing one year with another at a time of such rapid technological and cultural change.

There has always been an anti-growth tradition, harking back to Rousseau's simple savage. The romantic movement never liked factory regimentation, and the break with established and hallowed practices which the Industrial Revolution inevitably entailed. More recently, particularly from the left of the political spectrum, scepticism about the benefits of economic growth have materialised in a steady undertow of criticism of the same ilk. Targets have been the impersonality of modern production relationships, the alienation and loneliness of late twentieth-century lifestyles, the vapidness of much contemporary culture, and the unfairness in the distribution of the wealth and incomes which economic growth has produced.

No-one can deny that there are valid concerns about the impact of industrialisation and increasing output. This is a different matter, however, from putting forward a compelling case that humanity as a whole would have been better off, or would have preferred, given the choice, not to have had the benefits which the economic changes in the developed countries have produced. There is no evidence at all that most people would prefer a lower rather than a higher standard of living, as conventionally measured. On the contrary, it is overwhelmingly clear that being better off in material terms is a very high priority for almost everyone. Elections are won or lost on economic issues. The world abounds with pressure for economic migration from poor countries to those which are richer. Almost everyone wants to earn a higher wage or salary.

A reasonably high rate of economic growth is therefore clearly what most people would select, given the choice. Nor are the benefits to be secured, of course, private only to individuals. There is a large public dimension as well. Increased output generates the tax base for a wide range of goods and services which are more sensibly and practically provided collectively than individually. It makes it possible to run the kind of social security programmes which are the hallmark of cohesive communities. It provides the wherewithal for the construction and operation of public facilities, from schools to libraries, roads to parks, hospitals to swimming pools, which are the necessary and widely appreciated accoutrements of modern societies.

Contrary to what might appear to be the position at first sight, economic growth also provides the only realistic way to pay the costs of avoiding the degradation of the environment that a rising population would otherwise entail. The most pressing environmental issues across the world are the provision of clean drinking water, the building of adequate sewage facilities, and the removal and processing of rubbish and waste. Protecting water supplies and the water table, in both the Third World and the developed countries, is expensive. So are all the steps which need to be taken to stop waste building up and the environment being polluted.

In fact, as living standards rise and the economy becomes more advanced, there is a tendency for the raw material content of finished output to fall. This happens as products become more sophisticated and services become a larger component of final output. The result is that, with reasonably competent management, the average economy's capacity to cope with environmental problems should rise faster than its tendency to cause environmental damage. Rising living standards also tend to entail lower population growth, again improving the trade-off between expansion and ecological pressures. There is therefore no convincing case against growth on environmental grounds.

On the other hand, leaving aside the clear preference which almost everyone has for higher living standards, both in terms of private consumption and public provision, there are other reasons for believing that a reasonably high rate of economic growth is overwhelmingly important as a political and social objective. These overlapping considerations concern unemployment, social strains, fiscal imbalance and Europe's place in the world.

The unemployment issue is simple and straightforward. There is a marked tendency for the average level of productivity of everyone in employment to rise. This stems from a variety of causes, all of which are likely to continue. They include increased use of computers, better management techniques, competitive pressures on manning levels, better and more focused training and education, and technological advances. The impact of these changes is to increase output per person by perhaps as much as 2.5% per annum on average, even if investment levels are quite low, and the economy is growing slowly or not at all. The result, however, is a very mixed blessing. It means that a rate of economic growth of about 2.5% is required in any developed country just to keep all the existing workforce in employment. If the growth rate falls below this level, unemployment will almost inevitably increase. If the potential workforce is growing, an increase in effective demand of more than 2.5% will be required. Yet for many years the EU economies have not been growing at 2.5%. Indeed from the late 1970s to the early 1990s the average was per annum 1.7%, a full 0.8% less than a reasonable estimate of the increase in productivity. The effect was to increase unemployment by something like 0.8% per annum cumulatively for the whole of the period, as the gap between growth and productivity failed to close. This is the reason why both the claimant count registered unemployment figure is so high, why so many other people have dropped out of the labour force, and why some 17%, more than one in six of all those potentially capable of working in the EU, are not doing so at present.

The social impact of unemployment, caused by slow growth, has been enormously damaging. It has produced ghettos, especially in inner-city areas, where almost no-one has a job. It is hardly surprising that in this environment crime rates rise, educational standards fall, social cohesion evaporates, anti-social behaviour such as drug abuse proliferates, and high levels of social deprivation are passed down the generations. It has produced regional imbalances, where the less favoured areas have been unable to attract sufficient economic activity to keep the indigenous population in work. When the pressure of demand is high enough, employers have little alternative to siting their operations in less favoured areas, because the workforces they need are likely to be unobtainable elsewhere. If there is unemployment almost everywhere, no such incentives exist.

Together with unemployment goes resentment, particularly towards foreigners. If almost everyone is in work, it is hard to blame unemployment on those from outside. If many people do not have jobs, it is much easier to attribute lack of employment opportunities to strangers, particularly if they are willing to work for wages and in conditions which the resident labour force regards as unacceptable. It is a relatively short step for this kind of resentment to be channelled by political movements into policies with a heavy xenophobic and racial dimension. There are alarming signs of far right revivals in France and Italy, and even in Germany.

The fiscal consequences of high levels of unemployment are also immensely important. Not only are large sums required from public finances to pay unemployment benefits, now running at billions of ECUs in all EU economies, but large numbers of people out of work vastly increase the outlays required for many other kinds of state-funded expenditures, from health care and housing subsidies to policing. In addition, there are huge losses of revenue to the tax system. Those out of work receive benefits, but pay no income taxes. Because their incomes are lower, they generate less VAT revenue. The combined effects of higher needs for expenditure and lower amounts of tax collected largely explain the fiscal problems which almost all EU exchequers are now facing. Unfortunately, the remedy currently on offer to deal with fiscal imbalance, in the form of the Maastricht convergence criteria requiring reductions in deficits, is all too likely to make the position worse. The deflationary impact of expenditure cuts is likely to increase unemployment still further, exacerbating all the underlying pressures.

High levels of unemployment make particularly little sense in the context of the changing age profile of the EU population in all the countries of the Union. As a result of improved medical care, the increase in the average age of parents when they have children, and a low birth rate, there is a marked tendency across the EU for the number of those who are beyond normal working age to increase rapidly in relation to those who are still below sixty or sixty-five. There will then be far fewer people to pay the taxes required to fund the pensions expected by those in retirement, even if everyone of working age has a job. In nearly all EU countries, state pensions are not funded, in the sense that savings have not been made during the working life of those due to retire, and invested to produce an income flow when pensions are scheduled to start being paid. In almost all cases, pensions are now paid from current taxation, and are expected to continue to be financed from the same source in future.

Projections show that state pension liabilities amount to 98% of Gross Domestic Product (GDP) in France, 113% in Italy and 139% in Germany. Some other countries, particularly Britain where the figure is only 19%, are much better prepared, in that a higher proportion of pensions are funded. Across the EU as a whole, however, there will be very difficult problems to overcome. They will be serious enough even if unemployment is low. They will be very much more difficult to manage, however, if not only are there far fewer people of working age in the population than used to be the case, but also a high proportion of those who could work are not doing so. The dependency ratio between those not working and needing income support, and those who are working and paying taxes to support the others may become unbearably high. This is in danger of putting large numbers of elderly people into dire poverty. Lower unemployment and a higher growth rate are far the most efficacious solutions to this otherwise intractable problem.

There are also vital issues concerning the EU's place in the world which are intimately bound up with the Union's economic performance. In the last analysis, political influence is almost entirely a function of economic power. European countries were pre-eminent in the world in the nineteenth century because they were much more economically developed than those anywhere else, apart from the United States. Britain's exceptional position in the world during this period resulted almost entirely from its lead in industrialisation. The outcome of the two world wars in Europe had almost nothing to do with the merits of the war aims of the participants, or the nature of the régimes involved, and almost everything to do with industrial and economic capabilities ranged on either side. The hegemony of the United States in the post-World War II period was almost completely a function of its economic capability. So was the rise of Japan, and now the rapidly waxing economic strength of China.

Power relationships generally change relatively slowly. A difference in growth rate over a year or two of 2% or 3% is barely perceptible. Multiplied over a decade, let alone quarter or half a century, however, the position changes radically. A differential growth rate of 4% will cause one economy to double in size relative to another in about seventeen years. This kind of change in economic weight makes a massive difference to any country's or region's industrial, financial, military and diplomatic power, to its self-respect, and to its ability to look after its interest *vis à vis* other parts of the world.

What will happen to the European Union if its growth rate continues to average less than 2% per annum in the foreseeable future, while the average for the rest of the world continues to be perhaps as much as 4%, and the Pacific rim countries achieve anything between 6% and 10%? The outcome is bound to be a massive attenuation in the relative status in the area of the world covered by the EU compared to other parts of the world. The EU will be in danger of becoming the sick man of the world, mirroring the decline suffered by Spain in the seventeenth century, or the Ottoman Empire two hundred years later. Europe's ability to influence world events will steadily diminish, as will its ability to defend itself if the world slips towards military conflict. Its position in the United Nations will be eroded. Its capacity to deal with the pressing issues of the next century, some of which, such as population pressures and climate change, are already apparent, will be severely compromised and diminished. Is this what the people of Europe want? Surely not. It is, however, the way events are inexorably going to develop if current trends continue.

LOW GROWTH AND HIGH UNEMPLOYMENT IN EUROPE

Why has the EU growth rate fallen from well over 5% per annum in the 1950s and 1960s to less than 2% over the last two decades and more? Why have the electorates in the EU allowed unemployment to rise to its present level? Clearly, these developments were not by popular choice. Were they inevitable, however, and if so in what sense? Was there something special about the circumstances in the EU, leading to such poor economic performance, which no feasible policies could have avoided? Or was there something wrong, but avoidable, about the policies pursued, which led to such mediocre results?

The case put forward in this book is that there were, and are, alternative policies, which could and would achieve much better results. To come fully to grips with alternative proposals, however, it is necessary to examine the pressures which led to Europe's economic history since World War II unfolding the way it has, and to understand the framework of ideas which provided the driving force for European integration. It was this powerful ideal which shaped the formation of the European Coal and Steel Community and the establishment of the Common Market, and which led to the development of the European Union which we know today. The crucial question is whether the integration of the economies involved in these developments caused the slowdown in growth and rise in unemployment which has unquestionably occurred, or whether these highly undesirable developments would have happened anyway, policies to integrate the EU economies being largely irrelevant.

It is easy to understand the pressures which motivated Jean Monnet, Maurice Schumann and the other proponents of greater European unity in the early days after World War II. For the second time within living memory, Europe had been devastated. No doubt the proximate cause of World War II had been the rise of the Nazi régime in Germany. Few doubted, however, that the success which Hitler and his associates had achieved in attaining supreme power rested on mistakes made during the negotiation of the Versailles Treaty in 1919, compounded by financial mismanagement and the resulting slump and economic nationalism of the inter-war period. There thus appeared to be overwhelmingly strong arguments for building institutions to bind the countries of war-torn Europe together in ways which would make a third internecine general conflict in Europe impossible.

First steps towards European integration began with the European Coal and Steel Community in 1951. The Common Market, following the Messina Conference in 1955, came into being on 1 January 1958. During this period, the original six economies making up the Common Market – France, Germany, Italy and the Benelux countries – were growing extremely rapidly, judged by all historical standards. This high growth rate continued throughout the 1960s, as the Common Market customs union established itself. The success which was achieved, particularly when compared to Britain, which was not a member at the time, was very striking. It was therefore easy to conclude, as many in Britain did at the time, and many others not in the Community were to do later, that the formation of the Common Market and the closer integration it promoted were the causes of the high growth rate. It did not occur to them that the early outstanding economic performance of the original Common Market countries might have been the consequence of events which would have produced excellent economic performance with or without the Community being established.

Nevertheless, the result of the high growth rate achieved by the Six during the 1960s was to invest the Common Market with a magnetic attraction for those left outside it. The European Free Trade Area, established as a counterpoint in 1960, never achieved the same allure, partly because Britain, the largest member, had a perennially slow growth rate which dragged down the average performance of the EFTA members. The self-confidence of those responsible for running Britain gradually declined, however, mirroring the country's poor economic performance and the erosion of its diplomatic influence. These events triggered the abandonment of its imperial pretensions, and the urge to become a member of the Common Market became overwhelming. Britain joined in 1973, bringing in Ireland and Denmark, both major British trading partners, in its wake, but not Norway where a referendum produced a negative result. Greece joined in 1981, and Spain and Portugal in 1986. All were attracted not only by the high standards of living and relative economic stability of the northern European countries, but also by the Common Market's democratic credentials, which each was keen to reinforce, in contrast to their recent histories. The final wave of applicants, Finland, Sweden and Austria, small countries which had previously been EFTA members, brought nearly all the highly industrialised western part of Europe under the EU banner by 1995.

The idealism which led to the formation of the Common Market, and its subsequent development into the European Union, proved therefore to have a strong appeal over a long period. The commitment to the EU of those responsible for running the countries which joined also gave them an immediate and substantial interest in justifying what they had done. Once the main Common Market institutions were established, they rapidly developed a momentum of their own, providing a powerful and well financed focus for large numbers of influential people, all with a major stake in promoting the Community's future.

The political momentum which has driven the Community has therefore been very effective. The problem has been the widening gap between the aspirations of those responsible for developing and running it, and the level of performance actually achieved. The EU has been successful at building a vast panoply of interlocking governmental structures at a supra-national level. It has achieved a level of political integration across Western Europe of which its forebears might be justly proud. On the economic front, however, compared with the rest of the world, the more that integration has proceeded, the worse the economic performance has been, producing a mounting danger that faith in the whole EU project is going to be undermined by low growth, expenditure retrenchment and unemployment.

What has gone wrong? Why has the EU done so poorly in economic terms, not only for a relatively short transitional period, which might be understandable, but for a quarter of a century? It is particularly important to find convincing answers to this question in the light of future developments currently being planned. If the policies which have been pursued during the last two or three decades have not been nearly as effective as their proponents hoped they would be, are there really good grounds for believing that intensifying them and extending them further will produce better results? If not, how has it happened that over a whole generation a large majority of Europe's leaders have espoused a strategy which, in at least economic terms, has been, and still is, seriously flawed? The aim of the chapters which follow is to set out convincing answers to these questions. To set the scene, however, it may be helpful at this stage to outline in summary what seems to have gone wrong, and why the EU's poor economic performance was allowed to happen. There have been a number of principal causes.

One was the conjunction between the success of the economies which came together to form the Common Market during the 1950s and 1960s, and the establishment of the Community institutions. The widely drawn conclusion was that one depended on the other, and that therefore extending and expanding the operations of the Community would improve rather than hold back the economies which comprised it. The statistics show that this inference cannot be right. The original six countries which came together to form the Common Market were already expanding very fast before the Treaty of Rome was signed.

The high growth rate of the Six was not caused by the establishment of the Common Market, but owed its existence largely to miscalculations by the victors of World War II, who completely underestimated the recuperative capacity of Europe's defeated economies. American generosity in making Marshall Aid available to many European countries, and still more the currency decisions after the war, which provided highly competitive export markets to war-torn Europe, were the main reasons for the post-war growth success of the main European economies. The *Deutcheswirtschaftwunder* was not primarily the result of the wisdom and foresight of Ludwig Erhard, the German Chancellor, although unquestionably the competent economic management which he provided helped. It was mainly the consequence of decisions taken by the occupying powers to give West Germany, in particular, an exceptionally favourable exchange rate as post-war recovery got under way. This was not done primarily to help the Germans, but because the victorious allies were afraid that otherwise they would have to support the German economy with aid for the indefinite future.

The growth rates achieved by the original six Common Market countries averaged slightly more for the seven years from 1950 to 1957 than for the subsequent seven years. Not too much should be made of this comparison, because even over a reasonably long period such as seven years, many influences come to bear on economic performance which do not imply secular changes in trend. It is clear, however, that there was no dramatic growth acceleration after the signing of the Treaty of Rome. However fast the Six were growing after 1958 – and their rate of growth over that period was indeed impressive – it was not the establishment of the Common Market which caused it. The fairest assessment is that, during the early years, its impact on the growth of its constituent economies overall was roughly neutral.

To a large extent, therefore, the success achieved by the original Common Market members did not rest on the foundations on which at least some of its leaders appeared to think it did. It depended mainly on factors of which they were only partly aware, or which they often chose to ignore altogether. This made them singularly badly prepared to handle the dislocations of the 1970s, when the world's economy was thrown into turmoil by a succession of unforeseen events, each triggering the next. It started with inflation in the United States, caused by the way the Americans financed the Vietnam War, which led to the break-up of the Bretton Woods international monetary system. This generated currency instability, a huge commodity boom, and the quadrupling of the price of oil, following the Yom Kippur War of 1973. Boom and bust in a number of European countries, particularly Britain, led to a substantial increase in inflation in all countries. At the same time, the very large balance of payments surpluses piled up by the oil-producing countries in the Middle East were reflected in deficits for the countries of the industrial West, which each tried to pass on to another by a process of competitive deflation.

A lack of clear economic analysis unquestionably confused the picture, as faith in Keynesian policies faded. Increasing scepticism about any economy's ability to combine high levels of employment with low inflation was aggravated by the arrival of new economic theories. Monetarism appealed greatly to the instincts of many major participants in the economic policy making world, yet turned out to have remarkably little firm substance, and even less worthwhile prescriptive value. Monetarist ideas nevertheless took firm hold over much of Europe, exacerbating the deflationary tendencies already there as a result of the first oil crisis, which repeated itself at the end of the 1970s, adding yet further to Europe's problems with rising unemployment and inflation, the sour mixture which came to be known as stagflation. The reaction of European leaders was not, therefore, to re-establish the economic conditions which had been responsible for the sustained post-war boom. It was, instead, to use a combination of conviction that salvation lay in building stronger pan-European institutions and faith in monetarist theories to create a fiscal and financial structure for the European Community which, in the end, finished up by aggravating all the existing problems.

This book argues that Europe's history during the last quarter of a century could have been very different and much more prosperous if its leaders had adopted, as they could have done, alternative approaches in two critical overlapping areas. The first is that they allowed their enthusiasm for integrating the countries of Europe to cloud their judgement about the economic conditions which were really needed to produce high rates of growth and full employment. The second is that, as growth faltered, they allowed themselves to be persuaded that restrictive rather than expansionist policies were the solution to the economic problems confronting them. Hard-line monetarist policies have a particular tendency to flourish in countries which are doing poorly. The Member States of the European Community have proved to be no exceptions to this rule. Although they are exactly the opposite to what is actually needed, monetarist ideas are all too inclined to persuade those in power that more deflation is the appropriate remedy to be applied to poorly performing economies, even though it was contractionary policies which led to their lack of growth in the first place. The result is a vicious downward spiral in performance, as growth falters, productivity rises faster than output, and increasing unemployment is the inevitable consequence.

POLITICAL PRESSURES AND ECONOMIC IDEAS

If Europe's leaders had understood why the major economies of Europe had done so well during the 1950s and 1960s, it is hard to believe that they would have allowed their performance to deteriorate so greatly during the next quarter of a century. Failure to deal with this relative decline is partly attributable to their belief in explanations for the EU's poor economic performance which this book argues do not stand up to rigorous examination. It is also, however, the failure of the economists and policy advisors with the ear of those in government to produce more coherent and effective analysis of the real nature of the problems which needed to be tackled, and the solutions which needed to be applied. Europe's poor performance over the last quarter of a century is not just the responsibility of its politicians. Its root cause has been the failure of the EU's élites as a whole, in the academic, media and business worlds, as well as in government, to understand and explain convincingly what has gone wrong, and to provide clear guidelines to Europe's leadership as to what should have been done instead.

The most common explanation for the slow growth and poor performance of the EU's economies over the last quarter of a century is to attribute them to over-generous employee entitlements such as excessive job security, high social security costs, short working hours, long holidays and rigid labour markets. Yet over much of Europe during the last two decades, huge strides have been taken, for good or ill, towards less job security, weaker trade union organisation and more flexibility. The proportion of the labour force involved in the kind of activities organised effectively by trade unions has fallen everywhere, as manufacturing has declined in importance compared to services. The growth rate has not, however, improved. On the other hand, the Japanese economy grew for decades at 6% per annum or more with rigidities in the labour market which were far greater than those in Europe. Faced with this contrast, it never has been plausible to argue that employment conditions themselves have been the root cause of Europe's problems. Surely the correct implication is that good employment conditions can be afforded if the economy is competitive, as was the case in Japan. If, however, the economy is uncompetitive enough, as a result of misjudged macro-economic policies, no degree of job insecurity will make up the difference.

The lack of enterprise among European companies, particularly those involved in manufacturing, and their consequent inability to compete in developing and marketing successfully state of the art products, is another reason often cited for the malaise from which the EU economy suffers. It is frequently said that many of Europe's manufacturing industries are involved in yesterday's growth markets, and too few in those of tomorrow. These charges may have some substance, but it is much more plausible to argue that Europe's lack of competitiveness is the consequence rather than the cause of slow growth. If this is indeed the case, then the remedy is to use macro-economic policies to produce conditions which will improve the growth rate, not to resort to supply-side policy initiatives to solve the problem. There is no evidence that supply-side policy initiatives on their own can successfully be implemented to remedy competitive deficiencies.

Some have alleged that Europe's problems derive from high levels of taxation, excessive public expenditure, and too much public provision of goods and services. Unquestionably, at both the EU and national level, public money is wasted on inappropriate policies. Subsidies to inefficient and loss making national airlines are impossible to justify on rational grounds. So too is much of the expenditure on the Common Agricultural Policy. It is, however, a fallacy to believe that wasting money on badly conceived agricultural support policies is unique to Europe. Both the Japanese and American systems of support for their farmers, in different ways, have been equally or even more expensive and inefficient. All countries spend large amounts of money on unproductive economic activities – the Americans proportionately far larger amounts than Europeans on defence, and the Japanese on one of the most inefficient internal airline systems in the world. Nor have the EU countries, such as Britain, which have made the most determined efforts to privatise their public industries and to deregulate their economies, done conspicuously better than the low EU average. It is hard to believe that the root cause of the EU's poor economic performance can be explained in this way.

If it is more plausible to attribute the failings of the EU economies to poorly formulated policies at the macro level, rather than to labour rigidities, industrial mismanagement or overblown public sectors, why have there not been clearer analyses of these failings, and better policies which might be pursued? Much of the problem lies in the general failure of economic policy prescriptions to provide clear guidelines to political leaders responsible for dealing with the difficulties with which Europe is confronted. Because there are no agreed explanations as to what causes economic growth to take place or to falter, why unemployment is high in some places but low in others, and what inflationary price has to be paid for economic growth, there are no clear formulations to follow. Understandably, with a vacuum like this, log rolling is inclined to take over from rational decision taking. Too much political activity takes the form of battles for power rather than for the implementation of policies which are well thought through and therefore likely to work.

Humanity has a well documented capacity for believing that what is in its own interest will also be to the general advantage. When there is a lack of rational consensus, sectional interests are all too likely to prevail. Bureaucrats consolidate their power and influence. Bankers press the case for monetary restriction and expenditure cuts. Trade unions, if they are in a powerful enough position to do so, press for wage and salary rises unfunded by adequate productivity increases, thus adding to inflationary problems. Politicians bicker and disagree, while their electorates become more and more disillusioned with them. The European Union at present has too many signs of all these conditions. It need not be like this. Nor should it be. Europe has huge advantages compared to much of the rest of the world, and ought to be able to do at least as well, if not better, than others. It has a long history, providing a cultural coherence, common identity and social solidarity missing in many other parts of the world. It has a well educated labour force. It is exceptionally well endowed by nature. It is a civilised and attractive place in which to live. It could and should do a great deal better economically than it has done recently.

EUROPE'S CRITICAL CHOICES

In the near future, the European Union will have to take momentous decisions on the Single Currency. The extent to which the EU Member States aspiring to be in the first tier have complied with the convergence criteria laid down in the Maastricht Treaty is to be established by reference to their performance in 1997. The figures will be known early in 1998. The decisions as to who will qualify are scheduled to be taken, in the spring of 1998, at a Summit Meeting in Britain which will at this time hold the EU Presidency. The planned start date for the Single Currency is 1 January 1999. During the following three years, the euro will circulate in the participating countries in parallel with national currencies, which will be phased out in anticipation of the euro, the new EU currency, taking over exclusively by 1 January 2002.

A vast amount of work will have to be done to prepare for the new currency. Every organisation will have to change its accounting systems to a greater or smaller extent. For commercial companies, government departments, banks and other financial institutions, the upheaval and cost will be enormous. Every machine which takes or dispenses cash will have to be altered. Every computer accounting programme will have to be changed. Provision will have to be made for the impact of the currency conversion on every legal contract involving money. Everyone will have to get used to prices and costs being denominated in a new way. A large amount of training and re-training will be required to enable all concerned to be prepared for the new requirements.

Even if there is a lack of complete certainty that the Single Currency project will go ahead on time, no major organisation can afford to bank on its delay, let alone its abandonment. Inevitably, therefore, the project is gathering momentum, as more and more time, money and management effort is expended everywhere on ensuring that preparations are completed on time. The EU institutions have, of course, always been behind Monetary Union, and the full resources of the Commission are being deployed into urging everyone to comply with all the currency conversion requirements. In addition, a major propaganda campaign is planned, to persuade the populations of the participating countries that the Single Currency holds the key to the future.

At national level, extraordinary zeal is being exhibited by all the Member State governments which aspire to be in the 1999 first tier to comply with the Maastricht convergence criteria. Despite protests, marches, adverse opinion polls and electoral reverses, cuts in expenditure are being implemented to meet the parameters which have been set, or at least to get close enough to them for waivers to be granted. Leading politicians in many countries have nailed their flags to the Single Currency mast, and they are determined not to be deflected. Even in countries such as France, where there has been strong opposition to the public expenditure cuts required to meet the Single Currency criteria, there is still widespread popular support for the principle of currency union as a recent poll showed, indicating that 75% thought that France should participate. How membership of monetary union on the Maastricht terms can be combined with expansionary policies is not explained. The leaders in Europe are not, therefore, without support amongst their electorates in pushing ahead towards the Single Currency, but there are also warning signs that the support is fragile and much less universal than is sometimes supposed.

A substantial majority of those polled in Germany are worried that the euro will not be as secure and reliable a currency as the Deutsche Mark, particularly if countries such as Spain and Italy, with much worse inflationary records than the average, are included among the participating states. There are some politicians in each country who are not enthusiastic about the Single Currency, and who are getting an increasingly strong response from the electorate when they criticise the cost of monetary union in terms of deflation, lost output and rising unemployment. The manipulation of the convergence criteria in many countries, including Germany, enabling them to produce figures for 1997, the qualifying year, which they are most unlikely to be able to repeat subsequently, have disturbed the ranks of those who might otherwise have been strong supporters. Senior banking figures have broken ranks to criticise the extent to which the criteria have been fudged, expressing fear that the supposed discipline of the Single Currency is being undermined by political dealing. Two Member States, Britain and Denmark, have continually voiced serious reservations about European Monetary Union, and it is very doubtful that either of them will want to participate, at least in the initial phases. Even amongst those who support the Single Currency in principle, there is an increasing minority who believe that insufficient genuine convergence has been achieved between the aspirant Member States, and that it might be wise to delay implementation.

It is not, therefore, yet certain that the Single Currency project will proceed as currently planned. It is unlikely that it will be completely abandoned, at least in the immediate future. It is, however, possible that its implementation will be delayed, as too many difficulties and doubts crowd in about pushing ahead with it on the current schedule. If this happens, however, it may be the beginning of the end. The generation of European leaders now in power, almost all heavily committed to European Monetary Union, will not be there for ever. The current world boom, which is helping the EU to grow economically rather more rapidly than it has done for a while, will may weaken before long, worsening the conditions in which any future decisions about locking EU currencies together will have to be taken. The climate of opinion on economics, which has recently been becoming increasingly disillusioned with hard-line monetarist prescriptions, may well become even less inclined to treat deflationary policies as the only viable way of running Europe's affairs. The public is becoming more and more frustrated by endless calls for retrenchment. For all these reasons, if there is a delay on implementing the Single Currency, the momentum may never be regained.

Undoubtedly, there will be some people who have set their hearts on seeing a United States of Europe in their lifetime, who will greatly regret such a turn of events. It is very doubtful, however, whether such sentiments are in a majority. Most people in Europe certainly want to maintain good relations with their neighbours, to share responsibility for common problems, and to maintain the liberal open economic policies which have served the developed world well over the last half-century. They are much more doubtful whether uniting the EU's currencies is a step in the right direction. This book shares both this scepticism and the understanding that good relations between the nations of Europe, including those further east, are essential for the future.

2   The Historical Background

'Study the past if you would divine the future.'
                                                    Confucius

Industrialisation might have started during the period of the Roman Empire, but it failed to do so. Why was this? At first sight, it might appear that the Roman Empire had all the necessary requirements to enable a beginning to be made on applying technology to the perennial problems of economic shortage. For nearly four hundred years after the consolidation which took place under Caesar Augustus, it encompassed a large and varied area, where peace and order prevailed. There was a relatively efficient and impartial legal system. Although the Roman Empire was plagued by inflationary problems, trading and banking were well established, and there were substantial accumulations of capital. Interestingly, the Roman period is the only one when much of Europe was covered by a single currency.

Some industrial processes, such as smelting, were well known. An accumulation of theory about scientific matters, mostly developed by the Greeks, was available. Indeed, a steam engine of sorts, used as a toy, had been developed by the Greek polymath Hero in Alexandria, one of the centres of Greek learning. There was a substantial artisan class, capable of contributing practical knowledge and experience to new ideas about production methods. The standards of education, especially among the more prosperous classes, were reasonably high. And yet, despite all of these apparently potentially favourable circumstances, there was almost no technological development at all for hundreds of years.

There have been at least two other large empires with similar conditions to those in the Roman Empire. There is some evidence that in China, during the fifteenth century, something close to the beginning of an industrial revolution did occur, but it was snuffed out by the country's leaders, who turned back to traditional ways. India, on the other hand, never showed any more signs of sustained industrial development than the Romans, despite the ability of the Mughal culture to build the Taj Mahal, its high point of excellence both in design and execution. Nor were smaller empires any better at producing sustained economic growth. On the contrary, it was in Europe, divided into a large number of relatively small states, that there began to be a sustained increase in living standards, starting early in the current millennium, which eventually produced the Industrial Revolution.

The conjunction of circumstances required to trigger off industrialisation turned out to be remarkably complex. Certainly, both a well developed trading system and a trustworthy banking network were required, in addition to a legal and political system capable of ensuring that financial surpluses could not be usurped at will by those in political control. There also needed to be sufficient stability and peace to make it worthwhile for entrepreneurs to take more substantial risks, with the prospect of recouping their investment outlays over periods of years rather than months. Sufficient technical knowledge and scientific theory was required to enable the development of new processes to be guided by well established knowledge and scientific principles rather than by guesswork and trial and error. All these requirements, however, had been met, at least to a substantial degree, in other places, but had failed to produce results. What was different about Europe?

A key theme running through this book is that breaking new ground in the commercial and industrial world is extremely difficult, and requires exceptional ability. Once it has been done, it is comparatively easy for others to see how it occurred, though not necessarily obvious how to break in against established competition. The societies which successfully initiated the Industrial Revolution, and those who have been most effective at sustaining it, are therefore ones where a significant proportion of their most talented individuals were immersed in the manufacturing and commercial worlds. The Industrial Revolution began in Europe rather than elsewhere because there was a sufficient number of exceptionally able and gifted people who were interested in industry and commerce rather than doing something else. It is not kings or queens, politicians or professionals, churchmen or academics, soldiers or diplomats, who create economic resources. Only to a limited extent, too, do traders and bankers perform a significant role in wealth generation. Most of the increase in output which is achieved by modern methods of producing goods and services, at least in the early stages, comes from manufacturing, with agriculture making an important subsidiary contribution.

The unique contribution which Europe made, and particularly the Netherlands and Britain during the early stages of the Industrial Revolution, was to generate circumstances where sufficient able people began to apply themselves seriously, and on a reasonably large scale, to employing new industrial technology and to improving agricultural methods. Slowly the notion that there might be continuing opportunities to expand output, raise living standards, and increase productivity began to spread. Once this happened, the history of humanity was irreversibly established on the path of industrial advance.

Once set on the road to cumulative economic development, with all its advantages in terms of improving living standards internally, and increasing military and diplomatic power externally, it might be thought that sustaining the initial momentum would be a top national priority. No doubt it was almost universally intended that it should be, but in fact maintaining this momentum has proved to be extraordinarily difficult. The economic history of the last two centuries is littered with cases of countries which achieved high rates of economic growth initially, but which then slipped back and permitted others to overtake them. In the eighteenth century, the Netherlands provided its citizens with the highest standard of living in the world. The British economy did the same during the first half of the nineteenth century, but over the next hundred and fifty years Britain allowed itself to be overtaken by some twenty other countries.

The huge economic lead which the United States enjoyed at the end of World War II has been steadily whittled away since then. Japan's long post-war record of economic growth came to an abrupt end in 1991, and the Japanese economy has been in the doldrums for the last six years, with little sign of return to previous growth rates. Countries such as Taiwan, South Korea, Hong Kong and Singapore, on the other hand, have shot up the league table with phenomenal growth rates, now being exceeded by those achieved in China. It used to be widely argued that these countries were all so successful because they began with very low labour costs, with which the developed West could never compete. This view always ignored the well established theory, going back to the British economists of the early nineteenth century, which showed that countries at any stage of development could always trade with each other to their mutual advantage provided exchange rates were correctly positioned. It looks threadbare now that the standards of living in many Pacific rim countries are overtaking those in Europe, some with their growth rates still being maintained unchecked as their standards of living rise through the levels prevailing in Europe.

What accounts for these variations in performance? The answer lies in the reactions to wealth generation, and the processes involved in achieving it, which seem to have a capacity to replicate themselves across the world, thus producing similar trends everywhere. Being at the cutting edge of industrial and commercial development is a risky business, and humanity generally is risk averse. Industrial and commercial activity also involves a concentration on products and their development, promotion and sale which perhaps intrinsically does not have the cachet and glamour of other ways of making a living. There has thus been a universal tendency for most successful business classes to encourage their children into other less hazardous and more socially acceptable ways of making a living than being in trade and industry. However understandable this may be for the individuals involved, it has had dire effects on the performance of the economies where they live.

Other powerful forces have reinforced this tendency. Countries which have been initially successful industrially have tended to pile up balance of payments surpluses, which then had a marked tendency to generate high values for their currencies. These make it much more difficult for their industries to compete in the world against those in other countries without this disadvantage. With declining profits go reduced earnings and prestige. In these circumstances, investments abroad appear to have better prospects than those at home. Partly for these international reasons, and partly because of low industrial profitability domestically, bankers tend to gain in prestige and importance *vis à vis* industrial borrowers. Political power and influence is then inclined to seep away from industry, and to become increasingly concentrated in other parts of the economy, generally amongst people with little experience or interest in manufacturing and commerce.

An interesting insight on these processes is provided by those who for one reason or another have found themselves excluded from the mainstream of political life in the countries where they live. These groups have not had the same ability to urge their children into non-commercial or industrial ways of earning a living as other groups of people. The Quakers and Nonconformists in Britain, the Huguenots in France and Jewish communities everywhere have fallen into these categories. It is no coincidence that these groups of people have made disproportionately important economic contributions to the countries where they have lived.

In general, however, minority communities, however much they have contributed, have not been able to buck the general trend. The result has been that all countries experiencing industrial revolutions have tended to go through the same cycle of growth, relative pre-eminence and then slow relative decline. Unfortunately, the European Union now appears to be well established in the decline phase. Is it possible, however, by analysing carefully the way that leverage can be applied to the economy by using appropriate policies, to cause this process to reverse itself? This is an extremely important topic, central to finding a solution to the EU's recent poor economic performance.

INDUSTRIALISATION UP TO WORLD WAR I

The Industrial Revolution, which began in Europe in the eighteenth century, rested on a foundation built over hundreds of years. Since the Middle Ages, and at least since the fourteenth century, there had been a slow increase in output per head in Europe, set back from time to time by wars, pestilence and bad government. This growth had come about partly as a result of improved agriculture, partly as a result of increased trade, but mainly because of the application of new ideas, some based on novel technology, to a wide variety of production processes.

The advent of the printing press vastly reduced the cost of producing books, and thus of disseminating knowledge. The developments in ship design and navigation greatly decreased the costs of trading, while opening up large sections of the world which had previously been unknown to Europeans. The resulting exchange of products enabled gains from specialisation in the production of goods and agricultural products to be realised which had never previously been available. There was a steady improvement in the working of metals, providing the basis for the production of machinery. The Renaissance and the Enlightenment provided a ferment of ideas, some of which fed through to industry to provide a much clearer explanation of how industrial processes worked than was previously available. Not least of these were advances in mathematics, which made it easier for calculations relating to production processes to be done quickly and accurately. At the same time, there was a steady accumulation of practical knowledge acquired by increasingly skilled labour forces, capable of putting new ideas into operation.

The Industrial Revolution quickened and began to gather pace faster in Britain during the eighteenth century than elsewhere, allowing Britain to take over economic leadership from the Netherlands. Britain had moved further away from the feudal system of the Middle Ages than most other countries in Europe. There was a more highly developed system of contract law, and a less arbitrary system of government than generally on the continent. As a result of successfully developed trading patterns, there was a reasonably sophisticated banking system and an accumulation of capital which could be mobilised for risk ventures. There was stable government. Above all, there was an entrepreneurial class, much of it, characteristically, excluded from mainstream political life in the form of the Nonconformists, which was interested in commerce and manufacturing. There were also major agricultural interests, with much land owned by forward looking landowners, interested in exploiting new ideas in agricultural husbandry.

The Industrial Revolution thus got under way in Britain in textiles, pottery, mining and metal working, aided by improvements in communications such as the development of canals. A combination of outworking and factories led to big increases in output when production processes were broken down into individual specialised functions, as Adam Smith accurately noted in *The Wealth of Nations*. This extremely influential book, published in 1776, during the early stages of the Industrial Revolution, contained a remarkably powerful set of ideas about the changes taking place in the industrial and commercial worlds, and how government policy should be organised to take advantage of them. Not only did the early Industrial Revolution involve rising living standards on average for the British people compared to those elsewhere, but it also greatly enhanced Britain's power in the world. This enabled the British to build and maintain a dominant navy and to deploy and finance the coalition of land forces which eventually won them victory in the Napoleonic Wars.

While France had at least as high a standard of living as Britain in the early eighteenth century, and perhaps higher, many of the other circumstances needed to get industry moving were also in place. The French, however, were much slower to take advantage of the new opportunities available in industry. Partly this was the result of the arbitrary characteristics of the *ancien régime*, which lacked the contract legal system introduced shortly after the 1789 French Revolution. Partly it was a matter of social pressures, also related to the sense of values of the pre-Revolutionary period, which held industry and commerce in relatively low esteem. The result was that French manufacturers tended to concentrate on the output of individually crafted products, some of them widely recognised as being of exceptionally high quality, rather than moving to mass production methods. French furniture, tapestries, china and jewellery were internationally renowned, but the cottage industry techniques used for producing them are not the stuff of which industrial revolutions are made.

Germany also suffered from disadvantages, many of them similar to those in France, compounded by the patchwork of small states which made up the country, each with its own tariff and economic policies. The southern states of Europe, Spain, Portugal, Italy and Greece, were all much poorer, and in a weaker position to start industrialising, as indeed remained the case for a century or more. The Netherlands, which had grown richer during the eighteenth century than anywhere else, faltered as its trading success drove up the value of its currency, undermining its domestic industry – a story to be repeated many times in the years to come. It was therefore Britain which made the running for a long time into the nineteenth century.

Following the Battle of Waterloo in 1815, which ended the Napoleonic Wars, the British economy suffered a sharp decline until 1820. This was largely caused by the decision to restore the value of the currency to the same parity against gold as had applied at the beginning of the wars. The risk of invasion, and the consequent run on the provincial banks of the time, had led to a suspension of the Gold Standard in 1797. The pressure on the economy generated by the wars had led to significant price rises. By 1810, prices had risen by an estimated 76% compared with 1790. The issue confronted by *Report from the Select Committee on the High Price of Gold Bullion*, presented to the British Parliament in 1810, was the cause of the price rises. Had they occurred because of the financial laxity allowed by the suspension of the Gold Standard, or were they an inevitable consequence of the pressure of demand in a rapidly expanding economy, and the need to increase the money supply to accommodate a much larger volume of transactions?

Despite the protests of a vocal minority, led by David Ricardo, the majority supported the return to the 1797 parity. The deflation required to force prices down to their previous level was responsible for the post-war depression. This decision also left the pound sterling tied to a high gold value compared to the currencies of the other major countries in Europe, which had also been subjected to inflationary pressures during the wars. These other countries did not see the necessity, however, to revert to the previous parities, and left them where they were at the end of the wars.

The resulting relatively high cost of producing goods and services in Britain compared with the rest of Europe did not, however, hold back the British economy for long. During the first half of the nineteenth century, Britain was the only country which was industrialising fast. In consequence, the cost of goods produced in Britain fell rapidly compared with output elsewhere in Europe, making them very competitive despite the high gold parity. The British economy expanded by nearly 3% per annum on average for the whole of the period from 1820 to 1851, when the Great Exhibition was held in London, marking the high peak of British pre-eminence. From 1851 to 1871 the growth rate slowed to about 2%. Even so, the cumulative increase in wealth and the standard of living was without parallel with anything ever seen in the world before, except in the United States, far away on the other side of the Atlantic and heavily protected by tariffs, where high rates of growth were also being achieved.

With increasing confidence in its industrial capacity, the case made for trade liberalisation in Britain became stronger. The Industrial Revolution had started in Britain behind substantial tariff barriers, themselves a legacy of the mercantilist policies of self-sufficiency against which Adam Smith had preached in *The Wealth of Nations*. As the expanding population pressed on the domestically produced food supply, however, necessitating increased imports of corn and other foodstuffs, the case for keeping down the cost of living by removing import tariffs and quotas seemed to become stronger. Free trade arguments were also extended to manufactured goods, leading to the trade treaties negotiated in the 1840s and 1850s, culminating in the 1860 Treaty with France, which reduced the total number of dutiable items coming in to Britain to only forty-eight.

Unilateral free trade, however, makes any country's imports relatively cheaper than its exports, once the tariffs have been removed. Adopting free trade policies therefore had the same effect as raising the exchange rate, which was already very high. Free trade in consequence also contributed to Britain's undoing as the nineteenth century wore on. All over Europe, but particularly in France, Germany and the Benelux countries, British manufacturing techniques began to be copied. The initial impulse came primarily from railway development, as their construction got under way on a major scale all over Europe from the 1840s and 1850s onwards. This necessitated not only major developments in civil engineering, but also big investments in production facilities capable of turning out thousands of kilometres of rail, relatively sophisticated rolling stock, and complex signalling equipment. Characteristically, while in Britain all these developments had been financed entirely by the private sector, in France and Germany the state was heavily involved in railway construction from the beginning, underwriting a considerable proportion of the high risks involved. Differing perceptions about the role of the state *vis à vis* the private sector across Europe have a long history.

British production techniques were soon copied in railways, and in virtually all other fields. Other forms of communications, such as canals, were constructed. Mass production of textiles followed, particularly in north-east France to start with, but soon spreading throughout Europe. Iron and steel output, greatly stimulated by the development of railways, but also providing the basis for the production of metal goods for a wide range of purposes, began to grow rapidly, particularly in Germany. The output of steel trebled there between 1840 and 1860, and trebled again between 1860 and 1880. The economies of Europe became better able to compete with Britain for other reasons too. Germany was united first loosely under the *Zollverein* of 1834, and later more tightly under Bismarck, once Prussia had secured its position of leadership. Everywhere, although much more rapidly in some places than others, there were improvements in education, the legal system, the organisation of the professions and the training of skilled workforces.

A major turning point came in the 1870s, as the worldwide consumer and investment boom which followed the American Civil War and the Franco-Prussian conflict collapsed as a result of the fall in demand for armaments, and the slowdown in railway building. For the first time, Britain felt the full blast of foreign competition, and the British lead in industrial output became reduced. The growth rate of the British economy stabilised at 2.0% per annum for the last quarter of the nineteenth century, while that of Germany and the Netherlands increased to 2.6% and 2.3% respectively, though France did worse at 1.4% and Italy worse still at 1.2%. From 1870 to 1900 the economy of Germany grew by 125%, the Netherlands by 96%, Britain by 85%, Belgium by 82% and France by 56%.

The sources of their increases in output differed between France and Britain, which were falling back, and countries such as Germany which were pulling ahead. In Britain, in particular, more and more investment went abroad. In the slower growing economies, a rising percentage of investment went into housing and infrastructure, and a relatively low proportion into industry. Total investment as a percentage of GDP in these countries fell or remained static. Where investments were made in industry, more went into widening rather than deepening the industrial structure. In Britain, in particular, there was a vast expansion of the cotton industry and coal mining, both of which were labour intensive, but where large productivity gains were difficult to achieve.

In Germany, and to a lesser extent elsewhere on the continent, these trends were reversed. A higher proportion of investment went into new industries, such as the production of dyes and chemicals, sophisticated metal products, and later of motor vehicles and electrical goods. The significance of these industries was that the scope for increased output and improved productivity was much greater than in the kind of industries to which Britain was moving. The circumstances which had given Britain the advantage in the early part of the nineteenth century were reversed. It was Germany and the Netherlands which now had more competitive exports, and which were less prone to import penetration because of the strength of local manufactures. They could therefore concentrate production where the growth prospects were highest, and were in a position to reinvest productively a greater proportion of their national incomes in their own economies.

The result was that by the time of the start of World War I, the gap between the income per head in Britain and the rest of north-west Europe had largely closed. Whereas in 1850, the income per head had been twice as high in Britain as in the most advanced parts of the continent of Europe, by 1914 the difference was only about a quarter. Furthermore, in industrial capacity in many respects Germany was well ahead of Britain. German steel output had overtaken Britain's in the 1890s. By 1910, Britain was producing 6.5m tons of steel per year, but Germany was producing 13m. Just before the outbreak of World War I, Germany had twice as many kilometres of rail track as Britain and was generating six times as much electricity.

Why did Britain allow this to happen? Partly, it was because the reasons for Britain's relative decline were not understood, so there was no clearly articulated policy available for reversing it. In place of a determined and well formulated series of policies to keep the British economy on a high growth track, the social and economic pressures described above were allowed full rein. Those with accumulated wealth dominated the way the economy was run as against those striving to create new industries. Sterling was too strong, encouraging imports and discouraging domestic production. Too much investment went abroad. Too few talented people went into industry and commerce. Too many went into the professions, administering the empire acquired almost entirely as a result of Britain's earlier economic pre-eminence, and into academic life, the civil service, the church – anything, if they could avoid it, except industry and trade.

THE INTER-WAR PERIOD

World War I was a catastrophe for Europe in every way. Not only was there a huge loss of life and immense material destruction. Even worse than this, the relatively stable and secure social and economic systems which had been developed during the nineteenth century, which had stood Europe and the world as a whole in such good stead, were totally undermined. It took another World War and the passage of three decades before anything resembling the peace, prosperity and security of pre-World War I Europe would be re-established.

Approximately 8.5m people lost their lives in Europe prematurely as a result of World War I, and a substantial additional number, harder to quantify, in the influenza epidemics which struck down a weakened population in the immediate war aftermath. The damage done to towns and factories, though much less than in World War II, was still considerable. The national incomes of the countries of Western Europe fell precipitately between the period just before World War I started, and the early years after it ended when the demand for war-orientated production fell away. France's industrial production dropped by over 40% between 1913 and 1919, caused partly by the disruption and damage of the war, and partly by the post-war slump. It was 1927 before German GDP rose again to its 1913 level. Britain fared a little better, with the GDP staying more or less constant during the war, although it fell heavily, by about 20%, immediately the war finished.

Economic instability in Europe was greatly compounded by the Treaty of Versailles, negotiated between the powers which had won the war, and the humiliated Germans. The Americans had not come into the war until 1917, and insisted on the large debts run up by Britain and France for war supplies being repaid. Britain and France, in turn looked to Germany to make huge reparations, partly to pay the Americans and partly on their own account. All these arrangements, negotiated by political leaders under immense pressure from electorates only too interested in settling old scores rather than facing up to new realities, bore no relationship to the ability of the Germans to make these payments. Leaving aside the extent to which the German economy was already languishing as a result of the damage done to it by the war, the only feasible way for the Germans to pay the reparation bill was to run a very large export surplus. In the fragile state of the world economy in the 1920s, no country was prepared to tolerate a large German trade surplus, even if it could have been achieved. Payment of reparations on the scale demanded, whatever its electoral appeal, or the requirement of the United States to see debts to it settled, was never therefore a remotely realistic prospect.

Attempts to extract reparations, however, compounded with post-war political and economic disruption, caused havoc in Germany. The government, unable to raise sufficient revenue through the tax system to meet the obligations it had undertaken to fulfil, resorted to the printing press to create the money it was unable to raise in any other way. The result was the German inflation of 1923, which ended in hyperinflation and the total collapse in the value of the currency. The Reichsmark had already lost half its value during World War I. Now all those with savings denominated in money lost everything. This experience understandably scarred the German attitude to inflation and monetary rectitude, with reverberations which are still felt today.

Gradually, however, towards the end of the 1920s, some measure of normality began to reassert itself. There was a significant boom in France, where industrial output doubled between the post-war low of 1921 and 1928, although even in 1928 it was only 10% higher than it had been in 1913. Industrial output also rose in the late 1920s in Germany, peaking in 1929 at about 20% higher than it had been in 1913, while Germany's GDP grew cumulatively between 1925 and 1929 by a respectable 2.9% per annum. In Germany's case in particular, however, the recovery was fragile. It depended heavily on large loans flowing in from abroad, especially the United States, to enable reparation payments to continue at the scaled down rate agreed by the Young Plan in 1929, replacing the much harsher Dawes Plan of 1924. Nevertheless, in the late 1920s, Germany's unemployment was falling and living standards were slowly increasing.

Britain remained depressed, mainly because of a repetition of the same process which had taken place after the Napoleonic Wars. The link between the pound and gold had been suspended on the outbreak of World War I, and the pressure on the economy during the war had led to considerable price inflation. Nevertheless, on the recommendation of the Cunliffe Committee, in 1918 it was decided to restore the gold value of the pound to the same parity, $4.86, which it had enjoyed in 1914. Achieving this objective meant forcing down costs in Britain, which was attempted by imposing severely deflationary policies. The reductions achieved, particularly in labour costs, were nothing like sufficient, however, to restore Britain to a competitive position at the new parity. As a result, Britain spent the whole of the 1920s in the worst of all worlds, suffering from a combination of lack of competitiveness at home and abroad, leading inevitably to domestic deflation and slow growth in output and living standards

Europe therefore appeared to be very poorly placed to weather the slump which followed, beginning with the collapse of the United States stock market in 1929. The fragile American banking system was unable to cope with the unwinding of the speculative positions built up during the preceding boom years in the United States, and bank failures were widespread. Confidence drained away as the US plunged into depression, following the start of the world's economic crisis on 'Black Friday', 25 October 1929. The US GDP fell by 30% between 1929 and 1933. Industrial output fell by nearly half in just three years from 1929 to 1932. By 1933, a quarter of the American labour force was out of work. Nearly 13m people in the US had no job.

The most immediate effect of the American slump on Europe was that the flow of loans from the US to Germany dried up, plunging the German economy into a crisis of the same order of magnitude as had overcome the United States. Between 1929 and 1932, German GDP fell by nearly a quarter. Industrial production dropped by almost 40%. Unemployment, which already stood at 9.3% in 1929, increased to over 30% of the labour force by 1932. Unemployment during this year averaged 5.5m, peaking at 6m. In Britain, GDP fell, but by not so much as in the US and Germany. Industrial production dropped by 5%, but unemployment, which was already 7.3% in 1929, rose to 15.6% in 1932. Similar patterns to those seen in Britain were to be found in France and the Benelux countries. Mussolini's policy in Italy of keeping the lira at as high a parity as possible, mirroring the British experience, ensured that the Italian economy suffered similar disadvantages, although the proportion of the Italian GDP involved in foreign trade was much lower than that in Britain.

The crucially important lessons to be learnt from the 1930s derive from the different ways in which the major economies in Europe, particularly Germany, France and Britain, reacted to the slump which overtook all of them at the same time. The history of the years to come was indelibly stamped by the different reactions of the electorates and their leaders in these three countries.

In Germany, the collapse of the economy, coming as it did on top of the trauma of the lost World War I, the vindictiveness of the Versailles settlement, particularly the reparations clauses, the political instability of the Weimar régime, and the hyperinflation of 1923, provoked a wholly counterproductive response from the Brüning government. In July 1931, and again in the

34   *Europe's Economic Dilemma*

summer of 1932, the amount and duration of unemployment compensation was reduced. Instead of attempting to reflate the economy, Chancellor Brüning, supported by the SDP opposition, cut wages and benefits, making the economic situation worse, precipitating the German banking crisis of July 1931, which followed the Austrian Kreditanstalt collapse two months earlier. The desperate attempts by democratic, well meaning politicians to maintain financial respectability were their undoing, and that of the whole of Europe as the Nazis came to power. This mistake, on top of all the others, provided Hitler and his associates with their opportunity to take over the government in 1933.

The economic policies pursued by the new Nazi régime, however disastrous in leading Europe into World War II, and however much racist and fascist policies are to be condemned, were nevertheless remarkably successful in domestic terms. Unemployment, which stood at over 30% in 1932, was reduced by 1938 to just over 2% of the working population. Over the same period, industrial production rose over 120%, a cumulative increase of 14% per annum. The gross national product increased by 65%, a cumulative increase of nearly 9% a year. A substantial proportion of the increased output was devoted to armaments, but by no means all. Military expenditure, which had been 3.2% of GDP in 1933, rose to 9.6% in 1937. It then almost doubled to 18.1%, but only as late as 1938. Between 1932 and 1938 consumers' expenditure rose by almost a quarter. Nor were these achievements bought at the expense of high levels of inflation. The price level was very stable in Germany in the 1930s. Consumer prices rose by a total of only 7% between the arrival of the Nazi régime in 1933 and the outbreak of war in 1939.

How were these results achieved? Some of the success could only have been achieved by a non-democratic régime, with access to total power. In particular, some of the pressure exerted on holding down price increases, and some of the policies imposed to restrict trade, so as to increase Germany's capacity to supply all its essential needs internally, would have been difficult for any democratic government to implement. Unquestionably these policies also led to increasing distortions in the economy, with a price which would have to be paid sooner or later. All the same, there was plenty of new production with which to pay these costs.

The expansion of the economy was achieved partly as a result of vast increases in expenditures by the state, which nearly trebled between 1933 and 1938. An increasingly high proportion of these were spent on rearmament as the decade wore on, but during the earlier years most of it went on civil expenditure, such as building a road system far superior to anything there before, although this also had military capabilities. A substantial proportion of the rest of the rise in output, however, went on increasing the German standard of living, as rising spending power from both the public and the private sector worked its way through to German factories. Much of the initial increase in expenditure was financed by borrowing on a large scale, some of it through bonds, but much of it from the banking system. There was a large expansion in the money supply. Increased tax revenues, however, flowing from the greatly increased scale of economic activity, kept the finances of the régime in bounds, which was partly why inflationary pressures were subdued.

In Britain, the initial reaction to the advent of the slump was much in line with the economic policies previously pursued. The Labour Chancellor of the Exchequer, Philip Snowden, tried to persuade his reluctant cabinet colleagues that the only solution to the financial crisis overwhelming the country was to maintain a balanced budget by implementing the same sort of cuts in expenditure which had been the undoing of the Brüning government in Germany. Eventually, there was a revolt when an overwhelming majority of Labour Members of Parliament ceased supporting the government, by refusing to back any more cuts. They preferred to go into opposition, allowing a National Government to be formed with the support of the Conservative opposition.

The policies then implemented were a complete break from those previously supported. The pound sterling was driven off gold, and allowed to fall in value by 24% against all other major currencies. Far from the government thereafter making efforts to restore the previous parity, as it had after the Napoleonic Wars and World War I, and which was to be the mistaken response time after time after exchange rate falls in the future, policy was dedicated to ensuring that the new lower parity was retained. An Exchange Equalisation Account was established, with resources of 5% of the gross national product, to keep the pound at its new competitive level. There was a very substantial expansion in the money supply, which increased by 15% between 1931 and 1932, and which rose by a further 19% during the first half of 1933. Interest rates fell to almost zero. Tariff protection was added to reinforce the protective effects of the reduction in the exchange rate.

In Britain, as in Germany, the results were dramatic and positive. Far from living standards falling, as almost all commentators had confidently predicted they would, they started to rise rapidly. Industrial production also increased substantially, if not quite as fast as in Germany. In the five years to 1937, manufacturing output rose 58% to 38% above the 1929 peak. Unemployment fell sharply, as the number of people in jobs quickly increased. Over the period between 1931 and 1937, the number of those in work rose from 18.7m to 21.4m as 2.7m new jobs were created, half of them in manufacturing. Unemployment fell from 3.3m to 1.8m. The poor business prospects in the previous decade had left Britain bereft of sufficient investment in the most modern technologies. Now the ground was quickly made up, with new industrial capacity employing the latest improvements, as indeed was also happening in Germany. Nor was inflation a problem. Contrary to all the conventional wisdom, the price level fell heavily, partly reflecting the slump in world prices, until 1933 after which it began a slow rise. The British economy grew faster during the five years between 1932 and 1937 than for any other five-year period in its history, showing clearly how effective a radical expansionist policy could be, against the most unpromising background.

Towards the end of the 1930s, the growth in the British economy began to slacken off, despite increased expenditure on armaments, a delayed response to the German threat. The reason was a further round of exchange rate changes. The Americans had devalued the dollar by 41% in 1934. In 1936 they were followed by the gold bloc countries, France, Switzerland, Belgium and the Netherlands, which had hitherto been in the doldrums with low growth and high levels of unemployment. Incredibly, in the light of the experience of the previous few years, instead of devaluing with them to keep sterling competitive, the British agreed to support the new currency alignments with the Exchange Equalisation Account. The competitiveness which had enabled the British economy to recover so quickly and so unexpectedly from the slump was thereby thrown away. In 1948, the Economic Commission for Europe estimated that sterling was as overvalued in 1938 as it had been in 1929.

The French experience over the period of the 1930s was the mirror image of that of Britain. Until 1936 when, under the Popular Front government of Leon Blum, deflationary policies were at last abated, France, along with the other gold bloc countries, stayed on the Gold Exchange Standard, refused to devalue, depressing the economy further and further, and reaping the inevitable consequences. The French GDP dropped steadily in real terms almost every year from 1930 to 1936, falling a total of 17% over these six years. Industrial production fell by a quarter. Investment slumped. Unemployment rose continually.

French crude steel production fell from 9.7m in 1929 to 6.1m tons in 1938. In Germany, over the same period, it rose from 16.2m tons in 1929 to 22.7m tons. France produced 254 000 cars and commercial vehicles in 1929, and 227 000 in 1938, while vehicle production in Germany increased from 128 000 to 338 000. British crude steel production rose from 9.8m tons in 1929 to 10.6m in 1938, while vehicle output went up from 239 000 to 445 000. These figures show with crystal clarity how much the French economy weakened compared to that of Britain and particularly Germany over this critical period. The results of the war battles of 1940 were very largely determined by the economic policies pursued by the three main protagonists during the previous decade.

Much the most significant contrast between the three largest economies in Europe in the 1930s was the relatively successful results, at least in economic terms, achieved by Germany and Britain, and the disastrously poor outcome in France and the other gold bloc countries. These lessons are still highly material today. The problem with the European Union in the 1990s is that it has reverted back to the same policies pursued with such relentless and misguided determination by the French sixty years ago. The difference in experience between France, Britain and Germany is extremely striking. Then, as now, it was not financial rectitude which turned out to be the answer to low growth, high unemployment, and overburdened public finances. The solution was expansion. The ultimate disaster for Europe in the 1930s was that it was the non-democratic, Nazi régime which chose the mixture of economic policies which worked best, while most of the European democracies ploughed on into stagnation and decline.

The really interesting exemplar is the British experience, at least until 1936. Thereafter, reverting to type, the huge advantage of a competitive exchange rate, rapid growth and falling unemployment enjoyed by Britain for the first half of the 1930s was gratuitously thrown away. 1931 to 1936, however, showed what could be done by a democracy faced with daunting economic problems, when the right policies were chosen. Expanding the money supply, reducing interest rates, and making the necessary exchange rate adjustments were the key to success. Creating conditions where exports could boom, the home market could be recaptured from foreign suppliers, and where industry could flourish, all had an enormously positive impact on the country's economic performance. There are very important lessons to be learnt from this period, highly relevant to Western Europe's condition as the millennium moves to its close.

RECOVERY POST-WORLD WAR II

World War II was an even worse disaster for Europe in terms of loss of life and material destruction than World War I. Many more people were killed as a result of hostilities, and the increased destructiveness of the weapons used, particularly those involved with aerial bombardment, caused far more damage to roads, railways, houses and factories.

Of the major European economies, Germany was by far the worst affected. Constant bombing by day and night for the last half of the war had reduced most German cities to ruins. Coal production, which had totalled 400m tons in 1939, fell to just under 60m tons in 1945. Crude steel production, which had been nearly 24m tons in 1939, fell to almost nothing by the end of the war. The currency collapsed again, and many transactions were conducted by barter, or by using cigarettes as a temporary substitute for money.

When the war finished, Germany was divided into four zones by the allied powers. Although the American, British and French zones were soon amalgamated, the Russian zone remained separated from the rest of the German economy, adding to the dislocation. The German boundaries were redrawn, and large tracts of land to the east became parts of other countries, triggering a vast migration of German-speaking people to the west. During the period immediately after the war, not only was there a desperate scarcity of industrial raw materials of all kinds, but there was also a very serious food shortage. The German standard of living plummeted to a small fraction of its pre-war level, as the German people eked out a living as best they could amid their shattered country.

France too suffered severely during the war, but not as badly as Germany. The French GDP fell 17% in real terms between 1938 and 1946, and industrial production by about the same amount. Britain did a good deal better. British industrial output grew by about 5% between 1938 and 1946, while total GDP rose 16%. Paradoxically, however, the British emerged from the war in many ways much worse prepared for the peace than the continental countries, almost all of which had suffered defeat at some stage during the preceding years. Britain's world pretensions were still intact, whereas those of the continental countries were greatly reduced. Germany, in particular, was allowed no more than token defence forces, whereas the British still had millions under arms deployed all over the world. Britain had also run up substantial debts with supplier countries during the war, despite the large quantities of materiel provided by the US, though much of this was shipped across the Atlantic without payment being required. Although major quantities of British foreign investments had been sold during the war to pay for supplies, large debts remained. Paying off the so-called sterling balances was a major commitment for Britain, unmatched by any comparable obligations undertaken by the Germans or French.

The post-World War II settlement for Europe, after some initial aberrations, was generally a great deal more reasonable and considerate than the provisions of the Versailles Treaty after World War I. The Americans, in particular, showed outstanding generosity with Marshall Aid, peaking at 3% of US GDP, pouring into all the economies of Western Europe, underpinning the recovery which was beginning to take place. Currency reform in Germany in the summer of 1948 was followed by a substantial, and as it turned out, largely unnecessary 20% devaluation in 1949. In the same year, an excellent harvest did much to solve the food shortage, suddenly leaving West Germany in an extraordinarily competitive position. Even though manufacturing output in 1948 was still at only half its pre-war level, and output per head was even lower as a result of the large influx of refugees from the east, over the next fifteen months manufacturing output rose 57% to 87% of the 1936 level. Exports more than doubled from 19% to 43% of the pre-war figure.

The French economy also emerged from the immediate post-war period in a much more competitive position than it had been in before the war, and began to surge ahead. Starting from a higher base than the Germans, increases in output were still impressive. The French economy grew by 42% between 1946 and 1950, and while some of this increase reflected recovery from the dislocations of the war years, much of the rest of it resulted from heavy investment in new industrial facilities, triggered off, as in Germany, by rapidly rising exports and home demand. In Italy and the Benelux countries, too, there was a much swifter recovery from the war than had been predicted. Growth in exports and industrial output surged ahead, as all the erstwhile devastated economies in Europe began to recover much more quickly than the British and Americans had thought they would. By contrast, the British economy, whose wartime gross domestic product peaked in 1943, did not regain this output level until ten years later in 1953, while the US 1944 wartime peak was not reached again until 1951.

The British, in particular, were left heavily exposed by the rapidly increasing competitiveness of the continental economies, combined with war debts, worldwide defence obligations, and major commitments on the domestic front to the creation of the welfare state by the Labour government elected in 1945. The loss of income from foreign investments, caused by sales of assets to pay for war supplies, meant that Britain had to cover a much higher proportion of its import costs than previously by export sales. This proved to be an impossible task during the early years after the war, despite strenuous efforts by the government. Britain was caught in a double pincer. On the one hand, there was a big dollar gap, caused by a major balance of payments deficit between Britain and the USA. On the other hand, British exports were unable to hold their own against competition from the reviving export industries of Europe. The British dollar gap problem was largely solved by the devaluation of sterling in 1949 from $4.03 to $2.80, but as much of the rest of Europe devalued at the same time, the continental economies retained their competitive edge *vis à vis* British exporters.

The British problem was worsened by the outbreak of the Korean War in June 1950. British efforts to maintain its coveted, if mostly illusory, special relationship with the United States led to Britain embarking on a major rearmament drive, pre-empting industrial resources away from export markets, and adding to inflationary pressures. The economies on the continent of Western Europe, on the contrary, were largely immune from these commitments, and continued to expand both their domestic and export markets.

The continental European economies were thus poised for the enormous expansion in output which they achieved in the 1950s. Driven by highly competitive exports, and aided by high levels of investment and modest rates of inflation, between 1950 and 1960, the French economy grew by 56%, the Italian by 80% and the West German by 115%. The British achieved a much more modest 30%. France's industrial output over the same period grew by 89%, Italy's by 131%, and West Germany's by 148%, while Britain's grew by only 28%. Significantly, this was a lower percentage than the growth in the British economy as a whole, presaging problems which would be shared by the other more successful economies in future decades.

The results of the differential performance of the major economies in Europe during the 1950s was a massive shift in their relative rankings, reflected in share of world trade, income per head, and not least, in self-esteem and self-confidence. Britain, which in 1945 had seemed to be much the most successful country in Europe, gradually began to have increasing doubts about its economic strength and its military and diplomatic position in the world. The continental economies, on the other hand, began to see each other in an increasingly favourable light, as the traumas of World War II faded in peoples' memories.

Discussions about some sharing of transnational sovereignty had started early after the end of the war, culminating in the Treaty of Paris in 1951 which established the European Coal and Steel Community. Now seemed the time to embark on a more substantial and far-reaching venture. The Messina Conference was held in 1955. From it emerged the Treaty of Rome, signed in 1957, setting up the Common Market which came into existence, along with a number of other Community organisations, on 1 January 1958.

THE COMMON MARKET

The European Coal and Steel Community was the first major consequence of the vision of Jean Monnet and his associates of a Europe not only at peace with itself, but bound together by increasingly integrationist and federal arrangements. From the beginning, it was made clear that the intention was not just to link the countries of Europe together by expanding the commercial bonds between them, but to build supra-national political structures which might eventually become the framework for a United States of Europe.

These ideas received a ready hearing, particularly in the countries on the continent of Europe which were recovering so successfully from World War II. Almost everyone wanted to bury the enmities which, within the living memory of most of Europe's leaders, had led to the two world wars. Despite the deep ideological divides World War II had generated, there was a widespread feeling that European countries had a great deal in common. They were the inheritors and guardians of a common culture, and ought to bind themselves more closely together to cherish and look after it. The rise in power of the United States and the Soviet Union, and the divisions of Europe into East and West, made it look prudent to create a European polity as a counter-balance to the other superpowers. Furthermore, despite the successful rate at which the continental West European economies were growing, they were still divided from each other by remarkably high tariff barriers. Most of these countries had long histories of protectionism, but there were powerful arguments in favour of freer trade, with the creation of a customs union as a first step towards closer integration.

There were also further reasons why particular countries were keen to integrate themselves more closely together with others of like mind. Germany still had recent memories of the Nazi period, and had a strong desire – still evident today – to subsume its identity and nationhood as much as possible in a wider European federation. France, with memories of three German invasions in a little over seventy years, still harboured understandable fears of its powerful eastern neighbour, and had good reasons to bind Germany into a new peaceful relationship. The Benelux countries had always been close to the French and German heartlands. Italy, like Spain, Greece and Portugal a generation later, also had a political legacy to live down, and wished strongly to associate itself with its more prosperous northern neighbours, with their post-war democratic credentials.

Britain was offered membership of the European Coal and Steel Community but rejected it. The ECSC was set up to support production, research and development and the restructuring needs of the coal and steel industries in the countries which came together to form it – the same six countries as subsequently came together to form the Common Market. It fulfilled its function as a supra-national body, exhibiting for the first time the willingness of the participating states to give up some sovereignty for a common purpose, but in other ways it was less successful. The ECSC was essentially a cartel, whose primary function was to keep prices up to assist its members. Like all such cartels, the benefits to its constituents in enhanced revenues were clear enough. The cost to everyone else in the six countries covered by ECSC, in the form of higher prices for coal and steel than might otherwise have prevailed, were not so obvious. The benefits to the coal and steel industries were bought at the expense of all their customers, some of whom, competing in international markets, were severely disadvantaged by higher raw material and energy costs.

Nevertheless, the experiment with ECSC was sufficiently promising to encourage the participating countries to convene the Messina Conference in 1955. The main agenda was to consider integration on a more comprehensive scale. The outcome was the Treaty of Rome, signed in 1957, which brought the Common Market into being on 1 January 1958. The Treaty's immediate objective was to establish a customs union. It was clear from the beginning, however, that the signatories regarded this as only a start to a process which was expected to go much further. The preamble to the Treaty spoke of those establishing the customs union being 'determined to establish the foundations of an ever closer union among the European peoples'. There is no doubt that many of those involved saw the Treaty of Rome as the first step towards a much larger political goal.

Britain, much the largest and most important European economy not included among the original Six, was asked to participate at Messina. The British delegate attended the conference proceedings as an observer, and duly reported his findings back to London. The British, still sufficiently confident in their world role, the Commonwealth and their supposed special relationship with the Americans, declined to join the new organisation. An alternative British proposal, to set up an industrial free trade area in Europe without the political overtones of the Common Market and without the Common Agricultural Policy régime, was decisively rejected by the Common Market founders. They were not interested in just an economic union, As with so many of the decisions taken in Europe, which shaped the way the European Community developed, Britain's rejection of membership was also taken almost entirely on political grounds, with little thought to the economic consequences. In this respect the British mirrored their counterparts in Germany, France, Italy and the Benelux countries. The motivation for setting up the Common Market was almost entirely political, as was Britain's refusal to join. In both cases, the economic arguments were treated as secondary and subordinate – a potent precedent for the future.

In fact the case for setting up a customs union in Europe was never as clear cut as its proponents claimed it was. Nevertheless, a plausible justification could be made out for it, on the grounds that the conditions required for the advantages to outweigh the disadvantages were probably, on balance, fulfilled. The arguments for and against customs unions are well rehearsed in economic literature. Essentially they turn on whether more is to be gained through trade creation within the union than is lost by trade diversion away from cheaper and more efficient suppliers who, because of the union's external tariff, can no longer compete. The proponents of customs unions generally advance two arguments. The first is that the trade creation gains will outweigh the trade diversion losses. The second is that the extra margin of competitiveness generated by a larger market will increase the average growth rate of all the participants, thus producing positive dynamic as well as static benefits.

Critics of customs unions, on the other hand, point to the fact that even if there is an overall gain from trade creation, this may be unevenly spread among the participants. Severe losses among the losers may be more important than the gains to the winners. Furthermore, even if there are gains from trade creation, they tend to be relatively small in relation to the increase in output to be achieved from a high overall growth rate. Trade creation gains of the kind envisaged by the establishment of the Common Market tend, at best, to be one off, and only of the order of 2% of GDP. This equates to the benefit of only four months' increase in output in economies growing at 6% per annum. Critics also tend to be sceptical of the claims that customs unions will necessarily increase the growth rate. They acknowledge that this may happen if all the countries comprising the customs union benefit more or less equally from its establishment. If, however, some members are in a weaker competitive position than others, they may well find that the increased competition will run them into balance of payments problems, triggering deflationary measures which might otherwise not have been necessary. This will bring down their growth rate, and the resulting reduction in overall demand within the union may end up by decreasing rather than increasing the rate of growth in the union as a whole.

Furthermore, the Treaty of Rome did not just establish a customs union. It also set up a number of other subsidiary organisations, of which much the most significant was the Common Agricultural Policy. The CAP was intended partly to deal with the problems of transition away from the high dependence of most European economies on employment in agriculture even as late as the mid-1950s. It was also charged with ensuring the maintenance of reasonable consumer prices for agricultural products, as well as continuity of supply. In addition, it was part of a deal between France and Germany. France was only willing to provide duty free access to German goods in its heavily protected market if French agriculture was protected from world competition.

Agricultural support policies have always been prone to problems. The CAP was certainly successful in producing sufficient food for the Common Market. Indeed, it produced chronic surpluses which have been expensive to store and to dispose of through sales outside the Community. Dumping food surpluses on the world market has depressed world food prices, and reduced agricultural output in countries which badly needed to encourage it. The high price CAP régime, which is also particularly prone to fraud, has led to food costs in the Community generally being considerably higher than they needed to have been compared to costs elsewhere in the world. The major beneficiaries from the CAP have not been small-scale farmers but large-scale agri-businesses, while the flow of funds between Community countries as a result of the CAP has done little to even up overall income disparities. Major beneficiaries have been rich countries such as the Netherlands and Denmark. The CAP, therefore, from its early days, has continued to be a wasteful and expensive way of producing food, and a heavy burden on the countries of the Community. Perhaps the most important single consequence of the CAP, however, has flowed from the difficulties caused to its operation by exchange rate changes. These have led to the problems in managing the CAP generating strong pressure for currency stability, notwithstanding the impact that locking currencies together has had on destabilising Community economies on a much wider scale, as we shall see.

The Treaty of Rome stipulated that the tariffs between the economies of the Common Market at the beginning were to fall to zero over a transitional period of ten years, starting in 1959 and ending in 1969, while a Common External Tariff was established. In fact, the abolition of internal tariffs was completed eighteen months ahead of schedule in 1968. In the light of the conflicting arguments about the benefits of customs unions, the best test ought to be the growth rates of the constituent Six for the period before and after its establishment. Table 2.1 shows the comparative figures for the seven-year period prior to the start of the Common Market, and for the same number of years after it came into being.

There was a small fall in the growth rate for all the Six countries taken together. Most did better in the earlier than the later period, at the expense of the German annual average growth rate, which fell from 8.6% to 5.8%. Yet the most significant major influence on the relative competitiveness of the Six over the fifteen years covered by the figures were the double devaluations of the French franc at the end of the 1950s. These reduced the parity of the franc against the Deutsche Mark by a quarter, following five smaller devaluations of the franc which had taken place since 1949, evening up the competitiveness of the French and German economies. Thus the early success of the Common Market can be traced to a significant extent to the exchange rate flexibility which enabled all the constituent countries to grow at similar rates. They each preserved a broadly equal level of competitiveness, without some countries running into balance of payments problems *vis à vis* others. Maintaining these conditions was one of the vital keys that was thrown away in the 1970s, when attempts began to be made to lock Community currency parities together.

Table 2.1: Growth in the Original Member Countries of the Common Market for the Seven Years Before and After its Establishment in 1958

	1950–7		1958–64	
	Total	Per Year	Total	Per Year
France	38%	4.8%	46%	5.5%
Germany	78%	8.6%	48%	5.8%
Italy	53%	6.2%	49%	5.9%
Belgium & Luxembourg	24%	3.1%	39%	4.8%
The Netherlands	38%	4.8%	44%	5.3%
Average of the Original Six Countries	54%	6.3%	47%	5.7%

Source: Derived from OECD National Accounts.

During the same periods as those in the table above, the British economy had grown respectively by 20% and 29%, with average annual growth rates over each of the two periods of 2.6% and 3.7%, about half the average achieved by the Six. The contrast between the performance of the British economy and the Common Market countries was all too striking, provoking the first application for membership by Britain in 1961. This was rebuffed by Charles de Gaulle in 1962. A second British application in 1967 fared no better with the General, whose distrust of British attitudes and intentions remained undiminished.

The logic, as opposed to the emotion, behind Britain's membership application was, however, not easy to follow. It was widely assumed that by joining a union of fast-growing countries, Britain's growth rate would automatically be lifted to something closer to the average of those to whom it was attaching itself. Exactly how or why this should happen was not explained. Critics of Britain's application remained concerned that the root problem behind Britain's slow growth rate, which was its lack of competitiveness, would be exacerbated rather than improved by exposing Britain to more competition inside the customs union. Between 1963 and 1973, the total Common Market GDP rose by 58%, a cumulative annual growth rate of 4.7%, whereas the British GDP, protected by significant tariffs, had grown by only 39%, or 3.3% per annum. These sceptical arguments failed to win the day, however, leading to the third, and this time successful membership application by Britain in 1970. The European Free Trade Area, comprising Britain, Switzerland, Denmark, Sweden, Finland, Austria and Norway, established in 1960, had failed to provide the dynamism which Britain sought.

Britain became a Community member at the beginning of 1973, bringing in with it Ireland and Denmark, both major British trading partners, but not Norway which opted to remain outside the Community.

Up to 1973, therefore, the Common Market had been able to maintain most of the momentum established during the post-World War II recovery period. The growth rate had slowed a little since 1957, but not much. Unemployment throughout the years to 1973 was very low, averaging little more than 2% over the whole period in all Common Market countries. Inflation varied somewhat from country to country in the Community, but was maintained at an average of about 3%. Pride in the achievements of the last quarter of a century was understandable and considerable. An enormous increase in wealth and living standards had been accomplished. At the same time, generous welfare systems had been established, progress had been made towards making post-tax income distribution more equal, vast improvements had been made in housing and education, and political stability seemed assured. Few people, therefore, foresaw the scale and nature of the problems which were about to unfold.

3   What Went Wrong?

'Facts do not cease to exist because they are ignored.'
                                                    Aldous Huxley

During the period from its establishment in 1958 until 1973, the average rate
of growth among the Common Market countries was 5.1%, the average level
of unemployment was little more than 2%, and the average rate of inflation
was 3.9%. For the twenty years from 1973 to 1993 the growth rate averaged
2.1%, and the inflation rate 7.0%. The rate of unemployment fluctuated over
the period, but overall it has been on a remorselessly upward trend. The
average registered unemployment across the whole of the European Union
in November 1996 was 10.9%, a more than fivefold increase. Even then, the
claimant count, which this figure represents, substantially underestimates the
total number of people who would like to work if they had the opportunity
to do so at a reasonable wage. What went wrong?

If the whole world had plunged to a much lower growth rate after 1973,
it would be plausible to argue that Europe was part of a universal trend. It
is not, however, the case, that the world growth rate has fallen dramatically
since 1973, although it has been lower since 1973 than it was before, 3.2%
compared to 4.9%. This reduction is partly accounted for, however, by the
reduction in the EU growth rate, which is a significant proportion of the world
total. While some parts of the world, particularly much of Africa and the
erstwhile Soviet Union have done very badly over the recent past, their weight
in world GDP is comparatively small. Other parts of the world economy,
particularly countries in the Far East have done very much better, and some
of these economies are now large enough to represent a significant proportion
of world GDP. Excluding EU countries, the growth in world output has
maintained an average rate of 3.9% per annum since 1950.

In the case of the Soviet Union, it is easy to point to the reasons for the
fall in GDP which followed the collapse of the communist régime. Unwinding
the distortions and inefficiencies of the Soviet command economy, combined
with the political instability once communist rule came to an end, between
them provide a clear explanation why the GDP was likely to fall substantially
before it started to grow again. In some underdeveloped countries, high
birth rates, corruption, poor infrastructure, low educational standards and,
for a significant proportion of the population, unfamiliarity with the market
economy, provide convincing explanations why they have had difficulties
competing in the world. It is not surprising that their growth rates have been

low, and sometimes negative. The countries of the European Union, however, do not suffer to a significant degree from any of these problems.

On the contrary, the EU economies appear to be blessed with almost every imaginable advantage to enable them to compete exceptionally successfully. Most of them went into the period after 1973 with a record behind them of high growth, high net investment, and low inflation. For decades on end they were at peace, with low military outlays, protected through NATO by the United States. Their workforces were exceptionally well educated. All were stable democracies, with, in most cases, and on a world scale, comparatively minor problems of venality and corruption. The Community countries ought, it therefore appeared, to have been much better placed than most to weather the economic difficulties thrown up by the 1970s. The records clearly show, however, that they did so exceptionally badly.

Nor, unfortunately, is there any sign at present that there is likely to be a major change for the better. Expectations for the future, which were so bright a quarter of a century ago, have been heavily scaled down. Growth rates for EU economies of 2% or 3% are regarded nowadays as being about as good as can reasonably be expected, especially over more than a year or two. On the jobs front, there is very little talk of reducing unemployment significantly, and even less expectation that a change for the better will actually materialise. On the contrary, there is a widespread concern that the number of jobless will go on rising remorselessly, perhaps considerably more rapidly than it has in the past. Inflation rates in all EU countries are much lower than they were in the 1970s and 1980s, but fear that they may rise even a little more rapidly than at present has become something of an obsession.

Is it inevitable that these trends should have emerged? The rest of this chapter traces the history of developments in the European Union since 1973, as a backdrop to the prescriptions which follow. Subsequent chapters set out ideas about the process of economic growth, the causes of and solutions to unemployment, and the impact that these might have on inflation rates. The aim is to show what could be done to bring the EU economies back to the levels of performance most of them achieved in the 1950s and 1960s. The conclusion reached is that realistic policy options are available, which could reproduce the accomplishments of these earlier much more successful periods. They do not involve abandoning any of the practical and desirable ways in which the countries of the EU clearly need to co-operate with each other. They are not, however, compatible with the range of plans for the EU's future enshrined in the Maastricht Treaty. Significant changes in direction are going to be needed if the EU is to revert to growth rates of 5% or 6% per annum, in conditions of full employment with a sustainably low rate of inflation. The programme this book sets out shows how it could be done.

OIL, MONETARISM AND EXCHANGE RATES

Three major developments were responsible for the substantial sea change to the fortunes of the Community economies in the 1970s. The first was the oil crisis, caused by OPEC's quadrupling of the price of crude oil, following the breakdown of the Bretton Woods system and the 1973 Yom Kippur War. The second was the change in intellectual fashion towards a much harder line version of economic theory and doctrine, as monetarist ideas replaced Keynesian thinking among large sections of those responsible for running economic policy in the Community countries. The third was the political initiatives taken within the Community, intended to lead to closer integration by linking the currencies of the constituent economies together first of all in the Currency Snake, then the Exchange Rate Mechanism, and now with proposals for full-blown Monetary Union. All these three developments were reflected in changes to the institutions and the power structure within the Community which reinforced their influence on events, unfortunately in ways which turned out to be exceptionally damaging.

The oil crisis had its origin in the pressure put on the American economy by the Vietnam War. Even for the powerful US economy, the extensive hostilities in Vietnam were extremely expensive, despite the poverty and lack of resources of the enemy that the Americans were fighting. President Johnson, a long-standing big government Democrat, did not want the Vietnam War to hold up implementation of the Great Society programme on which he had been elected. This involved extensive increases to government outlays on welfare, education and other social objectives. Financing both the Vietnam War and the Great Society programme together, however, would have involved increases in taxation which it was judged that the American electorate would have found hard to bear. In consequence, much of the combined extra cost was financed not by increases in taxation but by borrowing. Much of the borrowing, in turn, was done from within the banking system rather than from outside it, and was not therefore matched by any genuine saving. The impact of the resulting increased demand on the American economy, which was already operating at close to full stretch, was to increase the US rate of inflation substantially, and to worsen the trade balance. By the beginning of the 1970s the US, which for decades had run a substantial trade surplus, was moving into deficit.

Part of the problem for the Americans was the reserve role for the world economy which the dollar fulfilled, underpinning the Bretton Woods agreements, reached shortly after World War II to provide currency stability. President Nixon, now in the White House, nevertheless decided that it was impossible to continue with the dollar linked to gold at its then current valuation. At the 1971 Smithsonian Conference, the dollar was therefore devalued. The consequence was to break up the Bretton Woods arrangements, leaving exchange rates without the anchor which they had previously enjoyed. The world's currencies began to float against each other.

Partly because of the unaccustomed freedom from the constraint of having to hold the value of each country's currency against the dollar, within a short period after the end of Bretton Woods, a major world boom developed. The world's money supply increased dramatically, fuelled in significant measure by a large increase in the volume of Euro-dollars available, stemming from the US balance of payments deficit. Commodity prices started to rise very rapidly. Many of them doubled and trebled. Inflationary pressures built up. As this was happening, Israel and the surrounding Arab states went to war. The result was a triumphant victory for the Israelis, but the price for the West was further alienation of the Arab countries responsible for producing most of the West's oil supplies. Seizing their opportunity to obtain a much higher price for their oil, the OPEC countries increased the price of crude petroleum from about $2.50 to $10 a barrel.

The effect of this price change on the economies of Europe, none of which at that time was producing any significant quantity of oil, was to shift about 2% of their GDPs away from their own populations to those of the oil exporting countries. With good management, and a well co-ordinated response, this should not have been an impossibly difficult situation to contain. The problem was that the oil shock came on top of other causes of instability, including, in some countries, a crisis in the banking system as the boom broke, and in all countries the main strain was taken on the balance of payments. The result was that everyone reined in at once, trying to shift the trade balance problems elsewhere. Growth rates fell back sharply as deflationary policies were implemented everywhere. Indeed the economies then comprising the Common Market collectively contracted by about 1% in 1975, before resuming a much slower growth trajectory than had previously prevailed.

If the real world events of the oil price hike and the breaking boom were the immediate causes of the deflationary policies which checked Community growth in the mid-1970s, the willingness of the authorities to persevere with them was greatly reinforced by the spread of monetarist doctrines. The second major change was the conversion of so many people in influential positions to monetarism. This was partly a reaction against the Keynesian approach to economic policy, which had not worked as well as many had hoped it would, particularly in the Anglo-Saxon countries of Britain and the US. Both had failed to achieve growth rates comparable with those of the more successful economies, including many on the continent of Europe as well as Japan. Monetarist ideas became fashionable, however, in many other countries apart from Britain and the US. They appeared to offer everywhere to those in charge of economic policy an alternative series of policy anchors at a time when the guideposts which had served most countries so well in the 1950s and 1960s seemed to have been swept away. The credit creation and inflationary excesses of the early 1970s provided the circumstances in which a policy framework of monetary restraint appeared to warrant careful consideration. In particular, there was a pressing need to bring inflation down from the dangerous heights to which it had risen in some countries during the mid-1970s. Britain's year on year inflation peaked at 24%, France's at 14%, Italy's at 19%, and Germany's at a much more modest 7%.

Monetarist ideas had a particularly strong appeal in certain powerful quarters. The Bundesbank had always had a strong anti-inflation tradition, harking back to the German hyperinflation of 1923. Understandably it welcomed ideas which reinforced its collective view of monetary priorities. Nearly all Europe's central bankers followed the highly respected Bundesbank's lead. Monetarist ideas also became very much the fashion in academic circles, and these convictions were reflected in the tone of an endless succession of newspaper articles, popularising monetarist ideas to a wider audience. No-one should underestimate the power of ideas, well founded or not, to become the conventional wisdom, accepted as though unchallengeable. Despite its intellectual weaknesses, which were apparent from the beginning, monetarist ideas were extraordinarily successful in implanting themselves right across Western Europe as the norm which few people were willing to challenge.

The third and major influence on Community policies over the last quarter of a century has been the drive to achieve further integration by locking the Community currencies together. The most significant characteristic of these efforts has been that they have been initiated almost entirely from political rather than economic motives. There is a case for monetary unions, but both theory and practice show that they only work to the general advantage if a number of conditions are fulfilled. Careful analysis as to whether the states comprising the Community and later the EU met these criteria, and were likely to continue doing so, was, however, almost entirely absent from any of the major pronouncements made by Community leaders about the need for moves towards monetary union. On the contrary, proposals for such developments were almost invariably initiated in high-flown declarations about the destiny of Europe. Hard-headed economic analysis was relegated to a secondary and subordinate role. The pressure for producing the best economic case which could be made to buttress political positions which had already been taken up then became overwhelming. Attempts to lock the currencies together were seen primarily as highly significant political initiatives, designed to move towards the 'ever closer union' envisaged in the Treaty of Rome. Good politics was assumed to be good economics – a fatally flawed presupposition.

The result has been that all the effort put into considering the economic implications of EMU by the EU authorities has been heavily skewed towards justifying a political position which had already been adopted, rather than considering with an open mind whether the economic arguments for monetary union stood up to scrutiny on their own merits. A great bandwagon has been rolling for a quarter of a century in favour of moves towards a Single Currency with remarkably little dispassionate official analysis of the likely consequences. In fact, the case for monetary union, in the context of the European Communities, has always been a weak one. This is exemplified by the slow growth rate and increasing unemployment problems in Europe while attempts to implement it have been pursued through the Snake, the European Monetary System and the Exchange Rate Mechanism.

Far from promoting prosperity within the Community, the evidence shows all too clearly that attempts to lock the currencies together over the years have been very damaging. They have reinforced all the deflationary policies which have been the bane of the Community ever since the mid-1970s. They have exacerbated the trends towards higher and higher levels of unemployment across the Union. Nor have they been successful even in their own terms. All the efforts so far to fix exchange rates in the EU have ended in failure. Unfortunately, and for fundamentally the same reasons, even if the Single Currency comes into being over the next few years, it too will very probably come to grief, breaking up on much the same set of economic rocks as its precursors have done. This is only likely to happen, however, after a further lengthy period of slow growth and rising unemployment within the EU economies. The EU urgently needs to consider alternatives to this prospect as its future.

MONETARISM IN THEORY AND PRACTICE

The appeal of hard money has a long history. Those with established wealth have always been keen that it should earn a high return. High rates of interest and low rates of inflation have an obvious appeal to them, a view of the world almost invariably shared by those with a banking background. A sense of prudence militates against deficit financing and easy money. Making life easy for manufacturers and exporters by having low interest and exchange rates and plentiful credit somehow seems a less obvious way to encourage their operations than submitting them to the rigours and discipline of a much less accommodating economic environment.

Nor is it just the well off who are inclined to favour the financial environment which monetarist policies generate. Many poorer people, particularly pensioners on fixed incomes, favour high interest rates, and therefore the relative scarcity of money which is necessary to ensure that high interest rates can prevail. A high exchange rate, which runs with high interest rates and a restrictive monetary policy, provides the benefit of cheap imports and holidays abroad, reinforcing the widely held perception that people should be proud of their currency if it has a reputation for being strong rather than weak.

Predilections of this sort were therefore widely prevalent before monetarist orthodoxies became fashionable. The change in intellectual view which occurred was the result of a number of important works, not least those of Professor Hayek, who had always opposed the Keynesian revolution. Monetarist ideas, in their standard form, would not have become accepted as widely as they were, however, without the theoretical and statistical underpinning provided by Milton Friedman and his associate, Anna Jacobson Schwartz, in their seminal book, *A Monetary History of the United States, 1867–1960*. In this book, they made three important claims which had a major impact on economic thinking all over the world. First, they said that there is a clear association between the total amount of money in circulation and changes in money incomes and prices, but not economic activity until approximately two years later. Changes in the money supply therefore affect the price level, but not, except perhaps for a short period of time, the level of output in the real economy. Second, these relationships have proved to be stable over a long period. Third, changes, and particularly increases in the money supply, have generally occurred as a result of events which were independent of the needs of the economy. In consequence they add to inflation without increasing economic activity.

The attractive simplicity of these propositions is easily recognised. The essence of the monetarist case is that increases in prices and wages can be held in check by nothing more complicated that the apparently simple process of controlling the amount of money in circulation. Ideally, a condition of zero inflation is achieved when the increase in the money supply equals the rise in output in the economy. Since both wage and price increase can only occur if extra money to finance them is made available, no rises in either wages or prices will take place if no more money is provided. Thus as long as the government is seen to be giving sufficient priority to controlling the money supply, everyone will realise that it is in his or her interest to exercise restraint, reducing the rate of inflation to whatever level is deemed acceptable.

These ideas have been summarised in the following words by an eminent economist, Professor Sayers, in the following terms:

> First, past rates of growth in the stock of money are major determinants of the growth of Gross National Product in terms of current prices. It follows from this that fiscal policies do not significantly affect GNP in money terms, though they may alter its composition and also affect interest rates. The overall impact on GNP in money terms of monetary and financial policies is for practical purposes summed up in the movements of a single variable, the stock of money. Consequently, monetary policy should be exclusively guided by this variable, without regard to interest rates, credit flows, free reserves or other indicators.
>
> Second, nominal interest rates are geared to inflationary expectations and thus, with a time lag, to actual inflation. Although the immediate market impact of expansionary monetary policy may be to lower interest rates, it is fairly soon reversed when premiums for the resulting inflation are added to interest rates.
>
> Third, the central bank can, and should, make the money stock grow at a steady rate equal to the rate of growth of potential GNP plus a target rate for inflation.
>
> Fourth, there is no enduring trade-off between unemployment and inflation. There is, rather, a unique rate of unemployment for each economy which allows for structural change and job search, but which cannot be departed from in the long term. Government policy will produce ever-accelerating inflation if it persistently seeks a lower than natural rate of unemployment. If it seeks a higher rate, there will be an ever accelerating deflation. The natural rate of unemployment cannot be identified except through practical experience. It is the rate which will emerge if the proper steady growth policy is pursued.

These prescriptions have attracted much support to the monetarist banner, although it has always been clear that the monetarist case had severe deficiencies. To start with, the theory begged the fundamental question as to what was the appropriate way to measure the money stock when so many different ways of determining it were available. It was, in any event, well known that the ratio between the stock of money, however defined, and the volume of transactions could vary widely, as the so-called 'velocity of circulation' altered. More recently, in addition, it has become widely accepted that the Friedman and Schwartz analysis of the relationship between money and prices in the US was statistically unsound.

As with so much else in economics, there is a major feedback problem with much of the monetarist position, making it difficult to distinguish between cause and effect. It may be true that over a long period the total amount of money in circulation bears a close relationship to the total value of the economy's output. It does not follow, however, that the money supply determines the money value of the GNP and hence the rate of inflation. It may well be, instead, that the total amount of money in circulation is a function of the need for sufficient finance to accommodate transactions. If this is so, then an increase in the money supply may well accompany a rise in inflation caused by some other event, simply to provide this accommodation. It need not necessarily be the cause of rising prices at all.

Common sense tells us that changes in the money supply are only one of a number of relevant factors determining rises or falls in inflation. Monetarists, however, not only reject this proposition, alleging that all alterations in the rate of price increases are caused by changes in the money supply some two years previously. They also claim that the future course of inflation can be guided within narrow limits by controlling the money stock. Empirical evidence demonstrates that this contention is far too precise and greatly overstates the predictive accuracy of monetarist theories.

For this amount of fine tuning to be possible, an unequivocal definition of money is required. It is one thing to recognise a situation where clearly far too much money, or, more accurately, too much credit is being created. Monetarists are right in saying that if credit is so cheap and so readily available that it is easy to speculate on asset inflation, or the economy is getting overheated by excess demand financed by credit creation, then the money supply is too large. This is a broad quantitative judgement. It is quite another matter to state that small changes in the money supply generate correspondingly exact changes in the rate of inflation. Yet this is the claim which monetarists put forward.

This claim is implausible for a number of reasons. One is the difficulty in defining accurately what is money and what is not. Notes and coins are clearly 'money', but where should the line be drawn thereafter? What kinds of bank facilities and money market instruments should also be included or excluded? Many different measures are available in every country, depending on what is put in and what is left out. None of them has been found anywhere to have had a strikingly close correlation with subsequent changes in the rate of inflation. Often, different measures of the money supply move in different directions. This is very damaging evidence against propositions which are supposed to be precise in their formulation and impact.

Another major problem for monetarists, referred to above, is that there can be no constant ratio between the amount of money in circulation, however defined, and the aggregate value of transactions, because the rate at which money circulates can and does vary widely over time. The 'velocity of circulation' is far from constant. It has been exceptionally volatile in Britain, where it rose by 7% between 1964 and 1970, and by a further 28% between 1970 and 1974, only to fall by 26% between 1974 and 1979. Since then it has risen by 82%. The Netherlands and Greece have also had large changes in the velocity of circulation, particularly during the 1970s. Some of these movements were caused by changes in monetary policy, but a substantial proportion, especially recently, have had nothing to do with alterations in government policy. They have been the results of radical changes to the financial environment, caused by the effects of deregulation on credit creation, and the growth of new financial instruments such as derivatives. Variations like this make it impossible to believe in the rigid relationship that monetarism requires. In fact, the statistical record everywhere on the money supply and inflation shows what one would expect if there was very little causation at all at work. Except in extreme circumstances of gross over-creation of money and credit, changes in the money supply have had little or no impact on the rate of inflation. The need to provide enough money to finance all the transactions taking place has, over the long term, proved to be much more important a determinant of the money supply than attempts to restrict it to control inflation, although some countries have certainly had tighter monetary policies than others. In the short term, there is no systematic evidence that changes in the money supply affect subsequent inflation rates with any precision at all.

It is not surprising, therefore, that the predictions of monetarists about future levels of inflation, based on trends in the money supply, have turned out to be no better, and often worse, than those of other people who have used more eclectic, common-sense methods. Monetarists have not kept their predictions, however, solely to the future rate of inflation. There are three other areas of economic policy, as we can see from Professor Sayers' synopsis of their views, where their ideas have had a decisive effect on practical policy over the last quarter of a century. These are to do with unemployment, interest rates and exchange rates.

The monetarist view of unemployment is that there is a 'natural' rate which cannot be avoided, set essentially by supply-side rigidities. Any attempt to reduce unemployment below this level by reflation will necessarily increase wage rates and then the price level. This will leave those in employment no better off than they were before, while the increased demand, having been absorbed by high prices, will result in the same number of people being employed as previously. Increasing demand only pushes up the rate of inflation. It will not increase output of the number of people in work.

At some point, as pressure on the available labour force increases and the number of those unemployed falls, there is no doubt that a bidding up process will take place, and wages and salaries will rise. This is an altogether different matter, however, from postulating that unemployment levels like those currently prevailing across the EU are required to keep inflation at bay. Nor is it plausible that supply-side rigidities are the major constraint on getting unemployment down. There is no evidence that these rigidities are significantly greater than they were in the 1950s and 1960s, and on balance they are almost certainly less. If, during the whole of these two decades, it was possible to combine high rates of economic growth with almost negligible rates of unemployment in Western Europe, while inflation remained stable at an acceptable level, why should we believe that it is impossible now for these conditions to prevail again? One of the unfortunate triumphs of monetarism has been to condition people to tolerating much higher levels of unemployment than would otherwise have been considered economically desirable or politically acceptable.

Monetarism has also had a considerable influence on interest rates. The tight control of the money supply which monetarists advocate can only be achieved if interest rates are used to balance a relatively low supply of money against the demand for credit which has to be choked off by raising the price of money. As we can see from Professor Sayers, however, this requirement is made to seem less harsh by suggesting that a positive rate of interest will always be required to enable lenders to continue providing money to borrowers. It is alleged that any attempt to lower interest rates to encourage expansion will fail as lenders withdraw from the market until the premium they require above the inflation rate reappears.

Yet again, we have a proposition much more strongly based on assertion than on evidence. For years on end, in many countries including all those in Western Europe, real interest rates have been negative, sometimes even before tax. Negative interest rates may well not be fair to lenders who may, and frequently do, complain bitterly when they occur, but there is very little that they can do about it. Their ability to withdraw from the market is generally limited. Shortages of money can in any event always be overcome by the authorities creating more money to replace any which has been withdrawn. It is undoubtedly the case, however, that high positive rates of interest are a discouragement to investment, partly directly, but much more importantly, because of their influence on driving up the exchange rate.

This is particularly paradoxical in relation to the third major impact of monetarist ideas on practical issues, which has been on exchange rate policy.

It is argued that no policy for improving an economy's competitiveness by devaluation will work, because the inflationary effects of devaluing will automatically raise the domestic price level back to where it was in international terms. This will leave the devaluing country with no more competitiveness than it had before, but with a real extra inflationary problem with which it will have to contend.

This proposition is one which it is easy to test against historical experience. There have been large numbers of substantial exchange rate changes over the last few decades, providing plenty of empirical data against which to assess the validity of this monetarist assertion. The evidence is overwhelmingly against it. As we shall see, there is example after example to be found of devaluations showing no sign at all of automatically leading to excess inflation, wiping out all the competitive advantage initially gained. On the contrary, there is ample evidence to indicate that exactly the opposite conclusion should be drawn from experience both in Europe and elsewhere. Devaluing economies tend to perform progressively better, as their manufacturing sectors expand, and the internationally tradable goods and services which they produce become cumulatively more competitive.

Countries which have gained an initial price advantage therefore tend to forge ahead, with increasingly competitive import-saving and exporting sectors. They often, too, experience less domestic inflation that their more sluggish competitors, while rapidly growing productivity and efficiency in the sectors of their economies involved in international trading make them more and more capable of gaining a larger share of world trade. In practice, monetarist policies have had pronounced effects on the exchange rates of the countries where they have been most effectively imposed, but invariably their impact has been to push the exchange rates up. The economies concerned then suffer the worst of all worlds – a mixture of sluggish growth, low increases in output to absorb wage and salary increases, and sometimes higher price inflation than their more favoured competitors.

Monetarist theories start by appearing simple and straightforward, but end by being long on complication and assertion, and short on predictive and practical prescriptive qualities. They pander to the prejudice of those who would like to believe their conclusions. They lack convincing explanations about the transmission mechanisms between what they claim are the causes of economic events, and the effects which they declare will necessarily follow. Where they can be tested against empirical results, the predictions their theories produce generally fail to achieve worthwhile levels of accuracy.

Monetarist theories have nevertheless reinforced everywhere all the prejudices widely held in favour of the cautious financial conservatism, which monetarism so accurately reflects. In practice, monetarist policies are

almost indistinguishable from old-fashioned deflation. By allowing themselves
to be persuaded by these misguided doctrines, far too many of those
responsible for running the EU's affairs have acquiesced in accepting levels
of low growth and high unemployment which they should never have
tolerated.

The result has been that policies which should have been rejected, because
they were failing to work, have continued to be accepted. Because expectations
have been lowered, the deflationary consequences of high interest rates,
restrictive monetary policies and exchange rate rigidities, have not caused
the outcry that might have been expected, and which they deserved. The
population of the EU has been lulled into accepting levels of economic
performance far below those routinely attained elsewhere in the world. If
higher levels of achievement are going to be reached, a much less complacent
attitude is going to be required, to ensure that the changes which are needed
are put in place.

THE SNAKE AND THE EXCHANGE RATE MECHANISM

The first steps towards locking the Community's currencies together were
taken a little over ten years after the Common Market had been established.
In March 1970, the Council of Ministers set up a high-level group to prepare
plans for full economic and monetary union, rather than just a customs
union, among the original six member countries. The chairman was Pierre
Werner, then Prime Minister and Minister of Finance of Luxembourg, who
gave his name to the report which was produced within a few months.

Characteristically, it did not discuss whether monetary union was desirable
or even feasible. Driven, as it was, by a political initiative, summarised at
the time by the French as 'la voie royale vers l'union politique', it left out
any serious analysis of the pros and cons of currency unions, and consideration
of the conditions which might have to be fulfilled for the advantages to
outweigh the disadvantages. Instead, the report concentrated on the two
principal routes which might be chosen to achieve the convergence required
to make monetary union a viable proposition. This involved an uneasy
marriage of Keynesian and monetarist approaches.

The Keynesians believed that there had to be convergence in economic
policies and the performance of the constituent economies first, with monetary
union to follow when these conditions had been established. The monetarists
believed that the best approach was to establish monetary union as quickly
as possible, on the grounds that its creation would itself create the convergence
which would be necessary for its successful operation. In the end the Werner

Group recommended a compromise. There was to be a three-year lead-in period when Keynesian-style policies would be used to achieve convergence, followed by the full rigour of monetary union to complete the process, using monetarist methods.

In March 1971 the Council of Ministers accepted the broad thrust of the Werner Report, and agreed that, as a first step towards its implementation, the exchange rates of the member currencies should be maintained within 0.6% of each other from 15 June 1971 onwards. Significant parts of the Werner proposals, however, were not confirmed. The supra-national concept of a single 'Centre of Decision', specifying and co-ordinating common fiscal and monetary policies was too much for the French. The German response was that if the French were as half-hearted as this in their commitment to the Werner plan, they would not commit themselves to financing the proposed European Reserve Fund beyond an initial trial period. Disagreements of this sort were hardly an auspicious omen.

The start date for the Werner proposals could not have been at a more awkward time, though this is not a good excuse for their subsequent abandonment. In May 1971 the dollar crisis began, leading to the break-up of Bretton Woods at the Smithsonian Conference, and abandonment of the existing IMF exchange rate bands. Major fluctuations in the European rates meant that that the new narrow bands for what came to be called the Snake were difficult to establish. These were the percentage limits either side of the central rate within which exchange rates were allowed to move while still staying in the system. In the end they were finally agreed and implemented in April 1972, with wider fluctuation bands, 1.125% either side of the central parities, than was originally proposed, but still half those of the new IMF 2.25% limits. A European Monetary Co-operation Fund was established, operated by the central banks, to keep market rates within these limits. In view of their impending Community membership, Britain, Denmark and Eire joined the new system, as well as the original Six.

The life of the Snake, however, was short and undistinguished. Speculative fever in the international money markets switched to sterling from the dollar, after its Smithsonian devaluation. Within six weeks of joining, the British authorities were forced to abandon attempts to maintain the agreed parity for the pound, which dropped out of the Snake, taking the Irish punt with it. Six months later, in January 1973, the Italian government abandoned its commitment to keep the lira within the required limits and withdrew. A year later, in January 1974, the French gave up the struggle and followed suit. The franc rejoined the Snake in July 1975, but the second attempt to keep to the agreed parity lasted no longer than the first. In March 1976 it left permanently. In less than four years, therefore, three of the four major

Community currencies had abandoned ship, unable to keep up with the Deutsche Mark. The Snake had been reduced to a Deutsche Mark zone embracing, apart from Germany, only the Benelux countries and Denmark. This first major attempt to bring together all the Community currencies had failed ignominiously. Phase two of the Werner plan, the originally proposed move to Monetary Union, was quietly forgotten.

It might have been thought that lessons would be learnt from this experience, so that similar problems could be avoided in future. It was not a convincing excuse for the failure of the Snake to say that its demise occurred because the time at which its régime was introduced was difficult and turbulent. If the Snake was worth having at all, it could surely be argued that it ought to be more useful in times of stress than in easier conditions. No such conclusions were drawn, however, and no worthwhile wisdom about the practical problems involved in linking Community currencies together was accumulated. On the contrary, within three years, at Summit Meetings in Copenhagen and Bremen, monetary union was back again at the top of the Community agenda. The initiative for this resurgence lay primarily with the Commission's President, Roy (now Lord) Jenkins. As his memoirs, *A Life at the Centre* (Macmillan: London, 1991) make clear, his reasons for relaunching proposals for European Monetary Union bore little relationship to well argued economic analysis. It had everything to do with the politics of the Community, which was perceived to be in the doldrums and in need of a new mission and direction. In his own words (pp. 462–3) 'The Europe of the Community was bogged down at that stage ... A new initiative was therefore manifestly necessary. But what direction should it take? ... I came firmly to the conclusion that the most open axis of advance for the Community in the circumstances of 1977 lay in proclaiming the goal of monetary union.' Careful and realistic consideration of the pros and cons of monetary union, to ensure that there was a reasonable chance that the benefits would outweigh the costs, is, however, lacking in Lord Jenkins' long, discursive and entertaining book.

The main argument put forward for monetary union was that the full benefits of the Community's customs union could not possibly be achieved in an environment of exchange rate instability and uncertainty. It was alleged that fluctuating rates were damaging to trade and steady economic growth. While this may have seemed an appealing argument, there was no evidence that it was true. Indeed a number of studies, including a particularly extensive one carried out by the Bank of England, had shown that exchange rate movements have little, if any, effect on growth rates. The fact that the Common Market countries had been growing up to then at unprecedented rates without having their currencies locked together was totally ignored. It was also alleged that floating exchange rates were inherently inflationary. Again, however, no concrete evidence was ever produced to show that this argument was correct, and as we shall see in Chapter 6, there is ample evidence to show that in most cases it is false. The truth was that the economic arguments put forward for moving again towards monetary union had very little substance. They were scarcely more than a smokescreen for the real reason for the new initiative, which was driven by the perceived political need for closer European integration.

Part of the politics was the appeal which monetary union had for the Germans. The weakness of the dollar meant that the Deutsche Mark had become an attractive haven for loose money. The dangers to the German economy from this were twofold. One was that too many people buying Deutsche Marks would push the exchange rate up, damaging Germany's export competitiveness. Both German industry and the Bundesbank were well aware, at the time, how important a competitive exchange rate was for the German economy. The second was that offsetting these purchases by money market operations would increase the German money supply beyond a safe level, thus potentially rekindling inflationary pressures. The Germans therefore had a substantial interest in binding the other Common Market currencies to the Deutsche Mark, to hold its value down. The combination of Roy Jenkins' and the Commission's requirement for a new initiative, and Helmut Schmidt's and the Bundesbank's need to keep down both the parity of the Deutsche Mark and the German money supply proved irresistible. In 1979, the Snake was reborn as the Exchange Rate Mechanism (ERM), as part of a new European Monetary System (EMS).

There were several new features to the EMS compared to the Snake. First, there was a new unit of account, the ECU, made up of a basket of European currencies, by reference to which the new exchange rate parities were to be calculated. Second, the fluctuation bands, at 2.25%, were wider than had previously been allowed. Third, a much more substantial volume of credit facilities was assembled by the central banks to protect the newly agreed exchange rates. Fourth, it was envisaged that a European Monetary Fund would be created, with which, on a rotating basis, each of the participating central banks had to deposit 20% of its reserves. When it began operations in March 1979, the new EMS therefore had at its disposal a substantially more potent battery of weapons to deploy against the markets than were available at the time of the Snake. In addition, special arrangements were made to help secure the acceptability of the proposed structure to the new, smaller country members of the Community, Greece and Ireland. Extra grants, subsidies and loans on soft terms from the European Investment Bank were made available to them, setting a successful Commission precedent, often to be used in similar circumstances in future.

The first phase of EMS had two main objectives. The primary task was to achieve a high degree of stability in the exchange rates of the participating currencies. The second was to achieve convergence in the performance of the constituent economies. In the light of experience over the next fourteen years, neither was successfully attained. In the decade following its inception, there were no fewer than twelve realignments of one or more of the central rates. Over this period the central rate of the strongest currency, the Deutsche Mark, appreciated by 18%, while the weakest, the lira, fell by 29%. The combined impact of these changes was that the parity of the lira at the end of the decade *vis à vis* the Deutsche Mark was 50% of its value at the beginning. The effect of the ERM was not to stop exchange rate changes occurring, but merely to delay them. Nor was any greater success achieved on convergence. There was little sign of it in the sense of living standards across the whole Community becoming more equal, which may be regarded as an impractical objective, although the Irish economy grew considerably more rapidly than the average. There was even less sign that variables such as inflation rates were coming together. For example, in 1981, the consumer price index increased by 6.3% in Germany, 13.4% in France and 17.8% in Italy.

The proposal to proceed to phase two of the EMS, when the currencies would be locked together without further ability for exchange rate changes, although originally scheduled to be implemented in 1981, was therefore never put into effect. Indeed it was quietly abandoned in 1983. The ERM nevertheless continued in operation, despite limitations which were clear even to its supporters. One was that there was a major European currency – sterling – which was not in the ERM, although it was included in the basket of currencies making up the ECU. This deficiency was eventually remedied in 1990 when, despite misgivings, Mrs Thatcher, shortly to depart as Prime Minister, was persuaded to join by John Major, soon to replace her. Another serious problem was that while all those managing the participating currencies in the ERM had a clear idea how to keep them within the agreed bands, there was no effective way of managing the collective ERM exchange rate *vis à vis* other currencies, particularly the dollar and the Japanese yen. If the Community currencies as a whole became less competitive, therefore, as increasing evidence showed that they were, there was no practical way of taking remedial action to stop this occurring.

Notwithstanding the failure of the EMS by 1990 to achieve either the currency stability which was one of its main aims, or the convergence which was another, and despite the problems of co-ordinating the joint enterprise in relation to the dollar or the yen, further moves were afoot to proceed to full monetary union. The drafters of the Single European Act had succeeded in having the achievement of monetary union embodied in the Treaty as a specific commitment, with a target date of 1992. In 1988 Jacques Delors, the then President of the Commission, had persuaded the Council of Ministers to give him the task of 'studying and proposing concrete stages leading towards economic and monetary union'.

While these proposals were being considered, and embodied in the 1991 Maastricht Treaty which set out the programme for moves to a single European currency, the ERM began to disintegrate. During the summer of 1992, market pressure began to attack the weaker members of the ERM, leading to the devaluation of the lira. In September 1992 a wave of speculation against sterling swept the pound out of the ERM. The franc's parity with the Deutsche Mark only just survived. The French had held firmly to their rate against the Deutsche Mark for many years, but only at very heavy cost in terms of unemployment and slow growth. They were nearly driven out of the ERM at the same time as sterling, and were saved in the end from the ignominy suffered by the pound only as a result of massive intervention by the Bundesbank. Finally the pressure built up against the whole ERM system to a point where it became no longer possible to hold it together. In August 1993, the narrow bands were abandoned altogether, and an almost meaninglessly wide fluctuation band of 15% either side of the central rate against the ECU took their place. Notwithstanding all the effort which had gone into trying to make the ERM work, and the concurrent drive to replace the ERM with an even more rigid and inflexible Single Currency, the pressure of events had left the ERM in ruins.

The real problem with the Snake and the ERM, however, was not that they failed to achieve the currency stability and convergence which they aspired to attain. Their major defect was that they were aimed to achieve targets which were, at best, of secondary importance. The primary objectives of economic policy are not stable exchange rates and uniform levels of inflation. They are growth, full employment and rates of price increase which may vary from country to country, but which remain within acceptable limits.

With currency stability as the primary objective, far more important goals were ignored. The effect of having exchange rate stability as the primary target was to lock the whole of the EU into a relatively deflationary stance. This happened because all the participating Member States were forced to try to run their economic policies sufficiently harshly to maintain their currency's parity with the most competitive currency, which was usually the Deutsche Mark. Instead of allowing the exchange rate changes which were required to enable the Community economies grow faster to take place, as had happened in the 1950s and 1960s, the Snake and the ERM did not stop them occurring. They merely delayed them until the deflationary price was too much to bear. In the meantime billions of ECUs of growth potential were wasted, and millions of people lost their jobs.

THE SINGLE MARKET

The economic policies pursued by the European Union have not solely been concerned with currency stability and monetary convergence across the Community. There has also been a large range of other initiatives designed to make the whole of the area covered by the EU into a Single Market. The objective has been to move well beyond merely having a customs union and a free trade area inside what is nowadays a very low Common External Tariff, averaging only about 5%. The intention is to create as much uniformity as possible across the whole of the Union, so as to maximise competition on as 'level a playing field' as possible.

The policies pursued to achieve this objective have entailed a vast amount of standardisation involving everything from hygiene regulations to the permissible weights for lorries, from standards for electrical products to specifications for pharmaceuticals. The justification has been the argument that differing standards constitute significant barriers to the free movement of goods throughout the EU. Harmonisation reduces, and should eventually eliminate, this kind of barrier. The framework for this initiative was embodied in the Single European Act, passed in 1986, which planned the creation of the Single Market across the whole of the EU by the end of 1992.

Although economic justifications for the Single Market were put forward, not least in the Cecchini report, produced for the Commission to quantify what the benefits might be, the main drive behind the Single Market proposals again came mainly from political motives. The Single European Act was seen by its proponents as another major step towards European integration. The SEA not only included many provisions affecting the Single Market, but also covered extensions of the powers of the European Parliament, provisions to increase qualified majority voting, proposals for extending co-operation between EU members on foreign policy matters, and increasing the EU's power in regional and environmental issues.

As with other attempts to integrate the economies of the EU together more closely, however, the rational economic case for taking such steps ought not to lie in the degree to which activities across the Union could be harmonised or standardised to a greater degree than previously. The test to be applied should be whether the result was a higher rate of growth and lower unemployment, combined with tolerable levels of inflation. As with so many other proposals for strengthening the EU, however, such straightforward economic objectives were always subordinate to the political goals. The economic advantages to be secured from the Single Market were never likely to be large, as became clear when efforts were made to quantify them even by the Commission. The eagerness for the Single Market, however, never really rested on an economic foundation. It was the political vision which supplied the energy and enthusiasm for it, as with so many other EU projects, providing a new range of opportunities to integrate more closely the EU Member States.

In fact the benefits foreseen by the Cecchini report, produced for the Commission on the potential gains to the EU from the Single Market, were comparatively modest, even by its own optimistic lights. Three distinct primary advantages were envisaged, which it was hoped would raise economic output within the Community collectively by between 4% and 5% of its total GDP within eight years. The first of these was to remove the physical obstacles to trade caused by customs controls and formalities. These, it was estimated, currently added about 2% to the cost of all cross-frontier consignments. The second was to reduce the paperwork associated with the VAT régime because VAT rates varied between member countries. A long-standing Community objective has been to standardise VAT rates across the EU, but opposition to this part of the SEA proposals led quietly to their abandonment at least for the time being. The third range of benefits was to be secured by the removal of the technical barriers to imports and the increase in the cross-border provision of services which it was hoped would result from the establishment of the Single Market.

As a result, reductions in supply-side costs were included within the Cecchini second round benefits, which the Commission estimated would represent more than half the total gain to be secured. These would arise from the economies of scale made possible by the larger market, and the impact on operational efficiency of the increased competition which would ensue from it. It was further calculated that the impact of the Single Market would not only achieve these once and for all benefits, but that their impact would lead to a faster cumulative rate of growth in the Community, thus adding substantially to the initial benefits secured.

As part of the creation of the Single Market, the Commission also envisaged increasing competition in other areas. More stringent rules were adopted requiring tenders for public procurement to be advertised across the Community, opening up competition to suppliers in other Community countries, although subsequent investigations showed that these were effective in only about 2% of cases. Even more importantly, the Commission foresaw substantial gains, estimated to be the eventual equivalent of 1.5% of

Community GDP, by removing or standardising regulations at the national level on banking and financial services.

The Single Market project thus involved a very major initiative, and there is no doubt about the energy with which the Commission embarked upon its implementation. The initial list of 300 proposals which the Commission submitted to the 1985 Milan Summit was quickly reduced to 279 draft Directives to be laid before the Council of Ministers. Four years later, at the end of 1989, 60% had been adopted. The impact on the Community, in terms of changes to the way in which vast numbers of production processes and transactions had to be conducted, was considerable. There is little doubt that standardisation of many economic activities across the Union was achieved.

The real issue, however, was whether all this effort was justified in terms of the main objectives of economic policy – a high and sustainable growth rate, full employment, and a tolerable level of inflation. Judged by this standard, the 1992 project has played a modest role, and a much less significant one than its adherents generally claim for it. The benefits projected by the Cecchini report depended heavily on dynamic effects for their realisation. Unfortunately such positive influences as the Single Market may have had were swamped by the impact of other EU policies, particularly those to do with monetary policy. The problem was that the deflationary impact of the ERM made most of the gains from the Single Market, dependent as they were on dynamic growth, unrealisable in practice. Between 1990 and 1993, during the period when the Single Market was being introduced, the growth rate of the EU was dismally low, averaging only 0.9% per annum for the first three years of the 1990s. It rose to 2.9% in 1994 and 2.4% in 1995, but it is hard to believe that this improvement had much to do with the establishment of the Single Market. Much more powerful influences were the surge in growth in world output, the elimination of the German balance of payments surplus following the uniting of East and West Germany, and the greater exchange rate flexibility possible after the demise of the ERM.

There may well be a case for removing some non-tariff barriers across Europe, and for some standardisation of products and services throughout the Community. There must be a role for governments in co-ordinating responses to commercial pressures to eliminate unnecessary barriers to trade. The notion that adopting such policies will make any significant difference to growth rates is, however, an illusion. The gains to be achieved are mostly 'one off' and small in relation to those obtainable by increasing the growth rate by changes in macro-economic policy. Strong evidence for this proposition is that the high rates of expansion achieved in the 1950s and 1960s in most of Europe were accomplished without anything equivalent to the Single European Act, indeed at a time when tariffs in most of Europe were very high. Correspondingly, the advent of the Single Market did nothing visible at the time of its introduction to increase the EU growth rate. The solution to Europe's problems of slow growth and high unemployment lies only marginally, if to any significant extent at all, in projects like the Single Market. It lies, instead, in large-scale changes to Europe's policies on interest rates, the money supply and exchange rate flexibility.

THE SINGLE CURRENCY

Notwithstanding the failure of the Snake in the early 1970s, and the foundering of the Exchange Rate Mechanism, after fourteen years of operation, into 15% wide fluctuation bands in 1993, the process of creating a full blown European Single Currency, as enshrined in the 1991 Maastricht Treaty, has been forging head. The implementation process has, however, involved a bumpy path. The Single Currency was rejected by the Danes in the first referendum on it, although narrowly agreed in a second, after substantial concessions had been agreed. The French referendum resulted in what was aptly described as a 'très faible oui'. The legislation required by Maastricht was only passed in Britain after a long and wearing parliamentary battle, despite the opt out clauses on implementation of Stage II of the Single Currency conceded to John Major during the Maastricht negotiations.

The Single Currency convergence terms, required to be observed by all EU states whether or not they have opt outs, have involved imposing yet more deflationary policies on economies already suffering from low growth and high unemployment. The result has been strikes and marches all over Europe, not least in France and Germany, the two countries at the heart of the Single Currency project. Opinion polls throughout the EU have shown increasing doubts among the population at large about monetary union. Particularly significant have been those in Germany, where mounting concern has been expressed as to whether it makes sense for the trusted Deutsche Mark to be subsumed in a wider European currency. Undaunted by any of these developments, however, the proponents of the Single Currency are still determined to proceed with it.

The Maastricht Treaty obliges all countries which meet the convergence criteria laid down in it to lock their exchange rates irrevocably on 1 January 1999, as the precursor to adopting a common currency, the euro, in 2002. There are five convergence criteria which each qualifying Member State has to observe. It must have an inflation rate within 1.5% of the average rate of the three states with the lowest inflation. Its long-term interest rate must be within two percentage points of the average rate of the other Member States with the lowest long-term interest rates. Its national debt must not exceed 60% of its gross national product. Its budget deficit must remain below 3% of its GNP. For two years, its currency must have remained within the fluctuation margins allowed by the ERM, although as the ERM bands have been widened to 15%, it is not clear what this condition means in practice. It is understandable that if a range of disparate countries decide to lock their currencies together there should be strict rules as to how the system should operate. All the same, it is extraordinary that all the chosen criteria should relate solely to financial variables, and none of them to the main objectives of economic policy which are, or ought to be, growth and full employment with inflation at an acceptable rather than necessarily at the lowest possible level. It also appears that some of the criteria at least are largely arbitrary. This criticism applies in particular to the link between the size of the permissible 60% national debt to GDP ratio and the 3% annual deficit. This link is designed to ensure that state borrowing does not rise in relation to GDP. Other ratios, however, would achieve the same objective, with less of a deflationary impact, yet all the economies in the EU are now bound to aim for those chosen, despite the enormous costs in terms of lost output and increasing unemployment which are involved.

At present, only Luxembourg genuinely fulfils all the Maastricht criteria. It is increasingly plain that not only will no other member country meet them in full during 1997, which is the accounting year to be used to establish compliance, but that most of them are moving further away from doing so. By far the most important reason for this is the huge and rising cost of unemployment, which is driving up fiscal deficits. As a result, the criteria are being fudged. Instead of having to meet them precisely, they are being reinterpreted. The public debt ratio, for example, may be deemed met if 'the ratio is sufficiently diminishing'. The budget criterion has now been adjusted to allow countries in if their deficit 'comes close' to the threshold.

Furthermore, all manner of devices are being employed, sanctioned by Eurostat, whose reputation for independence has been severely damaged in the process, to bring the deficits closer to where they are supposed to be. The French government has been allowed to credit to government receipts a cash payment of FFr 37bn from France Télécom in return for the government taking on future pension liabilities. Italy is using money set aside by state companies for severance pay on privatisation to reduce its deficit. It is taking rail and local authority subsidies off budget. It has introduced a special one-off Euro-tax, which the government says it will pay back from 'future' privatisations. Belgium has sold part of its gold reserves to reduce its debt, and has disposed of the Euro-parliament building and other property which it owns, crediting the proceeds to its current account. There have even been proposals in Germany, vehemently opposed by the Bundesbank, that the German gold reserve should be revalued, and the profit credited to the government's current account. All of these transactions are 'one off', and have nothing to do with complying with the underlying financial discipline which the Maastricht criteria are supposed to secure – yet another example of politics first and economics a long way second.

An extraordinary number of Europe's élites seem prepared to turn a blind eye to these stratagems. Others, however, have become increasingly concerned that the Single Currency project is being built on a foundation of false statistics and unsustainable trends, which are more and more obviously likely to undermine the project if it progresses. The Germans, in particular, fear that lax implementation of the disciplines required to give the project credibility will lead to the Deutsche Mark being subsumed into a euro whose record of long-term stability will be little better than that of the lira or the pound. For this reason, the Germans have insisted on there being a Stability Pact. At the December 1996 Dublin Summit, their initial proposals were watered down somewhat, primarily at the insistence of the French. Nevertheless, a draconian array of penalties for countries failing to comply on a continuing basis with the Maastricht convergence criteria was agreed.

Whether these are enforceable remains to be seen, not least because any country having to pay a heavy fine could only do so, in practice, by moving still further into deficit to meet the payment required. The German fears, however, may be well founded. The lax application of the criteria means that a much larger number of countries may now be able to claim compliance when decisions as to who qualifies for admission are taken by majority voting early in 1998. In addition to the core members, France and Germany, plus smaller states such as the Benelux countries and Austria, whose currencies have long closely been linked with the Deutsche Mark, Spain, Italy and Eire may well be candidates. It is possible, though unlikely, that Britain may be too. The situation is greatly complicated by the qualified majority voting procedure involved. The most plausible ERM contenders can muster only 42 votes, which is 20 short of the 62 out of 87 needed to secure the required majority, leaving Spain and Italy, neither candidates for the Single Currency favoured by the Germans, with blocking votes against a narrow EMU.

There is thus a likelihood that far from the new currency régime being a stable one when it is introduced at the beginning of 1999, it may start looking weak and liable to speculative attack. The rationale for the Single Currency has always been that its very nature would make it proof against this kind of assault because of its indivisibility. The currencies used by those joining monetary union in 1999, however, will not all be indivisible. For three years between 1999 and 2002, the existing national currencies will also be circulating in the economies of the participating Member States. If there is any sign of wavering, speculators may again exploit the one-way options which led to the collapse of the Snake and the ERM.

There are also going to be problems controlling the borrowing of Member States using the euro currency, particularly those with long-standing traditions of fiscal laxity, which paradoxically the Stability Pact, insisted upon by the Germans, may make worse. The fact that several EU states have large unfunded pension liabilities increases the significance of this possibility. The Maastricht Treaty makes it clear that each Member State will be responsible for its own liabilities, even if they are denominated in euros. Indeed the Treaty specifically forbids either governments or the European Central Bank coming to the aid of a potential defaulter. Thus if any state over-borrows, running the risk of default and having to pay an interest rate premium, it will be entirely responsible for its own salvation. The problem with the Stability Pact is that, by specifying more and more tightly what national governments can or cannot do, operation of the Pact's provisions may begin to shade into taking responsibility for their actions, thus making it less clear where final accountability lies.

All these problems are going to make the role of the European Central Bank, responsible for making the new monetary system work, more onerous and more important. The members of the governing body of the ECB, significantly all central bankers, will be nominated for eight years, and their appointments will be non-renewable. Their primary function will be to safeguard the value and integrity of the new euro currency. Their independence from democratic pressures, to enable them to perform this role, is enshrined in the Maastricht Treaty. Formally, they are not allowed to be influenced by the governments of Member States, the EU institutions, or even public opinion. Their role will be to maintain low inflation and currency stability above all other considerations. The Treaty gives the European Central Bank a uniquely powerful position compared to any other central bank. It will be under less democratic control, and it will have a clearer, if narrower, remit, than other central banks because its primary function is to keep down inflation regardless of the costs of doing so on output and employment. It will still, however, have an exceptionally difficult function to perform, because of the widely disparate nature of the EU economies and the deeply political environment within which it will have to operate, whatever the Maastricht Treaty may say.

The way the Single Currency project is developing, as with so much else to do with the formulation of EU economic policies, is indeed another triumph of political determination over economic practicalities. Without a common currency, it is not possible to turn the EU into a unitary political entity. The primary drive for monetary union comes from those who believe that there ought to be a United States of Europe. The economic case for monetary union is therefore a secondary one, but it has had to be made to justify the steps which are being taken, albeit very largely for other reasons. In the light of the way in which events are developing, what is this case, and how strong is it?

It is argued first that there are exchange costs involved in having a multiplicity of currencies in Europe, and that these could be reduced if there was only one currency. Unquestionably there are costs involved in changing money from one currency to another, although as a proportion of the EU's total GDP they are not large. Estimates of the total savings which might be achieved, assuming all Member States joined, amount to some 0.5% of EU GDP. Obviously, the fewer states which join the Single Currency, the smaller the benefits will be. If it is only a small hard core, the savings would probably be about 0.2%. Offset against these advantages to monetary union are the one-off costs of converting everyone's accounting systems, including bank processing systems and cash taking machines, to the new currency, estimated at as much as 3% of EU GDP. There is a potential gain to be secured, but not a big one, with something like a six-year pay-back period. These calculations do not, however, include a large additional cost for which provision may have to be made, which is that the Single Currency project goes ahead, but may then collapse. If this happens, or is even seen to be a serious risk, much higher costs will need to be incurred to ensure that all the conversion work which then would become abortive could be capable of being very quickly reversed.

Second, it is claimed that eliminating exchange-rate volatility will encourage competition within the EU, leading to higher levels of investment and increased output as a result of a more certain and secure climate for business activity. It has to be said that there is negligible evidence for this proposition. Businesses everywhere respond to increased demand by expanding output whatever happens to exchange rates. Their investment decisions flow largely from what they believe they will be able to sell in future. There is no systematic evidence from economic history that stable exchange rates promote faster growth. On the contrary, misaligned exchange rates, which ought to change, but which are precluded from doing so for whatever reason, are almost invariably the cause of deflationary policies which restrict growth.

Third, it is argued that the Single Currency will lead to lower interest rates than would otherwise prevail, and that these will stimulate investment and economic activity. This argument depends initially on a distinction being made between real interest rates, allowing for inflation, and nominal interest rates.

At present, the rate of inflation across the EU is very low by the standards of the 1970s and 1980s. Even though nominal interest rates are also low, however, the real interest rate, which is the nominal rate minus inflation, is now at a relatively high average level. If the major objective of the ECB is to keep inflation at low levels, it may be difficult to avoid high real rates of interest at the same time, especially before tax.

Even apart from this consideration, however, the claim that the Single Currency is required to achieve low real rates of interest should be treated with a good deal of suspicion. Any sovereign country can reduce interest rates if it wants to do so. It may have to increase the money supply, and it may see its currency depreciating in the international markets if its interest rates go down, but these are by no means necessarily disadvantageous developments. It might be argued that the euro would be able to enjoy the confidence of the markets in a way in which most national currencies would not. This might enable it to sustain a low rate of inflation and low real interest rates without concomitant changes to the money supply and the exchange rate, if these were thought undesirable. It is not easy to see that this would necessarily be the case however, especially in the light of the fiscal and financial records of some of the Member States which might be initial members, and the reluctance of core countries such as France to accept the continuing deflationary implications of the hard euro approach.

On the other hand, leaving aside much more radical proposals for improving the economic performance of the EU economies, the project for an EU Single Currency presents major problems which its proponents have not successfully rebutted. Far the most important one is strongly reflected in the inability of the Snake and the ERM to continue operating permanently. They failed to do so because the performance of the constituent economies diverged to an extent which in the end made currency realignments unavoidable. If these parity changes had not occurred, the levels of deflation required in the weaker economies to maintain their balance of payments positions would have become intolerable. The Single Currency, however, rules out parity changes. What, therefore, is to take their place? The answer is that if some areas within the Single Currency area do much worse than the average, they will have no way of responding other than to allow their living standards to fall, and their labour forces to move out, until some kind of equilibrium is restored. Bearing in mind the cultural and linguistic barriers within the EU, the strains thus engendered may be very large indeed. It is not at all clear that in these circumstances the deficit areas are going to tolerate the Single Currency indefinitely, if a more and more obvious solution to their problems is to revert back to having their own currency. This would provide them once more with the opportunity to overcome their lack of competitiveness by a devaluation, which by then would almost certainly be the only practical way out of permanent deflation.

All single currency areas, of course, are subject to problems of this kind, and in some large currency areas, such as the United States, the impact on disadvantaged areas has been very heavy. The US, however, is different to the EU in at least two important respects. The first is that the US is much more culturally and linguistically uniform than the EU, making it a great deal more practical for people to move from one place to another in search of work. The second is that the US federal government has large tax revenues at its disposal – approximately 20% of the US GDP – and these can and have been used extensively to mitigate the impact of adverse circumstances. The proportion of GDP which passes through the EU level tax and redistribution system is currently just under 1.25%, and therefore about one sixteenth of the US ratio. Half of this sum is deployed on funding the CAP, where much of the movement of tax resources is from relatively poor areas of the Community to relatively rich ones, such as the Netherlands and Denmark, both substantial net CAP beneficiaries. The EU is therefore very short of taxable resources to redistribute to less favoured areas.

Strains on the Single Currency may also arise in other ways, requiring either large fiscal transfers for which no resources exist, or exchange rate adjustments which the Single Currency is designed to preclude. The economies comprising the probable single currency area, particularly if Britain were to be included, vary substantially in their economic structure and institutions. As a result, changes in circumstances, many likely to be well beyond the control of any government, including that of the EU collectively, will have markedly differential effects on different countries. For example, a major alteration in the price of oil and natural gas would have the opposite effect on countries rich in these resources and able to export their surpluses from those which lack them and have to import them. The impact of interest changes also has a very different effect on countries where most loans are at fixed rates compared to others where variable rates are much more common. Again, the Single Currency provides no practical way of making the adjustments which might well be required.

Another major problem is all too likely to flow from the convergence criteria underpinning the Single Currency project. To remain within the criteria, even allowing for some latitude in their interpretation, would be difficult enough for most countries even if the relatively favourable conditions of 1997 continue. There is some economic growth across the EU, and the world economy and world trade are both increasing fast. Expansion of output within the EU, however, may well not continue for long. As each country has to reduce public expenditure to get within the Maastricht borrowing limit, growth, at least in Europe, is likely to slow down. As this happens, the pressures for increasing public expenditure, while tax revenues decrease, will become extremely strong. If all, or nearly all countries in the EU attempt these policies at the same time, however, each will export more deflation to the other. The cumulative effect could easily be a further fall in the EU's overall growth rate, and perhaps even a decline in output, making the convergence criteria impossible for many countries to achieve, however hard they try.

Some of these problems could be ameliorated if the EU were to be provided with much larger tax raising powers, a solution which many of those keenest to see the emergence of a unitary European state might well applaud. It seems extremely unlikely, however, that changes on anything like the scale needed will occur within the foreseeable future. The reforms required would be so enormous, and they would have to be made against what is likely to be such a discontented and unpromising background, that it is very improbable that they would happen.

Instead, it seems much more likely that the EU Single Currency will break up, for much the same reasons as sank the Snake and the ERM. The strains will become intolerable. Here another major difference between the US and the EU will become critically important. Even though some parts of the US have unquestionably suffered as a result of being part of the single currency dollar bloc, since the American Civil War there has never been any part of the US which conceived itself as being separable from the rest. There are no regional identities, with obvious enough boundaries and clear and exclusive common interests, to make it feasible to think of dividing one part of the country from the rest. In Europe the structure is completely different. In the EU, the nation state is still very much alive. While many people in most of these states are prepared to give up some sovereignty to build supra-national institutions which they think will benefit them, it is extremely unlikely that there will be a continuing majority in any of them in favour of arrangements which appear to be manifestly and permanently to their disadvantage.

This is why the Single Currency is such a gamble. Its success relies on so much going right, when historical experience suggests that at least a fair proportion will go wrong. It depends on all the constituent countries starting off and remaining for the foreseeable future roughly competitive with each other, with none gaining an undue advantage or falling badly behind. Its success rests on there being no shocks to the system – even quite small ones – to upset the equilibrium. For these conditions to prevail, there will have to be, within narrow limits, the same rate of inflation in all the constituent countries for as far ahead as anyone can see. Perhaps all these conditions will be fulfilled. Perhaps, on the strength of decades of successful currency stability and prosperity, the tax raising and spending powers of the EU will be increased enough to enable relatively minor differences in performance between the constituent countries to be ironed out sufficiently to make the whole project viable in the long term. It is just possible that all these favourable events will transpire. The odds against all these beneficent conjunctures occurring, however, look very poor, and the downside costs, if the gamble does not succeed, are potentially enormous.

POLITICS, ECONOMICS AND DEFLATION

This chapter has argued that the economic history of the countries of the European Union over the last quarter of a century has been clouded by policy errors. As a result, a huge opportunity has been lost. Instead of continuing to expand at the same rate as was achieved for decades prior to the 1970s, the growth rate has declined to little more than a third of its previous level. With the increases in productivity materialising amongst the workforce in every developed country, the rise in unemployment which the EU has experienced was then inevitable.

There are alternative policies which will change this performance, but they are not compatible with the proposals stemming from the Maastricht Treaty which currently form the basis for EU policy development. In particular, the Single Currency, far from being the salvation of the EU, is all too likely to be the cause of a further reduction in EU economic achievement. At best, even if everything its strongest adherents hope will happen materialises, it is difficult to see why the EU's growth rate should rise much, if at all, above the levels achieved over the last two decades. If this is the outcome, productivity among the employed labour force is likely to continue to increase more rapidly than total output. The consequence can only be that more people will be out of work, and greater fiscal problems will be experienced by all the countries involved. Why is this being allowed to happen? How have the political élites in Europe allowed themselves to run Western Europe's economic affairs so badly, and to be driving forward now with proposals which are all too likely to make matters worse?

Perhaps the simplest answer gets closest to the truth. The major problem is that much too much of the idealism which has gone into trying to build structures to unite the countries of Western Europe has been channelled into the implementation of political initiatives which have not made sense economically. Time after time, political resolution has taken the place of economic analysis. The European Coal and Steel Community was established primarily to build bridges between Germany and France, not to provide solutions to industrial over-capacity and restructuring problems, which might have been easier to solve at national level. The Common Market was created, as the Treaty of Rome makes clear, principally to secure the 'ever closer union', which was the real objective of its founders. The creation of a customs union was a step along the road to a united Europe. The Snake and the ERM all had similar, politically motivated reasons for their inception. The Single Market and the Single Currency again had the same provenance. In all cases, the primary goal was closer political integration, with better economic performance a secondary and subordinate objective, when it was seriously considered at all as an issue of significant importance. The economic justification for any of the major Community developments invariably came after the political decisions to initiate them had been made. The best available arguments were then used to support the steps being taken, irrespective of whether the case being made, on balance, had any real merit.

Economics is a difficult subject, full of feedback and ambiguities, and lacking in any of the certainty which controlled experiments provide to scientific studies. A plausible economic case can therefore be made out for almost any policy which political leaders, and others, want to see implemented for non-economic reasons. Economics is not, however, so malleable that it is incapable of providing guidelines which will work. Nor is it incapable of making distinctions between policies with a reasonable prospect of success, and those with a high chance of failure. The reason for the dismal performance of the EU economies for the last quarter of a century is that too often rhetoric took the place of analysis. Filling the vacuum thus created, too many political leaders took advantage of the opportunities which poorly articulated policies at EU level gave to them to further their national interests at the expense of the rest of the Community.

Part of the reason why this happened arose from the structures of the Community itself. Although members of the Commission are supposed to serve the Community, and not to favour the countries from which they come, not all of them have done so. Frequent examples of politicians and officials fighting for their country's corner, often dressed up in appropriate EU rhetoric and carried out with great sophistication, have damaged the whole. Much more importantly, the Commission itself has developed a Euro-centric culture, which has enormously slanted EU policy towards federal ends. The Council of Ministers has leaned in the same direction, favouring integration in almost all circumstances. Further pressure has come from other major components of the EU system, especially amongst those administering the CAP, whose natural proclivity has been towards currency stability, and all the institutional arrangements that go with it, to make their agricultural role more manageable.

Other Community organisations, which might have pulled in the opposite direction, have failed to do so. The European Court of Justice in Luxembourg has had a consistently federal bias in its decisions. The European Parliament, with few powers, but awash with Euro taxpayers' money, has turned out to be little more than an ineffective talking shop, despite the additional authority which it has recently acquired. The national parliaments, with a great deal to lose if power seeps away from them to Brussels, have sometimes been more willing to stand up for themselves, as have some individual leaders such as Charles de Gaulle and Margaret Thatcher. The general picture, however, has been one where the Commission has run rings round everyone else, leaving national delegations in Brussels, and even the meetings of the national leaders at the European Council, with little they could do except to accept whatever *faits accomplis* Commission officials had designed for them in advance.

Changes will be required if the future trends in the EU are to be different from those of the last two or three decades. The rest of this book sets out what these might be. The next chapter discusses the conditions which cause economic growth to take place, to provide a backdrop against which economic policies in the EU need to be reassessed. Chapter 5 looks at what needs to be done to bring unemployment down again to the levels experienced in Europe in the 1950s and 1960s. Chapter 6 reviews the impact that the kind of policies designed to achieve much higher rates of growth and lower rates of unemployment might have on inflation. Chapter 7 then looks at what reforms to the way the EU operates might be required to implement the alterations in policy which this book recommends. Changes would be needed, but none that cannot be relatively easily achieved. The transition to a new set of policies, much more likely to produce a better economic performance for the EU than those presently on offer would not be very difficult. They would be a small price to pay for extricating the EU from its present economic languor.

4   Achieving Economic Growth

'Civilization and profits go hand in hand.'
Calvin Coolidge

The economic history of Western Europe since the start of industrialisation has been remarkably patchy. Britain experienced a long period of rapid growth in the first half of the nineteenth century, but then slowed down between 1850 and 1900. Germany and the Netherlands did much better during the second half of the nineteenth century than the first, and better still during the early years of the twentieth century, leading to World War I. The 1930s were a particularly interesting and important period, with France languishing, Britain doing far better than previously, and Germany surging ahead at an astonishing pace. There have been decades when most of the main economies were growing very quickly, as they did in the 1950s and 1960s. After the post-war boom, in the 1970s, growth slowed everywhere in Western Europe. Britain's poor record for most of the twentieth century began to be emulated by everyone else.

Why should this have happened? Why was growth so much faster in some periods than others, and what can policy makers do to create the conditions where sustained increases in output are achieved? How can they avoid their economies slowing down? The objective of this chapter is to put forward a simple and clear explanation of what causes economic growth. This can then be used as a backdrop to seeing how a range of policies could be developed for the European Union, which would overcome its current problems of slow growth and high unemployment.

The starting point is to understand the circumstances which allow and encourage economic growth to take place. Growth is achieved by creating conditions where the output of goods and services rises. This is not necessarily the same thing as increasing productivity, at least among the existing work force. Higher total output entails greater average productivity per person if the same number of people are employed to produce more output. The same increase can be achieved, however, if the number of people working goes up without any extra output per person. If productivity increases in isolation from a general expansion of the economy it will not contribute to raising the growth rate. More productivity among some people will be counterbalanced by rising unemployment, while total output stays constant. This crucially important point, which has wide policy implications, runs through all the arguments which follow. The key to achieving high growth rates for the economy as a whole is to create conditions where increases in output will take place across the board, keeping all factors of production fully employed. This will then cause average productivity to rise, without increasing unemployment, which is the key combination of objectives which needs to be attained.

High growth rates are achieved by keeping all the factors of production, particularly labour and capital, in use as intensively as possible. The growth in output thus achieved will be reflected in increased output per head, which is how productivity is raised. At the level of the individual enterprise, this is accomplished in three principal ways. The first is by investing in machinery and equipment which makes it possible for the existing labour force to achieve increased production. The second is by better management and training of the workforce, and enhancing its skills and experience. The third is by increasing sales, so that all the available resources of labour and capital are used to maximum capacity.

The potential for improved production as a result of capital investment is a familiar concept. The power, dexterity and speed with which machinery operates made the Industrial Revolution possible. During the past two centuries, the development of a huge range of machines has been matched by many other inventions and technological developments which can be used to increase output, from internal combustion engines to electronics, from steamships to airliners, from new building techniques to plastics. All these developments make it possible to produce goods and services of greater value per labour hour. We shall see, however, that there is a huge variation in the return on investments. Some types of investment are very much more productive, and therefore conducive to high rates of economic growth than others. One of the ways of increasing economic growth, and making it much easier to achieve, is to create conditions in which the economy is biased towards the most highly productive investment.

The quality of management is extremely important in producing greater output. Many improvements in working practices which lead to more production, or changes in output designed to make it more attractive to consumers, involve little capital outlay but a great deal of management skill. Some of this comes from good education and training. An even more important factor is ensuring that the best available managerial talent is concentrated in those areas of the economy where it can be used most effectively to improve economic achievement. Where talent is actually concentrated depends critically on economic rewards, and the social status which follows behind them. The second element in improving economic achievement is to shift both rewards and social status towards those involved in running the parts of the economy where good management has the best chance of increasing performance.

The third vital component is to create enough pressure of demand on the economy to ensure that all the available resources of capital and labour are, as far as possible, fully utilised. To achieve most from capital equipment, it needs to be used as intensively as possible. To get the best out of the labour force, it needs to be fully employed. When there is a shortage of jobs, it may make sense to increase output by using relatively low productivity machinery and more labour. As supplies of labour run short, this no longer becomes a viable option. There is then no alternative to labour-saving equipment. At the level of the enterprise, a full order book at profitable prices is needed, with highly productive machinery used to capacity to produce goods which the market is hungry to buy, operated by a well trained and motivated labour force, led by able managers. These conditions exist now in Korea, Taiwan and the fast-developing parts of China, which is why these economies are expanding so rapidly. They were also replicated in Germany, France and Italy – indeed over nearly all of Western Europe in the 1950s and 1960s – when all these countries were growing much faster than they are now.

If the EU wants its constituent economies to grow much more quickly, and to employ all their labour forces, these conditions will have to be recreated. We turn now to seeing in more detail how this might be done.

COMPETITIVENESS

What are the conditions which enable economies to prosper? How is an environment created which encourages economic growth to take place? What can those responsible for the performance of the economies in the EU do to ensure that their growth performance is as good as that achieved with comparative ease in many other countries? It is often claimed that the solution is to concentrate on the supply side of the problem. The way to higher growth, it is said, is to improve European competitiveness by better education and training, by higher levels of investment, and by improving productivity. This will both make the EU economies more competitive, and increase their productive capacity, allowing more growth to take place. The problem with this approach, however, is that improving efficiency will not necessarily result in lower prices and greater competitiveness. It depends on the price charged to the rest of the world for the output which is achieved. Nor does increasing productivity necessarily result in rising total output.

A variation on the supply-side theme is to blame poor growth performance on production techniques and design sophistication which are not as advanced as those available elsewhere in the world, perhaps compounded by ineffective salesmanship, late deliveries and inadequate after sales service. There is evidence that this may be a significant part of Europe's current problem. European companies have not been particularly good at keeping up with innovations in some of the newly developing industries, such as bio-technology and the latest applications of electronics. More generally, it has been argued that Europe's industrial capacity is too heavily orientated towards yesterday's growth markets, and too little towards those likely to produce the biggest increase during the twenty-first century. If European industry is becoming uncompetitive for reasons of this sort, this is a major problem, and a solution urgently needs to be found, to enable it to compete again on equal terms with the rest of the world.

Of course, productive efficiency has some bearing on competitiveness, but actually surprisingly little. The higher the level of productivity, the more efficiently goods and services will be produced, but it does not necessarily follow that they will then be internationally competitive. High productivity is closely associated with high standards of living, but very poorly with competitiveness. This is why there is no observable correlation between the growth rates of rich and poor countries. It is, nevertheless, true that in any economy which is growing, productivity will be increasing. This leads many people to conclude that concentrating efforts on raising productivity will push up the growth rate. Unfortunately, this conclusion is not correct. Productivity is not the same as competitiveness. There are many examples, including all the EU economies, where productivity is increasing quite rapidly, but growth in output is slow. The result is rising unemployment and unused resources.

Striking confirmation of these propositions is provided by comparing the position of the United States and the tiger economies of the Far East during the period since World War II. After 1945, the United States labour force was vastly more productive than the largely peasant workforces of Taiwan and Korea. The levels of training and education in the US were far superior to those in most other countries in the world, while significant proportions of the Taiwanese and Korean labour forces were illiterate. The value of capital per head in the US was many multiples of the almost non-existent industrial capacity in Taiwan and Korea. Despite all these huge advantages, the US has been completely outpaced in the growth race since World War II by the Taiwanese and Korean economies.

It is not, therefore, productivity which is the key to making economies potentially capable of growing fast. It is competitiveness. It is the prices charged to buyers both in the home and export markets, compared to foreign suppliers, which count. This is partly a function of how productive the domestic economy is, but it is also a question of how much it charges the rest of the world for its output, whatever the level of productivity. This is determined by the exchange rate. Even if productivity is very low, and everything is wrong with the output of the economy, if it is cheap enough it will sell. However high the quality of the output, if it is too expensive, market share will be lost. In the end, it is price which balances out all the other quality factors. This is why the exchange rate is so critically important.

Other things being equal, the lower the exchange rate, the less the domestic economy charges the rest of the world for its labour, land and capital, and the more competitive, compared with the rest of the world, the domestic economy will be. This condition bears directly on the three requirements identified earlier for increasing both productivity and output. First, for all those economic activities which require capital investment to secure increase in output, the lower the associated labour and interest costs, measured in international terms, the higher the profitability of the capital investment, and the more investment will be undertaken. Second, the greater the competitiveness of the output produced, the easier it will be to sell larger amounts at a profit, and the greater the capacity utilisation. Third, the higher the profits thus generated, the more those sectors of the economy which are engaged in producing internationally tradable goods and services will be able to attract the most talented people into management positions. Exceptional profitability will also enable them to employ and make best use of the most competent people available to staff every level of the operations concerned.

Just as a company's competitive position is heavily disadvantaged if its costs are far out of line with the rest of the market, so it is the same for the whole economy. There is, however, one further important difference between companies and economies. If the exchange rate is too high, reducing it is an even more potent way of cutting costs across the board than anything an individual company can do. All companies have fixed costs which are impossible to cut significantly. This is not true of the economy as a whole. Changing the exchange rate carries with it the costs of every factor of production. No wonder countries with overvalued exchange rates suffer so grievously, and those with undervalued exchange rates do so well.

The relationship between productivity and competitiveness is therefore the reverse of what is often supposed. It is not increasing productivity which produces greater competitiveness. It is greater competitiveness which generates the conditions where increased productivity is most easily achieved, and with the greatest advantage. This is not a trite conclusion. It has profound implications for determining the conditions which will make economies grow, and the policies which need to be pursued to make this happen.

The significance of these exchange rate issues to the EU is that, for much of the post-World War II period, there has been a mismatch between the competitiveness of the German economy and most of the others in Europe, compounded by Germany's low inflation record. Germany was extraordinarily competitive immediately after World War II, although France and Italy were not far behind, especially after the French devaluations under de Gaulle at the end of the 1950s. Britain, by contrast, throughout this period had chronic competitive problems and its performance lagged accordingly. Given reasonable flexibility on exchange rate movements, there is no reason why the major continental economies should not have kept up their high growth rates, or resumed them immediately after the hiatus in the mid-1970s. Once it became impossible to offset lower inflation and increasing competitiveness in Germany by parity adjustments, however, as history shows, a slowdown across the whole of the Community became inevitable.

As soon as attempts were made to lock the exchange rates together, the differentials in competitiveness became a major problem. Shorn of their ability to keep up with Germany by devaluing, none of the unsuccessfully competing economies had any method of maintaining their balance of payments under control other than by reducing demand. This resulted in deflationary policies which slowed up the whole of the Community growth rate. Germany suffered too as its major trading partners all reduced their demand for German exports. Two thirds of German exports go to other EU countries. Now, mainly because of decades of relatively low investment, the whole EU bloc is becoming uncompetitive with the Far East, compounding the problems within the EU. Until the economies of the EU can overcome these constraints, the prospects will remain as unpromising as they are at present.

PROTECTIONISM AND FREE TRADE

It is sometimes proposed, particularly by those suffering from world competition, that the way to create favourable conditions for growth is through protectionist measures designed to shield producers from world competition. It is argued that a major restraint on growth in the European Union is excessive competition, particularly from the Far East, which only import tariffs or quotas will contain. The European Union may still have a balance of payments surplus with the Far East, but this is not necessarily going to last. A relatively high proportion of EU sales to the Far East consist of capital goods, which the recipient countries may well learn to make themselves before long, whereas the main EU imports from the Far East are consumer products which cost far less to make in the East than the West.

Difficulties in competing with consumer products from the Far East and other developing countries have already led to significant restraints on trade. The Multi-fibre agreement was one of the earlier examples. Restrictions on the imports of Japanese cars is another. Other major areas of the EU economies which are protected from outside competition are steel, shipbuilding, chemicals, electronics, footwear, various forms of fuel, and of course agriculture on a comprehensive scale. If there needs to be more investment in EU industry, and better rewards for those employed in it, then some degree of protection, it is claimed, is the best way of ensuring that these objectives are achieved. If this cannot be attained openly, by raising tariffs or quotas, then covert protection, making importing difficult in other ways, may be the solution. It is not too hard to specify standards which foreign suppliers find difficult to meet, to hold up imports with long-winded bureaucratic procedures, and to lean on foreign governments to restrict their exports. 'Orderly marketing arrangements' and 'voluntary export restraints' then become the appropriate euphemisms.

Buttressing these arguments are others which have been the common coin of economic debate for decades. By imposing a tariff, the domestic economy could tax the foreigner to its advantage. Because those selling to the domestic economy would have to lower their prices to compete in its protected market, the terms of trade would improve. The domestic economy would then obtain more imports per unit of exports than it did before the tariff was imposed, thus making itself better off. Furthermore, if the effect of putting on import duties is similar to reducing the exchange rate, having higher tariffs on some commodities than others may give the domestic economy advantages that would not be obtained by a devaluation. For example, if import duties are imposed on finished goods but not on raw materials, the domestic economy may be able to protect its manufacturers without raising their costs.

The countries in the EU had a long tradition of high tariffs before they were reduced first by the Common Market customs union, and then subsequently as free trade within Europe was extended as a result of successive GATT tariff reduction rounds. There are still many people in Europe, however, whose instincts hark back to the protectionism and mercantilism exemplified by Colbert and other statesmen like him. This is so notwithstanding the strength of counter-arguments which have in fact prevailed, leading to steady reductions in tariffs throughout the world. In modern conditions, there are strong arguments against reverting back to a protectionist approach, and indeed for moving further towards opening up EU markets to foreign competition wherever possible. The EU's record in trade negotiations has not been impressively liberal, nor has its ingenuity in raising non-tariff barriers been put to best use. The EU is more likely to improve the prosperity of its citizens by looking outwards rather than inwards. The arguments for free trade and keeping the EU's economies open to foreign competition are as important now as they ever were, provided they are not undermined by inappropriate exchange rate policies, which can all too easily generate protectionism which politicians find difficult to resist.

First, there are the traditional comparative cost arguments for foreign trade. The relative costs of producing a wide range of output varies from country to country. It pays countries to trade with each other if they swap those products where their relative costs are low for others produced elsewhere which could only be made at a relatively high cost domestically. It is important to note that the case for international trade for comparative cost reasons is independent of absolute levels of productivity. Countries with such low productivity that they produce everything relatively inefficiently can still trade with advantage with countries which produce everything more efficiently. It is the variances round the norm which make this trade worth while.

Second, there is the spur to efficiency produced by competition from abroad. Most people prefer a quiet life, and do not relish the prospect of having to adapt constantly to changing tastes and fashions, to new technology and methods of distribution. Provided it is not overwhelming, foreign competition keeps them on their toes. A copying process results as those who are behind the times replicate the trends set by the market leaders. They buy in or replicate foreign technology and equipment, management techniques and sales methods. It is possible to achieve high rates of growth behind tariff barriers, as for example Spain did for decades during the Franco régime. The output produced in these circumstances, however, tends to lack the quality of the goods and services available in countries which are more exposed to the world economy.

Third, there are great advantages in producing competitive exports if all the raw materials, intermediate goods and other inputs which have to be bought in from abroad can be obtained at the lowest possible price. One of the problems with either import tariffs or quotas is that they generally increase the costs of domestic production. It is now more difficult than it was to draw a clear distinction between raw materials and finished goods, with tariffs imposed on the latter but not the former. If the key to long-term improved economic performance is to increase the competitiveness of all the EU economies at home and abroad, it does not help to raise domestic production costs more than can be avoided, or to restrict access to raw materials and components.

Fourth, tariffs or quotas have a fundamental flaw if they are employed to deal with an underlying lack of competitiveness. The problem is that while it is conceivable that there should be relatively low import duties, or a limited number of products subject to quotas, as soon as the height of the tariffs gets beyond a fairly low level – about 20% – the distortions they entail become more and more difficult to justify. Administrative problems also mount rapidly when quotas increase in complexity. It is not possible to keep on raising tariffs or tightening quotas indefinitely without dramatically diminishing returns setting in. Economic distortions get worse, evasion becomes an increasing problem, and complicated appeals procedures are difficult to avoid. Though agricultural protection is not unique to Europe, the fraud and waste of the CAP has much to do with the large-scale price distortions which are intrinsic to its operation.

If the root problem, however, is lack of competitiveness on the export market, as much as too much import penetration – and of course the two go together – then either the tariffs will have to be increased, or quotas tightened beyond any realistic point. Alternatively, the real remedy needed, which is changing the exchange rate, will have to be adopted. This is because tariff protection will not increase exports, but a growing economy will need more imports. There is no way out of this problem short of eventual autarchy, which forces the protected economy to produce more and more of its needs in the home market, even though it would be much cheaper to buy them from abroad.

There are, therefore, political and economic arguments for maintaining economies in the developed world as open as is politically feasible, although there may be a practical case for some measure of protection because of the difficulties of ensuring that exchange rates are always correctly aligned. This is the justification for the EU's Common External Tariff, the North American Free Trade Area, and similar arrangements in South America, the Pacific area and elsewhere. Achieving equality in competitiveness between economies within a customs union area, which is a vital component of good economic management, may in practice, therefore, be easier to achieve behind a common external tariff high enough to contain an unmanageable volume of foreign competition.

In the real world, therefore, there is an argument for a degree of protection, but a weaker one for quotas than there is for tariffs, and a stronger case for low tariffs than for high ones. When there is unmanageable competition, there is always pressure for protection. The case to be made in these circumstances, however, almost invariably depends on exchange rates being in the wrong position in the first place. Protectionist policies are then all too readily inclined to become the justification for failing to correct the exchange rate fundamentals. There is therefore no valid argument for a retreat into further protectionism as a major plank of economic policy. There is a much more effective way of dealing with the problems of major trade imbalance, for which tariffs and quotas are not the solution. This is to make greater efforts to position exchange rates at the right level, and to allow them to keep adjusting themselves as circumstances change and relative competitive advantage alters, so that the need for protectionist measures falls away. A very major problem with the Single Currency is that it is designed to make this adjustment process impossible.

RECAPTURING HOME AND EXPORT MARKETS

So far we have looked at the conditions favourable to economic growth in a static context, but the process we are looking at is far from static. It is one where movement and change are essential elements. There are two particular features which need to be highlighted. The first is that rapid economic growth, once established, has a strong capacity to reinforce itself. On the whole, therefore, fast-growing economies tend to stay growing rapidly. The second is that this virtuous circle of fast growth cannot be taken for granted. It can slow down or even stop for a time altogether, as has been the experience across much of Europe. It is important to be able to explain both what causes growth to accelerate to a fast pace, and why it can slow down, stop, or even go into reverse. This means pinpointing the mechanisms involved in both the virtuous circle of import-saving and export-led growth, and the vicious circle of import-led stagnation.

One of the keys to understanding this issue is to appreciate a particularly important characteristic of a large proportion of the investment taking place in those parts of the world economy which produce internationally tradable goods and services. This is the large increases in output which investment of this sort is capable of producing at relatively low run-on costs. Indeed this characteristic provides the main explanation for the enormous growth in international trade which has occurred over recent decades. The result is a special feature of the production costs of internationally traded goods and services. They almost all involve steeply falling cost curves. This means that the cost of producing the first batch of any new good or service may be high, but all subsequent output is much cheaper. The average cost of production therefore falls quickly as the volume of output builds up.

This characteristic of internationally traded goods and services is highly significant. Any economy with macro-economic conditions making it relatively easy to sell the output from this kind of investment – in particular low interest rates, a plentiful supply of credit and a competitive exchange rate – will achieve rapid output growth. Once the initial investment is on stream, low marginal costs of production lead to competitive pricing and high profits, which are then available to finance the risks involved in subsequent waves of investment. High profitability also enables these enterprises to attract and hold the most able people in management positions, making it more likely that the next round of investment decisions will be shrewdly judged and efficiently carried out. The low cost of production makes it relatively easy to keep plants fully occupied as higher output leads to lower production costs and the capacity for even more competitive pricing. This virtuous circle thus tends strongly to fortify itself. Higher sales and greater profitability make it easier to finance research and development, and to keep ahead. They also provide the profitability needed to sustain high selling costs, so that new markets can be penetrated. The competitive position of successful enterprises is strengthened by better design, advertising and selling efforts, and after sales service, all of which are expensive. On the back of a large volume of profitable sales, however, they can be relatively easily afforded. Profitability remains high, making expenditure to produce increased output easy to finance. Both the savings ratio, and the rate of investment as a proportion of national income tend to be high and rising in economies with strong export sectors. With substantial rewards in successful enterprises go social status and political power, thus attracting and retaining more and more of the best talent. It cannot be stressed too strongly how important this talent is to achieving sustained growth. Creating the right economic conditions for the virtuous spiral of import-saving and export-led growth may be the precursor to economic success, but there is no substitute for the highest possible standard of efficiency at the level of the firm. This is where management quality is as critical as any other factor, perhaps the most critical of all. Sustained high growth rates can only be achieved by the difficult processes of making good judgements about increasingly complex problems, managing more and more complicated organisations, dealing with rapid and frequently technically intricate change, and assessing and sometimes anticipating accurately market trends, often covering the whole world.

The crucial question then is what makes it possible to break into the virtuous circle of import-saving and export-led growth? What are the conditions which cause import-led stagnation? The exchange rate is the most critical determinant, for reasons which Table 4.1 makes clear. This table shows in schematic, but not unrealistic form the costs and pricing options available to companies competing in international trade in three different economies, one with a parity in line with the world average, one with an exchange rate undervalued by 20%, and one with an exchange rate which is overvalued by the same percentage.

The costs of manufacturing companies are made up of a number of components, some of which are determined by world prices, and some locally. In the table, raw materials are shown as 20% of world prices for the firm's output in the averagely competitive economy. There is a world market for nearly all raw materials, but favourable selling conditions for exporters tend to go with efficient and low-cost raw material suppliers in economies whose manufacturing base is expanding rapidly. There is also an understandable tendency for economies with strong export sectors to lack significant tariffs or other import restrictions on raw material imports, whereas economies with weak balance of payments positions are more prone to try to protect their remaining industries with import constraints. Raw material costs are therefore likely to be lower in highly competitive economies than in those which are uncompetitive. The figures in the table show a 5% spread round the average.

Table 4.1: Options Available to Companies Producing Internationally Tradable Goods in Economies with Parities at Varying Levels

	Countries with Average Parities	*Countries Undervalued by 20%*	*Countries Overvalued by 20%*
Costs fixed in World Prices			
Raw Materials	20	19	21
Capital Depreciation	10	8	12
Total Internationally determined Costs	30	27	33
Costs fixed in Domestic Prices			
Labour Costs)			
Local Supplies)			
Land & Premises)			
Interest Charges)	60	48	72
Total Costs	90	75	105
World Prices for the Company's Output	100	100	100
Trading Profit or Loss at World Prices	10	25	–5

Source: Derived from OECD National Accounts.

Second, there are capital costs, which, when depreciated over output achieved in the average economy, are shown as 10% of selling prices. These costs, however, are even more likely to be considerably lower than raw materials in highly competitive economies, and higher in those which are uncompetitive. Not only do the competitive economies tend to have cheaper and more efficient suppliers for capital equipment than elsewhere, but they also benefit from potentially much higher levels of capacity utilisation. The result is that the cost of capital depreciation per unit of output tends to be much lower in companies in competitive economies than in those which are uncompetitive, a factor further reflected in the figures in the table.

Third, there are all the costs which are incurred locally. An overvalued currency implies that the average wage costs per hour, adjusted for local productivity, are necessarily above the world average by a similar proportion to the overvaluation. Indeed, it is the costs which the domestic economy charges the rest of the world for its labour, adjusted for productivity, which substantially determines whether the currency is over- or undervalued in the first place. Since labour costs make up some 60% of total charges incurred in developed economies, this factor makes a large difference to the prospects for the average firm. Higher labour costs per hour, adjusted for productivity, affect not only the labour costs the firm directly incurs, but also the labour component in all the goods and services it buys in from local suppliers. Furthermore, in an economy with an overvalued currency, interest charges will also almost certainly be higher than average, and high interest rates tend to push up the cost to the firm of land and premises, as well as borrowing. Taking all these locally determined costs together, they are shown as accounting for 60% of the selling prices for manufacturing companies in averagely competitive countries. These costs, however, measured against world prices for the firm's output, will be proportionately 20% higher in economies with overvalued currencies, and 20% lower for those whose currencies are undervalued. Finally, the table shows the firm in the averagely competitive economy making a 10% net profit on sales.

Now consider the options available to companies operating in the economy with the undervalued currency. If these companies sell at world prices, even with normal capacity utilisation, they make huge profits. This happens because their locally determined costs are 60% × 20% less than the world average, giving them a 12% cost advantage, in addition to the 10% net profit which has already been allowed for. An alternative strategy, which would still give them a 10% net profit on turnover, would be to sell at prices some 15% lower than the world average, providing them with an enormous cost advantage. They can then use their capital equipment much more intensively, reducing its depreciation charges as a percentage of selling costs by perhaps a fifth, the ratio used in the table. They can do this by relying on the large volume of orders which can be obtained at lower prices to achieve very high capacity working. In practice, the evidence from all the rapidly growing economies is that once they are making reasonable profits on turnover, companies which are highly competitive tend to go for lower prices and higher volumes of sales, rather than trying to keep prices up. This leads to even more rapid export-led growth than would otherwise occur.

The companies in the overvalued economy, on the other hand, face very different prospects. Their higher domestically incurred costs amount to 12% of the world selling prices for their output. These excess costs are more than the 10% net profit made by their competitors in the averagely competitive economies. The higher locally incurred costs wipe out all profitability for firms in countries with heavily overvalued currencies, if they sell at normal world prices, leaving them trading at a loss. They then have two choices. They can cut their current costs by paying lower wages and salaries, worsening employment conditions, cancelling investment projects and abandoning research and development programmes. Steps such as these may help in the short term, but are fatally weakening for the future. Alternatively, they can try to sell at higher prices. If they do this, however, unless they are in niche businesses which are not subject to normal competitive pressures, orders are bound to fall away, leading to lower and lower capacity working, and higher depreciation costs per unit of output. To make a 10% net profit on turnover, allowing for lower capacity working, the firms shown with the cost structure in the table in the overvalued country would have to charge prices nearly 20% above the world average. It is clearly impossible to compete at such high prices, especially against aggressive companies in the undervalued economies. All they can do is either withdraw from the market altogether, or persevere with prices which are the best compromise they can find between total lack of profitability and holding on to some market share.

It is all too clear which of these three examples is closest to the recent experience of much of Europe, particularly those confronted with competition on consumer goods from the Far East. Faced with the familiar problem of being uncompetitive, however, why cannot these companies increase their productivity to whatever level is required to be competitive with the world average, as all those who advocate industrial strategies and wage restraint are essentially trying to achieve?

Some companies can and will succeed in doing so. These are the ones which will survive even in the harsh conditions portrayed in Table 4.1 for companies in uncompetitive countries. Critical, however, to economies as a whole is not the performance of exceptional companies. It is the average achievement which counts. The required change might be made if it were possible to engineer a sudden huge increase in productivity across the board which competitors could not emulate, without any of the increase in output being absorbed in extra wages and salaries. One has only to look at these conditions, however, to see how completely unrealistic they are. It is far more difficult to increase productivity in slowly growing economies, with depressed levels of investment, low capacity utilisation, and relatively poorly paid staff, than in economies which are already growing fast, and where productivity will inevitably already be increasing rapidly. It is impossible not to share increases in output with the labour force to a substantial degree. What may be possible in isolated companies cannot be done across the board in all companies.

In economies with overvalued exchange rates, the more perspicacious managers of manufacturing companies do not persevere with attempts to improve productivity when they realise that they will never achieve sufficient increases in performance to be able to compete. They conclude that the safest, most profitable and rational strategy is to abandon manufacturing in the domestic economy. Some of them decide to buy from abroad whatever their sales forces can sell, perhaps reinvesting the proceeds from selling off factory sites and installations into manufacturing facilities in other parts of the world. Others sell out to multinational companies, who then use ready-made channels to distribute their output. The less perspicacious plough on until their companies go out of business. One of the paradoxical reasons why industrial strategies will always fail in economies with overvalued currencies is that the better the management in industry is at seizing profitable opportunities, the faster the process of deindustrialisation is likely to be. This is why many industrial companies with the best performance records in slow-growing economies are those which have closed down their manufacturing operations fastest, and moved them to other countries where costs at the prevailing exchange rates are much lower.

RETURNS ON INVESTMENT

A characteristic of much of the investment which tends to occur in rapidly expanding economies strongly reinforces the virtuous growth spiral. This investment is found mainly in manufacturing, especially in light industry, and also some parts of the service sector, where the returns are not only high but also tend to be very rapid. This is an extremely important component of the success of fast-growing economies, not least because it explains clearly why some countries have been able to go from being poor economic performers to being extremely successful very quickly. How did Taiwan and Korea manage to move from decades of stagnation to fast growth almost overnight? If it is possible to explain how this happened, and to show that it would be relatively easy for economies such as those in the European Union to recreate the conditions which would allow them to grow fast again, a further important policy plank available to the governments of the EU will have been laid.

The reason is that the return on nearly all successful capital investment is much greater than the proportion which comes back either as dividends or interest to the people who put up the money to pay for it. The 'private' rate of return on investment, which investors typically receive, is seldom above about 10%, even in those economies which are doing very well. However, it is by no means only investors who benefit directly from the projects for which they put up their money. Many others do as well.

The management and the employees in the enterprises where the investment has been made, whose productivity rises in consequence, almost invariably share in the benefits by obtaining salary or wages increases. The state also obtains a share through increased tax receipts. In addition, the consumer, who is provided with a better product or service, or a lower price, or both, is also a gainer. If the total rather than the private rate of return is taken into account, then across a wide swathe of much of the investment in fast-growing economies, the total return to the economy is much higher than 10%. This is not a particularly difficult ratio to calculate from national accounts. It is often 40% or 50% per annum, and sometimes higher still.

From the point of view of the investor, the build-up period for an investment is not normally particularly important. This is the time between when the investor starts to forgo the alternative uses to which his or her financial resources could be put, and when the investment comes on stream, starting to produce output and income. It is the time taken to build or construct the project into which the money is being invested. The investor's concern is that once the project is in operation, it should be able to provide a sufficient return to cover the interest charges during the build-up period as well as to produce a reasonable private return subsequently. For everyone else in the economy, however, and indeed for the economy as a whole, the build-up period provides no return at all because the investment project is not yet producing anything. There is no additional output to defray the private rates of return, or to contribute to the total rate of return, until the investment is physically in use.

It is extremely significant that investment projects typically found in rapidly growing economies combine the following characteristics. First, they have a high total rate of return. Second, they have a short build-up period, often of the order of six months, or even less. Third, they tend to be used fully once they are in place, because of the high level of demand which fast growth entails. When these three factors are put together, a truly astonishing cumulative rate of return on investment projects of this type becomes relatively easy to achieve. Investment projects which produce a total rate of return of 50% or more in six months or less, if the return on all the new output thus created is saved and reinvested, can produce a cumulative rate of return in excess of 100% per annum. This makes it possible for the whole of that part of the economy where this type of investment is taking place not only to double its output every year, but to generate all the investment funds required for this to happen. This kind of increase can be seen in some parts of the economies of countries such as Korea, Taiwan, and Hong Kong and, until recently, Japan, and now in the fast-developing parts of China. The huge returns on investment in the production of internationally traded goods and services, and the tendency for them to be reinvested, explain why rapidly growing economies have such high savings ratios, and why their industries have relatively few financing problems.

These very large rates of return cannot, however, be attained across the board. It is impossible to obtain 100% returns on investment in the social infrastructure, housing, public works and the like, except in very rare and unusual circumstances. Many private sector investment projects do not fit the bill either. Anything which takes a long time to build, whether, to take two major European projects over the last few decades, it is the Channel Tunnel or the Concorde supersonic airliner, will inevitably have a low cumulative total annual rate of return. These are not the projects which produce fast economic growth. Those that do, however, are exactly those with which the most profitable and rapidly growing international trade is concerned.

This is so because they have the same characteristic significant initial costs, with falling cost curves as production builds up and rising productivity comes through. Here, then, is another essential element in the strategy for achieving rapid economic growth. It is to pitch the exchange rate at a parity which enables fast export expansion and import saving to be achieved. This policy is needed not only because it creates and expands sectors of the economy where productivity growth will be very high. In addition, the total rate of return it can achieve is so large that it can generate the whole of the saving required to finance its own expansion, even if this entails doubling its output every year.

Two extremely important conclusions flow from these considerations. The first is that the lower the parity, the more chance there is of achieving not only self-sustaining but self-financing growth at a high rate. The increase in exports which is thus likely to be achieved is more than sufficient to take care of any increased import requirements there may be. Since any import restraints will make the exchange rate higher than it otherwise would be, the case for as few and as low tariffs as possible is reinforced. The second is that the large increase in productivity and output makes it much easier than might be supposed to deal with the inflationary pressures caused by rapid growth. We return to this important point in Chapter 6.

CHANGING THE EXCHANGE RATE

Is it possible for the exchange rate to be influenced by policy changes? Or is the parity entirely determined, as monetarists claim, by market forces over which the government of the day has little or no control? This is an extremely important issue for the Single Currency. If it is really market forces which control exchange rates, and governments are powerless bystanders, then attempts to lock the currencies of essentially separate states together are likely to fail. If, on the other hand, the policies of governments can have a powerful impact on their countries' parities, then the scope for maintaining a currency union of the type proposed for the EU will be stronger. Part of the problem for EU policy makers, paradoxically, is that for much of the time they profess conviction that monetarist tenets provide the solution to many of the Union's economic problems, but on the Single Currency they have to be ignored.

Indeed, one of the tenets of the monetarist school is that the exchange rate is entirely fixed by market forces, so that no action taken by the government to change it will make any difference. Monetarists have built up an elaborate theory which is intended to prove that there is an equilibrium exchange rate towards which every parity has a strong tendency to return. The traditional form of this theory was known as the Law of One Price, and the modern form is sometimes referred to as International Monetarism. It states that if attempts are made by the authorities to move to a parity different to the one which market forces will have established as the equilibrium point, then differential rates of inflation will soon pull it back to where it should be.

In particular, it is argued that any attempts to make the economy more competitive by devaluing will automatically cause an increase in inflation which will rapidly erode away any increased competitiveness temporarily secured. This will leave the economy not only as uncompetitive as it was before, but with an extra inflationary problem to boot. It is also contended that if, as a result of a temporary disequilibrium, the currency is overvalued this will exercise a strong downward pressure on the price level, thus reducing the rate of inflation without sacrificing competitiveness except perhaps in the short term. There is little doubt that many people in powerful positions in the European Union believe this theory to a greater or lesser degree. What is there to confirm that this proposition it is correct?

The evidence that devaluations always produce a corresponding increase in inflation will be reviewed in detail in Chapter 6. Suffice to say for the moment that the empirical evidence for the monetarists' contentions is extremely weak, and that there are good reasons, both theoretical and practical, for believing that on this issue they are wholly wrong. At this stage all that needs to be done is to look at what has happened to exchange rate changes across the world to see whether there is any evidence of an iron law which determines that parities cannot be altered without differential inflation rates at once starting to bring them back to equilibrium again. The plentifully available evidence shows beyond any reasonable doubt that monetarist contentions that exchange rates are entirely a function of market forces over which governments have no control cannot be correct. Without question, governments can and have changed both the nominal and the real exchange rates of the economies for which they were responsible by very large amounts. A conspicuous case was the huge rise in the rate for sterling which took place at the end of the 1970s and the early part of the 1980s. This was a direct result of the tightening of the money supply and the rise in interest rates which began under the Labour government of the time, and which was continued and reinforced by the incoming Conservative administration after 1979. As a result, the nominal value of the pound rose on the foreign exchanges from $1.75 in 1977 to $2.33 in 1980, an increase of 33%, and against the Deutsche Mark from DM3.85 in 1978 to DM4.56 in 1981, an increase of 18%. This happened despite far above average inflation in Britain over this period, thus enormously decreasing the country's competitiveness. In consequence the real exchange rate rose by 25%, with calamitous results for British manufacturing.

Another telling example comes from the early part of the Reagan presidency when the US talked up the nominal value of the dollar by no less than 60% against the Deutsche Mark (from DM1.83 to DM2.92) between 1979 and 1985, although the inflation rates in the two countries were broadly similar. A current example of a currency being held at a rate which is far from a market clearing rate is the *franc fort* policy pursued by the French. The cost to the French economy in holding the rate for the franc against the Deutsche Mark has been enormous. Growth has languished, investment has slumped, and registered unemployment has risen to one in eight of the labour force, while the economy has had to be forced by deflation to run a balance of payments surplus without which the *franc fort* policy would collapse.

Governments can also bring down the external value of their currencies if they want to do so. Between 1982 and 1989 the nominal rate for the US dollar against the yen fell by an astonishing 45% (from 249 to 137 yen per dollar), while the rate for the dollar against the Deutsche Mark went down by 38% (from DM2.84 to DM1.76) in just four years, from 1984 to 1988. Of course, there is a limit to the extent to which governments can resist market pressures, as Britain discovered when sterling was forced out of the ERM in September 1992, despite the government's best endeavours to the contrary. There is still, however, considerable scope for monetary authorities in any country to choose whether they want to be at the high or the low end of what the market will accept.

Nor does a longer perspective do anything to improve monetarist theory's credibility. One of the most striking cases of a successful devaluation was that of France at the end of the 1950s. The government of Charles de Gaulle, faced with increasing competition from Germany as the Common Market became established, devalued the French franc twice, by a total of 25%. The French inflation rate rose sharply for a few months, but by nothing like as much as the devaluation. Within a year the rate at which prices were increasing dropped back to where it had been before. French competitiveness *vis à vis* the German economy was established. The result was a long boom which took the French average growth rate to 5.5% per annum for a decade and a half, more than doubling the national income in fifteen years.

The evidence clearly shows that it is well within the power of any government to choose from a spectrum of possibilities where it wants the real exchange rate to be, and over long periods to hold it there within reasonably narrow margins. Of course there will be short-term fluctuations, but these are not so important. It is the medium-term trend which counts. What are the policies which any government can pursue to change the exchange rate, and then hold it at or near the preferred level? A considerable number are available, all of which need to be used in a co-ordinated fashion.

First, and underlying all else, is the monetary stance adopted by the government. There is overwhelming evidence that tight monetary policies, and the high interest rates which go with them, pull the exchange rate up, and that more accommodating monetary policies and lower interest rates bring it down. Study after study has shown that interest rates have a powerful effect on the exchange rate, significantly greater than other changes, such as the advent in Britain and the Netherlands of North Sea oil and gas.

Second, the actions and stance of both the government and the central bank in dealing with the foreign exchange market have a major influence in markets where expectations and opinion are almost as important as the underlying realities. If the government has a clearly expressed view that the exchange rate is too high or too low, the market will respond, as it did for example in the United States during the 1980s. The operations of central banks in buying or selling foreign exchange can and must be made consistent with other government policies.

Third, the government should have a definite plan as regards foreign trade balances. In the short term fluctuations are unavoidable, but in the longer term these can to a large extent be ironed out. If balance of payments surpluses are allowed to accumulate, as has happened in Japan, there will be strong upward pressure on the exchange rate. The converse is clearly the case, reinforcing the arguments for taking a liberal view on protection, and in general avoiding impediments to imports. The balance of payments is also a function of the level of domestic activity. Deflation produces a larger payments surplus or smaller deficit, and upward pressure on the parity, and reflation the opposite. The level of domestic demand is therefore a further important determinant of where the exchange rate goes.

Fourth, the government has a considerable degree of control over capital movements, with or without formal exchange controls. Any policy which encourages repatriation of capital and discourages capital outflows will push up the exchange rate, and vice versa. One of the problems which may occur if a policy of growth based on increased competitiveness is successfully pursued is that capital may be attracted in undesirably large quantities. This may make it more difficult to keep the exchange rate down. The answer to this problem is likely to be lower interest rates, if these are feasible, or not funding the whole of the borrowing requirement, to discourage an inward flow of funds. Domestic sources of capital funds can also be encouraged by concentrating economic activity as far as possible in those parts of the economy which can generate their own savings and investment at a high rate. If there are enough domestic savings to finance all the economy's investment needs, there is no merit in stopping any surplus being invested abroad. Still less is it sensible to insist on capital being repatriated which is not required, unless circumstances are such that it is necessary to get the exchange rate up. If the exchange rate needs to be kept down, there are, on the contrary, positive advantages to capital exports.

Finally, allowance needs to be made for the well known 'J' curve effect. If the value of the currency falls, there is a tendency for imports to stay at more or less their previous volume while the domestic revenue from exports falls because the exchange rate has gone down. This produces a worsening in the balance of payments position until the volume of exports increases in response to lower prices. If the value of the currency falls slowly, a succession of 'J' curve effects flows from each successive move downwards in the exchange rate, giving the impression that no improvement is in sight. The United States had something of this experience in the mid-1980s. The reverse tendencies are to be found if the exchange rate appreciates, giving the false impression for a few months, until market forces work their way through, that making exports less competitive does not make the balance of payments position worse. Part of the reason for the 'J' curve, however, is the belief by importers that any reduction in the profitability of their imports will shortly be reversed by an appreciation of the exchange rate. If it is clear, however, that a radical change in exchange rate policy has taken place, which is very unlikely to be reversed, it is possible to alter the behaviour of importers much more quickly.

With the battery of policy instruments available, governments can therefore determine the level of the exchange rate within wide limits. There is ample empirical evidence of government instigated exchange rate movements which have been successfully accomplished. Obviously it is impossible for all countries to move towards being competitive with each other simultaneously, although it would be possible for the world economy as a whole to adopt more expansionary policies. The evidence shows that it is practical for any individual country to decide where, within wide bounds, on the spectrum of international competitiveness, it wants to be, and having chosen that position, to stay fairly close to its preferred location.

Is it true, therefore, that the markets can be bucked? They do not need to be. There are internally consistent policies which any government can adopt which will hold the exchange rate down at least to a level which allows the current account to be balanced in conditions of full employment and at a sustainable rate of growth. These include low interest rates, an accommodating monetary strategy, keeping the economy open to imports which are competitive with domestic supplies, and encouraging capital exports. There are also other policies, currently adopted for example by the French, which will hold the parity at a high level. Provided the markets are satisfied that the policy stance taken up is one which the government is determined to continue, stability can be achieved over a wide band of different degrees of exchange rate competitiveness. It is not then necessary to buck the market. This is why, by choosing the right policy mix, it is always possible to choose a macro-economic stance which will ensure that external balance is combined with full employment and rapid growth.

The conclusions to be drawn in connection with the Single Currency proposals is that governments have wide, but not inexhaustible powers to control exchange rates. As happened with the Snake and the ERM, it is possible to restrict and control parity movements. Establishing the Single Currency, even against the pressures of market speculation, if these should occur, may well turn out to be feasible. As the currencies are locked together, however, without the redistributive powers across the EMU area which are available to the nation state, the cost of maintaining the currency intact may start to rise sharply. A political revolt against deflation and unemployment in the disadvantaged areas may take the place of the speculative attacks to which currency unions are prone while national currencies still circulate. The power of governments to control exchange rates is not unlimited, either against market or political pressures. Locked parities, even those in a Single Currency as long as there is still the possibility of constituent members reverting back to the *status quo ante* with their own currencies again, cannot be maintained against insupportable pressures.

EU POLICY MISTAKES

We have seen that rapid economic growth takes place in economies which are competitive in world markets and which start with the advantage of costs at least as low as their competitors. This enables them to expand their exports, without suffering from excessive import penetration, thus providing their economies with opportunities to grow without the constraint of balance of payments problems. Internal demand can then be kept at a high and rising level, without undue inflationary pressures developing. These conditions were established and maintained for all the original Common Market members in the 1950s and 1960s. They also applied to most of the rest of Western Europe – excluding Britain, which grew much more slowly – during the quarter of a century after the end of World War II and the immediate post-war recovery. During this period the economies of southern Europe were also growing fast, Portugal at 5.5% per annum, Spain at 6%, and Greece at 7.5%. The reason why such sustained growth was achieved, why living standards much more than doubled in the course of less than two decades, why unemployment barely existed, and inflation was stable, was that the macro-economic conditions were right.

To achieve high exports, every economy has to sell at home and abroad both the output of its labour and of its other factors of production taken together at competitive prices. If it does so, it will be able to achieve import-saving and export-led growth. If it fails to do so, especially by a wide margin, it will plunge into import-led stagnation. The only practical way of making any economy competitive is to position the exchange rate correctly. This is why the parity of the currency is so critically important. There is no other feasible way in which any country can change the price it charges for the whole of its output sufficiently to make the necessary difference.

The more exposed a country is to world trade, the more critical it is that its exchange rate should be correctly aligned *vis à vis* its competitors. As the Common Market was established, and subsequently a wider measure of free trade involving all the countries of Western Europe was put in place, so the volume of trade between them rose sharply both in absolute terms and as a percentage of each country's GDP. Probably all countries in Western Europe gained more than they lost from lower tariffs during the 1950s and 1960s. During this period, the gains from freer trade, as the tariffs came down, were not lost as a result of some countries becoming appreciatively more competitive than others, at least on the continent. Britain, the major exception, remained uncompetitive and refused to devalue, as became increasingly necessary, until 1967. The depreciation which occurred then was not only too late but too little, restoring the country's competitiveness, as government figures showed, merely to the same position as in 1962, which was not enough. The costs to the British economy of this mistake were huge.

The reason why the 1970s were so critical was that the impact of the break-up of Bretton Woods, the American devaluation, the early 1970s' boom and the oil shock, and the subsequent increase in the rate of inflation, were very unevenly spread among the West European economies. Germany, in particular, succeeded in weathering the storm with far lower price increases than prevailed elsewhere. The result was that Germany's competitive edge, already substantial, became greater still, and too much for the other economies of the Community and the rest of Western Europe to stand without taking defensive measures. These had to take the form either of exchange rate adjustments or deflation.

It was just at this time that the Snake was introduced. Instead of allowing the necessary exchange rate changes to take place, which were all the greater because of the turbulence of the time, it put off the adjustments which were needed. The inevitable result was that, in the end, the Snake proved unable to take the strain. The cost of fighting against the changes that were needed, however, is clearly marked in the growth rate of the countries involved. The economic expansion of the nine Community members, which had averaged about 5% over the previous decade, plunged to almost zero from the beginning of 1974 to the end of 1975. In 1976, the year after the Snake finally expired, it bounced back to 4.9%, and remained at an average of about 3% for the remainder of the decade. Of course the general economic instability characterising the early 1970s made policy management more difficult, but if the Snake was worth having, it ought to have helped to achieve the adjustments which were needed, or made them unnecessary. Instead, it left parity changes just as unavoidable as they were before, while delaying them at heavy cost in deflation, lost growth and rising unemployment.

In 1979, the Exchange Rate Mechanism was introduced, and exchange rates were again locked together. Thereafter, adjustments did take place, but invariably later than they needed to be, because of the ERM. Before they occurred, all the usual deflationary processes had to be put in train by the countries trying to defend their balance of payments positions against unmanageable competition. Again, the results on the EU growth rate are clear to see. For the whole of the period from the introduction of the ERM 1979 until its demise in 1993, the EU growth rate averaged only 1.7%, while the rest of the world achieved about 3.2% cumulatively. There was almost no net growth in output at all in the EU for the last three years before the ERM was effectively abandoned. Unemployment over this three-year period soared, reaching almost 11% across the whole Union by 1993. Yet again, when the effort to lock EU currencies together was temporarily abandoned in 1993, there was some resurgence in EU growth rates though still to much lower levels than had been seen in the previous halcyon days. The increase in EU GDP was 2.9% in 1994 and 2.4% in 1995. Unemployment at least stopped rising, although there was insufficient increased demand for labour for it to fall.

The fundamental problem throughout was the fact that the German economy was prone to less inflation than the average, and was therefore chronically inclined to become more competitive, with the results inevitably being reflected in the trade balance. Without exception, Germany has had a massive visible trade surplus every year since the immediate post-World War I period, only partly offset by deficits in services. Only recently, with increased imports after unification, has Germany had its first overall trade deficits. The previous large surpluses had to be mirrored by deficits in Germany's trading partners' foreign trade balances, most of which, weighted by the volume of trade, were in Western Europe. When they reined in to protect their balance of payments position, and to preserve the value of their currencies, as demanded by the Snake and the ERM, the result was that Germany's main export markets faltered, bringing down the German growth rate to little better than the average.

If the will had been there, it might have been possible for the EU to have broken out of this straitjacket, at least in part, by pursuing a general policy of reflation. The problem, again, was Germany, partly in the form of its competitiveness, but partly also in the guise of the Bundesbank, with its long-standing and determined anti-inflationary tradition. To reflate the economies of all of Europe, there had to be a major monetary relaxation in Germany, which would certainly have been perceived at the time to have involved significant risks with the price level. The Bundesbank would not allow this to happen. Without this stimulus, starting in Germany, it was impossible for other economies in Europe to reflate on their own, as the French rapidly found out when they tried their experiment in unilateral expansion after the election of the Mitterrand government in 1982. They soon discovered that they were faced with the familiar choice between retrenchment and devaluation. Delors, the then French Minister of Finance, fatefully persuaded his cabinet colleagues that deflation was the better option.

The low growth rate across the whole of Europe not only produced much lower living standards than might otherwise have prevailed, and much higher levels of unemployment, but it also had another very serious consequence.

The proportion of the EU GDP devoted to investment fell. Between 1965 and 1973, the proportion of GDP among the countries now making up the EU devoted to gross capital formation averaged 26.2%. Between 1986 and 1993, this ratio had fallen to 20.6%, a reduction of almost a quarter. There is no doubt that much of the missing investment which might have taken place, but failed to materialise, lay in the fastest growing tradable goods sectors, the seed corn for future competitiveness. Because of this, the ability of Western Europe to compete successfully with the whole of the rest of the world also gradually became undermined, reflected in a steady fall in the EU's share of world trade. Measured by exports from the twelve countries which were in the Community until the advent of Sweden, Finland and Austria, to countries outside it, the EU world trade share fell from 26.8% in 1963 to 19.9% in 1983, and on down to 17.5% in 1994.

These figures tell a depressing story for the almost 400m people living within the EU. It is one of lost opportunities, and relative decline in relation to the rest of the world. These trends have not materialised, however, for reasons which are beyond human control. They have happened because of policy errors which should not have been made, and which are still comparatively easy to rectify. With clarity of vision and appropriate policies, it would not be very difficult for the EU economies to return to the growth rates, full employment and modest inflation rates of the 1950s and 1960s. It would surely be hugely in the interest of everyone in Europe, and beyond its boundaries, for this to be done.

5 The Goal of Full Employment

'Without work all goes rotten.'
Albert Camus

An extraordinary change has taken place across the whole of the European Union over the past quarter of a century. It has been the huge growth in unemployment, matched by the fatalism with which this has been accepted by most of the population. When pollsters ask what respondents think is the most important problem facing the EU, the majority put unemployment high on the list, and often at the top. There is, however, little sign that this concern is being translated into effective action at the policy level. Indeed, there are ominous signs that unemployment problems across Europe may well be on the point of becoming even worse than they are at present.

The public are surely right to regard unemployment as a major evil. Its costs are enormous. Unemployment is a personal tragedy for everyone who wants to work and to make a useful contribution to society, and who is denied the opportunity of doing so. It is an economic disaster for those without work, whose incomes suffer accordingly. It is extremely expensive for the taxpayers who have to foot the bill for unemployment and related benefits. The indirect financial costs of having millions of people out of work is, however, very much higher than this. Those who are unemployed are much more likely to need the assistance of health and social services, and other welfare benefits, than they would if they were in work.

Nor are the financial costs of unemployment simply to be counted in the payments to those who are out of work. In addition, the economy forgoes the output that they could have contributed if they were working instead of being idle. In 1995, the average gross value of the output of every person in employment in the European Union was about 42 000 ECUs, equivalent to around $55 000. Even assuming that the average output of those just coming back into employment was rather less than this, the lost production of goods and services from having millions of people capable of working, but not doing so, runs into many billions of ECUs.

There is also a huge social as well as personal and financial cost to be taken into account. Innumerable studies show that there is a correlation between high levels of unemployment and crime, particularly theft. It is hardly surprising that it is difficult to get the more disadvantaged teenagers to concentrate on their studies if there is little prospect of a job when they leave

105

school. It is equally difficult, therefore, to avoid the conclusion that there is a strong association, reflected in international comparisons of educational achievement, between poor job prospects and low levels of literacy and numeracy among a whole generation of young people, many of whom have never been employed at all.

High levels of unemployment cause major fiscal problems. A large proportion of the taxable capacity of the EU Member States has to be deployed into paying for unemployment benefit, and all its associated costs. At the same time, the tax base shrinks because millions of people, who could be working and paying taxes, are instead drawing benefits. The major reason why governments across the EU have been unable to reduce the proportion of the national product spent by the public sector, and thus to contain or reduce the overall level of taxation, has been the inexorable rise in the cost of social security payments, for which high levels of unemployment are very largely to blame.

Furthermore, having millions of people who would like to work, but are unable to do so, makes less and less sense when the demographics of the EU are considered. The position varies across the Union, and is particularly acute in Germany, but there is a marked tendency everywhere in Europe for the number of people of working age to decline, particularly in relation to those who are retired. This inevitably means that the burden of supporting non-earning fellow citizens is going to have to rise for those who are working. It is absurd, in these circumstances, to have large numbers of people of working age who would like to work but cannot do so.

Nor do the published unemployment figures tell the full story. The headline unemployment rate measures only those who are actively looking for work. It excludes all those who would like to work, if the opportunity for doing so existed, but who have given up, temporarily or permanently, trying to find a job because the prospects look hopeless, or because they would be no better off in than out of work. The ratio between active job-seekers and those who could work, but are not trying to do so, varies across the Union. The average for the EU as a whole, according to Eurostat figures, is that for every 100 people who are registered as unemployed, about another 45 would like to work if they could.

The total number of people who would like to work, given a reasonable opportunity to do so with acceptable levels of remuneration, is therefore far higher than the number of registered unemployed. International Labour Organisation figures show that there may be as many as 30m people in the EU who could be drawn into employment if the conditions were right. No doubt many of them are currently working in the black economy, so the potential gains may not be quite as large as appears possible at first sight, but they would still be very substantial. So would be the fiscal gain from bringing them back into the tax system. Furthermore, there is considerable scope for increasing the amount of work done by those who count as being employed, but who are only working limited hours and who are not employed on a full-time basis. Some people, especially those with family responsibilities, may prefer to work part-time, but there are many others who would rather work longer hours for more pay.

There is thus an overwhelming case for increasing the amount of work available to the workforce, and reducing the amount of unemployment both of those on the register, and those who are not counted in the total. Why is this not being done? What is so different about conditions in Europe now than in the 1950s and 1960s? Why do some countries which are similar to those in the EU, such as Norway with only 2.5% of its labour force out of work in the spring of 1997, have proportionately much less unemployment? Why do other countries, such as France and Spain have even worse problems than the average? In France the percentage registered as out of work at the beginning of 1997 was 12.4%. In Spain it was a horrifying 21.6%. The corresponding figures for people under twenty-five were 28.2% in France and an almost incredible 40.7% in Spain. For the EU as a whole it was 21.3%.

This chapter is concerned with explaining both why unemployment now is so much higher in the EU than it used to be, and what can be done to reduce it on a sustainable basis to the rate which existed for two decades, in the 1950s and 1960s, when inflation was also comparatively subdued. Before doing so, however, we need to turn to the most commonly accepted conventional explanations for the high levels of unemployment which have been experienced in Europe for a decade and a half. This needs to be done to explain why nearly all of them are either only partly true, or plainly wrong. Many of the remedies for dealing with unemployment currently on offer do not and will not work. If the diagnosis is faulty, the prescription will almost certainly be wrong too.

FALSE ANALYSIS

When faced with the enormous number of people without a job across the entire European Union, almost everyone's instinctive reaction is to resort to essentially supply-side explanations for this state of affairs. Many different reasons are advanced to explain the high levels of unemployment which now prevail, and in consequence a wide range of remedies is on offer. It is not at all clear, however, that any of the explanations usually put forward to account for the high level of joblessness in the EU have any real credibility. If this is so, the solutions they entail are unlikely to do anything effective to resolve the problem.

First, there is a widespread tendency to blame unemployment on technical progress. It is clearly the case that much modern equipment can replace men and women with machines, which can do the necessary work far more quickly and accurately than any human can manage. Perhaps the greatest fears are of computers, with their ability to replace armies of clerks, accountants and secretaries. It seems logical at first sight that if machines can replace human labour, then the result must be fewer jobs and more people out of work.

This is of course a line of argument which has been current since the beginning of the Industrial Revolution, when mechanisation started. It is wrong because it depends on the 'lump of labour' fallacy. This is the assumption that the total demand for the output of labour is fixed, so that if part of a given amount of work is done by a machine instead of by human labour, unemployment must be the result. There is, however, no reason why the amount of output for which demand is available should be static. The history of the economically developing world has been one of rising demand ever since the Industrial Revolution began. Provided there is a steadily increasing amount of purchasing power available to buy the expanding output from mechanisation and technical improvements, there is no reason why involuntary unemployment should increase. The benefit from technical change will then appear as rising productivity and higher living standards. Problems will only occur if inadequate purchasing power is available to mop up all the new output potentially available.

Second, current levels of unemployment are not caused by the social and economic changes on which they are often blamed. Neither more women in the labour force, nor more part-time workers, nor shifts away from basic industries to light manufacturing, nor from manufacturing to services, nor any other changes in working patterns are responsible for more people being out of work. It is true that many of the new jobs which have been created recently in Europe have been part-time, especially in the service sector, and that women have been in many cases more willing to adapt to them, and to work for lower pay than many men have found acceptable. It is also true that the pattern of work available has shifted away markedly from employment where physical strength was at a premium to office and service activity. This has left large numbers, particularly of older male workers, with skills and experience which have been difficult to redeploy into the modern labour market. In this sense, there are mismatches in the labour market between the skills and abilities for which employers are seeking, and those which a significant number of applicants have to offer.

This cannot, however, be a satisfactory overall explanation for high levels of unemployment. The changes which are taking place in the labour market today are not so different from those which were occurring all over Europe in the 1950s and 1960s when no such problems were apparent, at least to anything like the same degree. The real problem is a different one. It is that there is not enough work to go round. In these circumstances, employers will inevitably choose the people who are most obviously suited to the work they have to offer, who are most adaptable and who will work for the lowest pay. With insufficient work for everyone, those who are least obviously fitted for the available employment, whether because of their locations, skills, ages or attitudes, will inevitably finish up without a job. If there were full employment, these problems would disappear.

It is often argued that so many people, and particularly young people, are out of work because their educational skills are inadequate, they are poorly trained, lack technical capabilities, and are not well motivated. There is little doubt that large numbers of younger people right across the EU lack good education and training. It is hardly surprising that many of them lack motivation if they are brought up in a culture where so many leaving school fail to find a proper job. It does not, however, follow from this that they are incapable of being employed. As with other categories of the labour force, the difficulty is that they are not those most obviously suitable for whatever employment is on offer, so they get left at the back of the queue. The problem, again, is that there is not enough work to go round, and in these circumstances the most disadvantaged are the most likely to finish up without jobs.

A different line of argument is that unemployment in the European Union is caused by high wages compared to those in many other parts of the world. It is assumed that it is therefore impossible for the EU to compete with places like China and Malaysia, where the standard of living is far below the level in Western Europe. An added twist to this argument is that generally in Western Europe, and particularly in countries such as Spain, France and Germany, employers have to pay heavy labour oncosts in the form of national insurance contributions, holiday and pension entitlements, and job security, which make labour costs even more expensive. In these circumstances, it is claimed, a large amount of work is bound to move to where the labour is cheapest, leaving European factories closing down, unable to provide jobs for their erstwhile employees. Nor, nowadays, is it just factory work that is affected in this way. If you ring up to book an airline seat, you may find your call being taken in a Third World country.

It is, however, a fallacy to believe that work always goes where labour is cheapest. It is also a fallacy to believe that rich countries and poor countries cannot trade together to their mutual advantage. The critical factor is not the amount that labour is paid per hour, but the cost of labour per unit of output, taking account of how productive it is and the rate at which it is charged out to the rest of the world through the exchange rate. If labour's productivity is high enough, it can compete comfortably in the world even though it is very well paid. We used to be told that it was cheap labour that made the Far East economies competitive. Now, however, the tiger economies have incomes per head approaching, and in some cases exceeding those in Europe, but their economies are still growing fast. Hong Kong currently has a standard of living which is higher than much of Europe, and its economy is still growing at about 7% per annum.

Variations in the cost of producing different goods and services explain why rich and poor countries can trade together to their mutual benefit, even if the poor country makes everything less efficiently than the rich one. In each case, the rich or the poor country will produce some output relatively more efficiently. For example, a low productivity Third World country may be a much cheaper place in which simple assembly work can be carried out. A rich country, in turn, may well be able to design complex products at far lower cost than might be possible even with the lowest paid labour in the poor country. It is these so-called variances which make it worth while for both countries to trade with each other. Each gains, and is better off than it would otherwise have been, as a result of the exchanges which trade makes possible.

For trade of this sort to take place to everyone's advantage, however, another important condition has to be fulfilled. The trade has to be in rough balance. Of course in the modern world where almost every country buys from and sells to every other, it makes no sense to try to make sure that trade between each pair of countries is symmetrical. It is each country's overall trade balance with the rest of the world which counts. If this is out of kilter, in particular because any country cannot sell enough to the rest of the world to pay for its imports, and therefore has to depress its economy to keep them down, thus putting people out of work, then its economy and its people will suffer from unemployment. This is not an argument, however, for abandoning the advantages of free trade. It is one for ensuring that the exchange rate is correctly positioned to enable it to hold its own with the rest of the world.

High unemployment is also sometimes blamed on those in jobs who work for excessively long hours, thus depriving others of the opportunity to work at all. This perception is the source of the pressure coming from some trade unions and other employees' organisations to cut down the maximum working week, to enable the available work to be spread out more evenly.

The Coates Reports on an Action Plan on Employment Policy, prepared with Stuart Holland for the European Parliament, takes the same line. There is some evidence that high levels of unemployment put pressure on those in jobs to work longer hours, but it does not follow that reducing working hours will increase the overall amount of work available. This is the 'lump of labour' fallacy in another guise. The solution is to increase the total demand for labour, and the way to do this is to make the whole economy more competitive. The problem with restricting working hours, apart from the fact that this does not appear to be most people's preference, is that such a policy is all too likely to raise costs, thus making the economy less rather than more competitive, and worsening the overall unemployment problems.

A different explanation advanced for high levels of unemployment is that the welfare state has blunted the need to work, and that therefore large numbers of people do not try to get jobs. It makes more sense to sit at home collecting benefits, the argument runs, than incurring the costs of being at work, especially if the pay is low. There is some truth in this assertion, especially for some people on low incomes. The effects of relatively high levels of income tax on low wages, combined with benefit withdrawal, can produce high effective rates of tax on people with low incomes. There are also particular problems for married couples, where one spouse working for low pay can reduce family entitlements by more than the income gained if the other remains out of work.

As a general explanation for high levels of unemployment, however, this argument is also unconvincing. First, large numbers of people who are out of work do not suffer from these kinds of income-trap problems. Second, at least some of these problems arise from the fact that there is so much unemployment in the first place. So many jobs are on offer at low pay because there are large numbers of people competing for the smaller quantity of unskilled jobs available nowadays. Third, and perhaps most importantly, much of the income-trap problem is itself directly the result of the huge cost to Member States of having very large numbers of people involuntarily out of work. There is acute strain on the tax and benefit system, largely because of the massive loss of income tax revenues from unemployment, combined with the heavy costs in benefits of having millions of people without jobs. The resulting high levels of tax on those with low earnings causes much of the overlap between taxes and benefits for people on low incomes. If the EU economies could rid themselves of the incubus of high unemployment, and as a result increase their tax takes while reducing the number of people in need of benefits, the income-trap problem would not disappear completely, but it would be greatly reduced.

MISGUIDED SOLUTIONS

Widely held perceptions of the reasons for high levels of unemployment are that large numbers of people are out of work essentially for the 'supply-side' reasons set out in the previous section. It is therefore hardly surprising that the government's response, in almost all countries with high unemployment, is to tackle supposed supply-side deficiencies. The objective is to make the economy more competitive, and thus better able to secure enough of the world's purchasing power to keep a higher proportion of the labour force employed. This activity is frequently devoted to efforts to improving productivity in the hope that this will make the economy more competitive.

The scale of much of this activity is enormous. France, afflicted by unemployment rates of more than 12% of its labour force, has recently been spending almost 0.75% of its entire gross national product on training schemes. Sweden and Denmark spend even more – over 1% of their GNPs. Nor do efforts to improve competitiveness cover only training. Higher levels of investment are also perceived to be a key factor, especially if the investment can be orientated to producing products with high value added. This often shades into claims that high technology is the key to improving productivity and competitiveness, generating state initiatives to move economies in Europe away from relatively 'low tech' activity to the 'higher tech' end of the spectrum, where it is thought that it would be easier to compete with elsewhere in the world.

This generally requires substantial capital expenditure, so another plank in the policy platform is then to encourage more investment, particularly in manufacturing industry. Fast-growing economies reinvest a much higher proportion of their national incomes than the relatively slow-growing economies of Europe. It is therefore assumed that if investment were increased this would tend to lead to high rates of growth. It is also argued that the state has a major role to play in enhancing the infrastructure to make the economy more competitive. Improving the road and rail system and developing more advanced telecommunications, proponents of this type of investment claim, will improve the capacity of EU firms to export and to compete in the world.

Unfortunately, evidence for the overall efficacy of any of these policies is almost totally lacking. Of course, more training gets some people into jobs which they might not otherwise have been able to secure, and it is certainly the case that wilting levels of investment weaken any economy's capacity to compete in the future. This is a different matter, however, from being able to show that all these state-driven supply-side efforts to cope with unemployment have been successful, despite their widespread adoption across the EU. Clearly they have failed. The EU still has well over 18m people claiming unemployment benefit, and a far larger number in total who would like to work but have given up hope of being able to do so. Furthermore, unemployment in Europe is on the rise again in most Member States.

These policies have failed to work because none of them begins to cope effectively with the real reason why there are so many people out of work in the EU. This has little to do with supply-side problems. On the contrary, it has everything to do with lack of sufficient demand for the goods and services which EU economies are capable of producing. When looked at in this light, it becomes comparatively easy to see why all the huge efforts currently being put into unemployment reducing measures are not going to work in the absence of changes in overall economic environment.

The fundamental problem with trying to use education and training programmes, and increased investment to make the economy more competitive, is that it is much easier to run such programmes successfully in economies which are already growing rapidly than where they are static or growing only slowly. EU economies are not the only ones with education and training programmes. Every developed country has them, and so, too, do developing countries. Furthermore, in countries which are growing quickly, with buoyant tax revenues and rapidly expanding and profitable enterprises, high quality education and training can be afforded relatively easily both in academic and on the job environments. The incentive for everyone to improve his or her skills is also clearly evident. With full employment, everyone can find a job, so time spent on training courses is seldom wasted. As a result, the effort and money spent on education and training has an immediate pay-off for almost everyone concerned.

In countries with high unemployment, the cards are stacked the opposite way. First, it is impossibly difficult to increase the skills of the labour force as quickly in a slow-growing economy as in one which is growing fast, because the opportunities for using increased skills are so much less. Slow-growing economies thus progressively slip further behind, and become even less competitive. Second, because there is still not enough work to go round, much of the education and training that takes place is wasted, since those on the courses cannot obtain work where they can use their new found skills once their training is completed. Even if they can, all too often they do no more than displace someone else, who then finds his or her way either on to the dole queue, or back to another training course. This is much too close to being an expensive and dispiriting zero sum game.

Nor is the encouragement of investment any more of a panacea in the absence of overall economic changes. As with education and training, it is far easier to implement successful investment projects in economies that are already growing fast than in ones which are static or growing slowly.

Profitability is much higher, making them easier to finance. Wages and salaries in the enterprises making them are relatively high, attracting able entrepreneurs and managers, who are likely to make good decisions. When mistakes are made, which inevitably they will be, it is easier to pay for them. As wave after wave of investment takes place, so the experience in managing the highly skilled process of operating a successful investment strategy becomes honed. It is extremely hard to compete against economies which have accumulated this kind of expertise. Far from it being easier in high-tech industries, furthermore, it is likely to be more difficult. Running high-tech operations successfully usually involves accumulating years of experience managing rapid technical change. The chances of companies anywhere being able to move into these fields from scratch and to compete successfully are not good. Logic and experience strongly suggest that it is generally easier to compete in industries where the technology is well established, and where the risks and skill requirements are lower, provided that the overall cost base is favourable.

The reality is that it is not high levels of savings and investment which produce high growth rates. It is high growth rates which produce high levels of savings and investment. The key to better economic performance is not to subsidise and cajole reluctant investors into putting more money into investment projects than they would if left to themselves. It is to create the macro-economic environment where high rates of growth are strongly encouraged by rising effective demand. Investment will then follow, as profitable opportunities open up. The reason for relatively low levels of investment in European manufacturing, compared to the fast-developing areas of the world, is that the prospects for making money out of new plant, machinery and factories in fast-growing economies tend to be much better than in those like EU countries which are growing much more slowly.

This fact cannot easily be discovered by looking at the results of large European based companies with worldwide operations, because many of them have substantial manufacturing facilities outside the EU. Figures from Britain, however, tell a story which is almost certainly replicated right across the Union. These show that the returns on investment in manufacturing have averaged just over half – 53% – that of the rest of the British economy over the whole of the period from 1970 to 1994. The average rate of return on investment on manufacturing over the whole of this quarter of a century averaged 5.0%, compared to 9.4% for the rest of the economy. Indeed, for twenty-two of the twenty-five years between the beginning of 1970 and the end of 1994, the British bank base interest rate, which averaged 10.6% per annum over the whole period, was higher than the average return on investment in British manufacturing. It is hardly surprising that the percentage of GDP spent on manufacturing investment in Britain, where the economy has long been run in a way which is hostile to manufacturing interests, is lower than almost anywhere else in Europe.

A widely trailed remedy to some of the EU's unemployment problems is the Union wide investment programme, discussed at a succession of Summits, originally at the instigation of Jacques Delors. The proposal is to spend large sums of money to enhance the infrastructure across Europe, particularly by improving transport facilities and telecommunications, financed by Eurobonds so that they do not impact on the Maastricht convergence criteria on government spending. If plans for the 500bn ECUs, which it is proposed should be spent over a period, all materialise, it is calculated that this may reduce joblessness in the EU by 1m, or at least offset increasing unemployment on this scale which might otherwise result from implementation of the Maastricht criteria.

Keynesian style reflation along these lines no doubt would create a significant number of extra jobs, although there have been substantial difficulties in delays in getting the planned infrastructure projects under way, so their potential impact should not be exaggerated. There is, however, a fundamental problem with reflationary projects of this kind, which greatly reduces their likelihood of making a major difference to the unemployment level. Whether they are financed by either borrowing or taxation, they tend to reduce expenditure in other parts of the economy, providing a substantial offset to the increased demand which they are designed to achieve. Very large programmes are therefore required, to secure even comparatively modest results. In the present constrained environment for public spending in the EU, it is therefore doubtful whether they are likely to play a major role in solving the Union's unemployment problems.

There is also a broad issue as to what strategies are worth pursuing when there are millions of people out of work, which relates to both investment and training as approaches for tackling the problem. Both involve improving skills and output, but does it really make any sense to try to improve productivity in these ways in conditions where there are very large numbers of people with no jobs? Is it so naive to reason that if 12% of the labour force is unemployed, everyone would be better off if productivity fell by 12%, so that no-one was without a job? In the real world so simple an economic rebalancing is no doubt impossible. The result is that high unemployment continues. Nevertheless posing this question points the way to some important and widely believed fallacies about productivity and supply-side remedies. Do they really have anything at all to do with competitiveness, and hence to improved economic performance? If asked what needs to be done to improve the EU's growth rate, the stock answer from most quarters is that the only solution is for the EU's industries and the economies of the Member States as a whole is to raise investment, productivity, quality, innovation and value added. Is any of this true?

As we have already seen, productivity is not at all the same as competitiveness. If it were, the richest countries would always successfully out-strip the poorer ones. This is clearly, however, not the experience of much of the world today. Nor has it ever been in the past. The reason is that productivity has everything to do with the standard of living, but almost nothing to do with competitiveness. It is the exchange rate – or more accurately the prices each country charges the rest of the world for the combined cost of all its factors of production – which determines whether the economy grows fast, or slowly, or remains static. Increasing productivity to make the economy more competitive will only work if it can be done fast enough to reduce prices more quickly than the world average, without reducing profit margins. Achieving this objective from a position where economies are growing more slowly than the rest of the world is an impossibly difficult task, and attempts to achieve it are virtually bound to fail.

Of course quality and innovation are important. No doubt, the better the quality the higher the price which can be charged. What can be done, however, if any economy starts from a position where quality is poor, and the products sold are old fashioned? Making them better is expensive, and everyone else in the world is trying to improve their products at the same time. The companies which are likely to succeed are those which are already profitable and expanding – in fast-growing economies. Those in slow-growing economies are much less likely to be so profitable, and thus cannot afford improvements nearly so easily. Again, producing conditions which trigger off fast growth is the route to quality improvements and innovation. Trying to use quality improvements and innovation as a way of increasing competitiveness and growth, rather than seeing them as by-product of an expanding economy, is again to set an impossibly difficult target which will almost certainly not be achieved.

Value added has similar characteristics to productivity. The total value added in any economy is roughly equivalent to total output. If the total output of the economy does not go up, and the economy does not grow, total value added will stay the same. If it then increases in some parts of the economy, it will have to go down in others. This is the root problem with trying to increase value added and productivity without tackling the macroeconomic environment. Even if successful in those parts of the economy where the policies are effective, if there is no overall output increase, the result has to be a corresponding reduction in performance in other parts of the economy which the policies have not touched. Increasing average productivity while the economy stays the same size does no more than guarantee increasing unemployment. The worst of all worlds will be achieved if productivity is increased, but the level of demand on the economy remains the same. The truth is that the connections between productivity, quality, innovation, value added and improved economic performance are very significant, but different from those normally perceived. It is not improved productivity or any of the other quality measures of output which produces more growth. The sequence is the other way round. This does not, of course, mean that productivity and related measures of economic performance are unimportant. On the contrary, they determine the standard of living, and are thus of vital significance. It is the output per employee which multiplies up to the gross domestic product. Whether an economy has a high or low standard of living, however, tells us nothing about whether it can compete in the world and whether, therefore, its total output, and with it productivity, quality, innovation and value added will increase or not. The economy's growth is determined by an altogether different factor, which is whether its output is competitively priced in the home and export markets. This is an exchange rate issue, and not one where any realistic policies on improving productivity, quality, innovation and value added, in isolation from macro-economic policy changes, have a chance of being successful on their own.

As with so many other economic matters, feedback makes it difficult to distinguish between cause and effect. In this case, as elsewhere, is all too easy to confuse symptoms and root causes. Determining the direction of causation is, however, critical to formulating policies which are going to work. Many millions of ECUs can be spent on supply-side policies designed to improve competitiveness and growth by increasing investment, productivity, quality, innovation and value added. Little or nothing will be achieved. No money needs to be spent, however, on implementing the policy which will actually achieve the results which otherwise will appear so elusive. Bringing down interest rates, increasing the money supply, and positioning exchange rates correctly, so that effective demand is increased, all cost nothing. Much more rapid growth will then follow, bringing increased investment, higher productivity, improved quality, innovation and greater value added effortlessly in train, as market forces drive expansion.

REFLATION AND THE TRADE BALANCE

The most important reason why the European Union suffers from such high levels of unemployment is not that there are supply-side difficulties which any practical policy is capable of surmounting. The real reason so many people are out of work is that there is insufficient demand for the output that they could produce to keep everyone in employment. Until this deficiency is remedied, unemployment will remain an intractable and insuperable problem. Trying to overcome unemployment by using education, training and investment programmes on their own will never work, however desirable all of them may be in a more favourable context. Nor will any of the EU level initiatives, designed to boost economic activity through the multiplicity of organisations under its umbrella, such as the employment structural funds, the European Investment Bank, the European Investment Fund, and European Regional Development Fund, fare any better. In the absence of major macro-economic changes, they will suffer the same fate as those implemented at national level.

The reason is that countries which are growing faster than the EU economies will always be able to use education, training and investment to increase output and employment more easily and rapidly than static or slow-growing economies ever can. The only solution to unemployment is to raise the level of demand for the output which all the EU economies are capable of producing to a sufficient extent to get almost everyone back into a job. How much demand is missing? The calculations are not particularly difficult, and they are set out below. It is easiest to start from a hypothetical country to illustrate the principles, and then to apply them either to individual countries within the EU or to the EU as a whole.

The starting point is to consider a country whose level of unemployment is at a higher level than is regarded as acceptable. If the reason for lack of jobs to keep everyone in work is insufficient demand, total demand within the economy will have to be increased until unemployment has been reduced to a level which is regarded as reasonable. How much extra demand is needed? If the potential output per head from those out of work was the same as those in work, the answer would be easy to work out. The increase in effective demand would have to be proportional to the increase in employment that was needed. For example, to reduce 12% unemployment to 3% would require an increase in demand to lift the proportion of those in work from 88% to 97% of the potential labour force, an increase of 9 divided by 88, or about 10%.

It is clear, however, that this is much too simple, even if we are only looking for broad approximations rather than exact figures. There are three major adjustments which need to be taken into account to produce approximately reliable results.

First, there is substantial evidence that to reduce the registered unemployment rate by, say, 100 000 people, much more than 100 000 new jobs need to be created. The reason for this is that increased unemployment opportunities attract back into the labour force many people who would not otherwise register as unemployed. The ratio varies, depending on a variety of circumstances, but the average across a number of EU countries during the major changes in unemployment rates which took place in the late 1980s, indicates that for every 100 000 people taken off the unemployment register, roughly 150 000 new jobs have to be created. This is likely to be a fair approximation for the ratio concerned across the whole of the EU.

Second, increasing demand is bound to lead to higher remuneration for the existing labour force, as the demand for labour tightens, even without hourly wage increases. More shift work will be needed, increasing overtime and payments for working during unsocial hours. People now counted as employed, but involuntarily working part-time, may take on full-time work. As a result, the average remuneration for all the existing labour force is likely to increase. Clearly the larger the increase in demand, the more pronounced this tendency will be.

Third, it is unlikely that the output per head of those currently unemployed will be as high as the average if they are reabsorbed into the active labour force. It will almost certainly be lower by a significant margin. Furthermore, the higher the level of unemployment from which we start, the larger this discrepancy is likely to be. We are not dealing with exact figures here, but within reasonably narrow limits it seems probable that this and the previous adjustment are likely to cancel each other out. Making this assumption then provides a relatively simple formula for calculating the increase in effective demand needed to increase employment by any given percentage. If registered unemployment is 12% and the target is to reduce it to 3%, effective demand has to be increased by the 10% already calculated, multiplied by an additional 50% to take account of the extra people drawn into the labour force. The total demand increase needed, therefore, will be approximately 10% times 1.5, which comes to 15%.

How can demand be stimulated to achieve much lower levels of unemployment? It has to be done both by both increasing the money supply and by expanding import-saving and export-led demand. The credit base needs to be increased sufficiently both to stimulate greater activity and to accommodate the new and higher volume of transactions which will need to be financed as the economy expands. The ratio between the money in circulation and the volume of transactions tends to fall as money becomes cheaper and more plentiful, and more idle balances occur. As a result, the increase in the money supply is likely to have to be significantly greater in percentage terms than the proportionate rise in domestic demand which will be needed.

It is not possible for any economy to increase demand by a significant percentage without regard to the impact this change would have on its balance of payments position. The next stage is therefore to calculate the balance of payments and exchange rate implications of a large increase in domestic demand. Again, it is easier to consider a hypothetical economy first, and then to apply the conclusions to the real world.

Suppose that the economy we are considering had a trade balance within acceptable limits before domestic demand was increased, and by way of illustration, suppose that a 15% increase in total demand was needed to reduce unemployment to the desired level. Again as an approximate estimate, the result is likely to be that exports of goods and services would stay the same as they were before, but imports would rise by the same proportion as the increase in domestic demand. A balance of payments deficit would therefore be created. How would this be corrected? There would have to be a devaluation. How much depreciation would be needed? Again, this is not difficult to calculate.

Large numbers of studies have been done into the sensitivity of the imports and exports of developed countries to price changes. All these studies show results that cluster round the same values. These are referred to as the price elasticity of demand, and the studies show that both imports and exports have elasticity values (ignoring their signs) of about one.

This means that if any economy, with these elasticities, devalues its currency, the volume of exports will rise by 1%, while the volume of imports will fall by 1%. If, again as an approximation, but not far from experience, import prices are set by world prices, and export prices are set in the domestic economy, a devaluation of 1% will have the following effects:

The value of imports, measured in the domestic currency will stay the same as they were before. This will happen because they will rise in price by 1%, but fall in volume by 1%, these two changes cancelling each other out.

The value of exports, measured in the domestic currency, however, will increase by 1%. This happens because their price, measured in domestic currency stays the same, but their volume increases by 1%.

The overall effect of these impacts on imports and exports taken together is that a 1% devaluation will improve the trade balance of the devaluing economy by 1%. This ratio then feeds straight back to the change in the trade balance required from the increase in domestic demand. If a 15% increase in demand is needed to reduce unemployment to acceptable levels, as a first approximation, this will need to be accompanied by a devaluation of the same size. This will both provide the stimulus needed to trigger off more growth and investment to sustain it, while also ensuring that there is no balance of payments constraint to check progress. These relationships remain the same whether the economy concerned has a large or a small proportion of its output involved in foreign trade. The sums of money involved in financing a trade deficit, compared with total GDP, however, would obviously be smaller if the economy had less of its GDP concerned with the import and export of goods and services. How would the devaluation be achieved? The answer is that the same policies are required to bring the exchange rate down as are needed to increase the money supply. More plentiful credit and lower interest rates, backed up by appropriate action by the central bank, would engineer the changes which would be required. It is not possible for the monetary authorities in any country to buck the market by trying to impose exchange rate régimes which the foreign exchange markets regard as unrealistic. There is no reason, however, why they cannot use the wide range of monetary policy instruments at their disposal to produce changes in exchange rates which clearly fit into a pattern which the markets can see makes sense.

It is important to stress again that the calculations set out above are approximate, and that they involve assumptions and simplifications which mean that the conclusions drawn are rough and ready rather than exact. These qualifications do not mean, however, that the orders of magnitude have been wrongly assessed, or that, allowing for margins of error, it is unsafe to rely on these results within broad limits. On the contrary, they point clearly to the direction in which policy needs to be moved, and they provide a reasonably reliable quantified indication as to the size of the changes which need to be made. It is significant that they are not by any means out of line with the scale of the exchange rate adjustments which have occurred frequently in the past, a further indication that the orders of magnitude have been correctly calculated.

If we now apply these conclusions to the situation in the EU as it now exists, it immediately becomes apparent that the changes in macro-economic policy required to bring the EU back to full employment are substantial, but far from unmanageable, both as between different Member States within the Union, and between the EU as a whole and the rest of the world. We turn now to seeing what these might be.

EXPANDING DEMAND

The calculations set out in the previous section indicate the orders of magnitude of the macro-economic policy changes which need to be made in the European Union. The current level of unemployment in the EU, at 12%, indicates that an increase in effective demand of approximately 15% would be required to bring unemployment down to 3%. This needs to be accomplished both by substantial parity adjustments between EU Member States, and by a reduction in the exchange rate of the EU currencies as a whole *vis à vis* the rest of the world from recent levels by about the same percentage, to deal with the balance of payments problems which would otherwise materialise.

Interestingly, some of these changes are already occurring. The Deutsche Mark has fallen significantly against the dollar, by about 10% over the last year, bringing down the value of all the other European countries currently linked to it. There has also been a much larger increase in the money supply in some EU countries during the last year than has been the case recently. In the year to August 1996, the German money supply, measured on the narrow M1 basis, rose by 10.8%, while the broader M3 rose by 7.7% – both larger increases than in the value of German GDP over the same twelve months, which rose by 4.0% year on year. The same sort or relaxation occurred in the Netherlands and Britain, and a number of other smaller EU countries, though not, significantly, in France. This may presage a better performance for the EU economies over the next year or two than might be expected in the light of the fiscal deflation which those attempting to meet the Maastricht criteria will have to meet. Nevertheless, the problems to be confronted look extremely difficult to solve permanently within the monetary and fiscal policy framework which the EU authorities are currently operating. There are two main reasons. Both fly in the face of all the major Single Currency policy proposals currently on the agenda.

First, it is clear from the different levels of unemployment across the EU that major exchange rate adjustments between Member States are going to be needed to bring unemployment down to an acceptable level across the Union as a whole. The first column in Table 5.1 shows the levels of registered unemployment in the EU states as of July 1996, the latest date for which they are all available at the time of writing on a consistent basis. It is clear from these figures that some countries, particularly Spain, Finland, France and Italy, have a far more serious unemployment problem than others, especially some of the smaller countries such as Luxembourg, Austria and Portugal. If no exchange rate changes take place within the Union, it is certain that some of the EU economies will become grossly overheated before others bring unemployment down anywhere near 3%. At best, therefore, a general reflation in the EU would have to be accompanied by significant parity changes at the same time, if its impact is to produce a general cure for unemployment across the Union. The second column in Table 5.1 shows the parity changes which would have to have been made in the summer of 1996 *vis à vis* the Deutsche Mark to enable all the EU economies to reduce unemployment to about 3% together. The third column shows the parity changes required, country by country, as against the rest of the world.

Table 5.1: Registered Unemployment Rates in the European Union by Country in July 1996 and the approximate Parity Adjustments required *vis à vis* both the Deutsche Mark and the Rest of the World to achieve 3% Unemployment throughout the EU

Country	Unemployment %	Parity Adjustment needed vis à vis *DM*	Parity Adjustment needed vis à vis *RoW*
Austria	4.1%	9%	–2%
Belgium	9.7%	–2%	–11%
Denmark	6.4%	5%	–5%
Germany	8.9%	0%	–10%
Greece	9.1%	0%	–10%
Eire	12.2%	–7%	–16%
Finland	15.5%	–14%	–22%
France	12.3%	–7%	–16%
Italy	12.2%	–7%	–16%
Luxembourg*	3.1%	11%	0%
Netherlands	6.7%	4%	–6%
Portugal	7.4%	3%	–7%
Spain	22.1%	–30%	–37%
Sweden	10.0%	–2%	–12%
United Kingdom	8.2%	1%	–8%
EU Average	10.9%	–4%	–13%

* Luxembourg uses the same currency as Belgium.

Second, even assuming that all the necessary exchange rate changes were made to enable unemployment to be reduced across the Union during the immediately forthcoming period, updated from those in Table 5.1, it is very unlikely that further parity adjustments would not be required in future. On the contrary, it is highly probable that there will be a tendency for the competitiveness of the constituent states to drift apart again, requiring more parity adjustments to avoid the same problems which are manifest now from recurring in the future.

The European Union's fundamental monetary and economic problem is that its proposals for locking currency parities together remove exactly the flexibility which is required to enable all the economies of the Union to prosper together. The fiscal transfers which the EU is capable of producing are small now, and unlikely to become sufficiently sizeable to deal with the inevitable divergence between Member States which will occur in future. The Member States themselves have sufficient tax and spending capacity to iron out, within reason, disparities in performance between regions within their own economies, but the EU as a whole does not have this ability. This is why there is no credible solution available to the Union's unemployment problems within the framework of the Single Currency.

Table 5.1 does, however, indicate that the exchange rate changes needed to deal with unemployment within the EU, given an environment where needed parity alterations can be made, are not unmanageably large. Some of them have already been made, particularly the reduction in the value of the Deutsche Mark, and with it all the currencies attached to it, *vis à vis* the rest of the world. Will this reduction be sufficient to increase the EU growth rate substantially? We turn to this question in the next section. Even if it were, however, there would still be a substantial remaining problem inside the EU about how to stop some economies overheating before others had returned to anywhere near their full employment targets. Exchange rate flexibility is just as important between EU countries as it is between the EU as a whole and the rest of the world.

LONGER-TERM SOLUTIONS

It is now possible to see the twin problems of slow economic growth and high levels of unemployment in the same context. The solution to them both has a substantial overlap. The policies for all economies suffering from slow growth and high levels of unemployment have to be changed in two vital respects. Their internal level of demand has to be expanded to a point where unemployment falls to whatever is regarded as an acceptable percentage. Their exchange rates have to be positioned at a level which enables them to shift to a much higher rate of growth. We need now to explore in more detail the conditions needed not only to achieve a spurt of growth while unemployment falls and underused resources are brought back into commission, but also to maintain a high growth rate for the foreseeable future.

The only way to do this is for a high and rising level of demand to be sustainable at whatever growth rate is considered desirable, without the economy running into either capacity constraints, or – the other side of the same coin – unacceptable inflationary problems. These conditions can be achieved, but to understand how to attain them, we need to revert to some of the issues discussed in Chapter 4. Bringing the exchange rates of the EU economies into line with each other, so that unemployment falls everywhere to around 3%, is certainly a very important first step to achieve the economic conditions needed in the Union. Accomplishing this objective is not, however, a sufficient condition for ensuring that the EU economies return to the vigour and stability they exhibited in the 1950s and 1960s. Other steps will have to be taken to ensure that these conditions are regained.

Certainly, a major one is to make sure that the European economies as a whole not only remain in balance with each other in terms of competitiveness. They also need to maintain collectively a sufficient competitive edge to keep the average growth rate of the EU as a whole at a level at least as high as the world average, and perhaps higher. To do this, the EU economies will have to obtain and keep a sufficient share of the investment and production which has the falling cost curves and large returns characteristic of international trade. This means that the costs of production in Europe, allowing for different productivity levels, will have to be as low as the world average. If this does not happen, footloose investment and production of both goods and services will migrate to other parts of the world. To make sure that this does not occur, the exchange rates of the economies of Europe will almost certainly have to drop, *vis à vis* the major currencies of the world, such as the dollar and the yen, further than would be required just to restore full employment in the EU. The extent to which further parity adjustments will be needed will depend heavily on developments elsewhere in the world. They include changes in competitiveness in the United States, Japan and elsewhere on the Pacific rim, as well as in other parts of the world, which are bound to unfold over the coming decades, and which are hard to foresee in advance.

It is, however, possible to predict with a high degree of certainty what will happen to the competitiveness of the EU economies if they continue to grow much more slowly than the world average. If their growth rate is less than that of the rest of the world, it is inevitable that this will be reflected in rates of gross investment below those of the economies of the world which are expanding more quickly. It is then equally inescapable that the proportion of the investment which takes place in the EU of the highly productive internationally tradable kind will be lower than in rapidly growing economies. The unavoidable consequence is that the EU as a whole will become progressively less able to compete in the world, unless more exchange rate adjustments take place.

Indeed, a general rule can be promulgated which applies to the economies of Europe as much as to anywhere else. Any economy which is growing at less than the world average rate, which is currently around 3.5%, will find its ability to compete falling away, while any growing faster than the world average will find its competitiveness increasing. This is a direct consequence of the self-reinforcing tendency for economies with exceptionally competitive international tradable sectors to grow more rapidly than the average, as they attract more and more investment, and their competitiveness increases. Exactly the reverse happens to the weaker economies whose ability to compete steadily diminishes, a reflection of rising costs, making them progressively less attractive sites for more investment.

There is thus a universal tendency for fast-growing economies to develop currencies which become stronger and stronger, while those of slow-growing economies weaken. They are then faced with the all too familiar choice in Europe – to deflate or to devalue. If devaluation is ruled out, the deflation which follows will progressively worsen their condition, as their investment ratios and competitiveness fall further and further away. The appalling levels of unemployment in Spain, and the not much better figures in many other EU countries, show only too clearly where this process leads if it remains unchecked.

Even a consistent growth rate of about 4% per annum, a little above the current world average, is still quite low by the standards of the Pacific rim countries, or in comparison with the achievements of many European economies in the 1950s and 1960s. Would it be possible for the EU members to move up to growth rates of 8% or more, if they wanted to, as are regularly achieved in the Far East? It would be, but still greater downward movements in exchange rates would be required, to enable the EU economies to achieve the super-competitive status that would be needed to put them into the same growth league as Taiwan, South Korea and China. If only to show how 8% or more rates of growth could be achieved, however, it is worth exploring the structural changes which would be required to bring the EU economies up to the Pacific rim level of performance, and to see how such high growth in output could be obtained. The figures in Table 4.1 (see p. 90), combined with historical experience of major parity changes which have triggered high growth, such as Germany achieved shortly after World War II, suggest that exchange rates in Europe might have to drop by perhaps another 20% *vis à vis* those in the Far East to do it. How would the returns on investment then produce the very high growth rates which the Far East economies achieve?

Consider again the total returns achieved by different types of investment projects, encompassing all the increases in income received by everyone in the economy as a result of investment. These include higher wages, better products, greater tax receipts, and higher profits, as well as the returns to the investors who put up the money. The returns on investment projects vary enormously. In some of the private sector, and much of the public sector, they are little more than the rate of interest, and sometimes lower. This is typically the total rate of return obtained on investments, for example, in housing, and many roads and public buildings. At the other end of the spectrum in some light manufacturing and parts of the service sector, the total rate of return is often far higher. It can be as high as 100% per annum in favourable cases. In the middle are investments in heavy industry, which typically produce total rates of return of around 20% or 25%.

Investment projects with exceptionally high total returns are characteristically those involved in international trade in goods and services. They therefore tend to be heavily concentrated in countries with low exchange rates, and strongly discouraged by high currency values. Furthermore, the high total returns on these investments both produce large resources for reinvestment, and ample opportunities for new profitable projects. The result is that a much higher proportion of the national income goes into investment than in slow-growing economies. Now consider two examples:

Country A has total gross investment of 15% of GDP, Two-thirds of this – 10% of GDP – produces an average total return of 10%, and one-third – 5% of GDP – produces an average total return of 20%. This economy will have a growth rate of (10% × 10%) + (5% × 20%) – a total of 2% per annum.

Country B has a total gross investment of 35% of GDP. In terms of GDP share, 15% produces an average 10% total return, 10% produces a 20% total return, and 10%, in the highly competitive internationally traded sector, produces a 50% total return. This economy will have a growth rate of (15% × 10%) + (10% × 20%) + (10% × 50%) – a total of 8.5% per annum.

Of course this is an oversimplified model, but this does not prevent it from demonstrating an important insight into how economies produce different growth rates, and how their structures adapt to, and reinforce the opportunities which their foreign trade relations open up for them. With an 8.5% growth rate, and gross investment running at 35% of GDP, productivity rises rapidly. The competitiveness of the internationally tradable sectors grows fast. Education and skill levels increase exponentially. The problem which these economies have is to avoid the growth of export surpluses, and the appreciation of their currencies, eroding away the competitiveness which makes such high increases in output possible.

Should the economies of the EU aim for as high a growth rate as this? Difficult decisions would be required. The social and environmental strains entailed by very rapid economic expansion are substantial. On the other hand, the increase in living standards and the extra ability to cope with novel developments which exceptionally rapid growth opens up are potentially very exciting. Also, with a fast-growing economy goes a corresponding increase in power and influence in the world, which may be of crucial importance. The point to grasp is that it is possible for these kind of choices to be made. It is not inevitable that the members of the EU should be left to languish at the bottom of the growth league, while other countries take advantage of their opportunities and make decisions precluded to EU electorates. If EU economies wish to revert back to growing as fast as Germany did in the post-war period, they could do so. They should be allowed to choose the future they desire, not shackled together with an average growth rate of 2% per annum or worse, as they are at present.

6   Living Standards and Inflation

'Beware of false knowledge; it is more dangerous than ignorance.'
George Bernard Shaw

There is a widespread fear that exchange rate changes automatically generate inflationary pressures in devaluing economies. It has always been a major tenet of the monetarist position that any benefits secured from depreciation will at best be temporary. They will soon be lost, it is argued, as a result of increasing inflation in the devaluing country, leaving the economy concerned in no more competitive a position than it was before, after a short adjustment process, but also with a legacy of an enhanced level of inflation.

It is also widely believed that a devaluation necessarily produces a fall in the living standards of any economy the external value of whose currency is falling. There are two reasons usually advanced to support this proposition. The first is that if a country devalues, there will inevitably be an adverse movement in its terms of trade. This means that, after the fall in the parity, the amount of imports which can be purchased for each unit of exports is bound to fall, depressing the national income. The second, which overlaps with the first, is that to make up for the reduction in the terms of trade, more room will have to be found for goods and services to be sold abroad. The only way of achieving this objective is to shift resources out of current living standards into exports, thus lowering average real incomes, and depressing the real wage.

There can be little doubt that the almost axiomatic strength of these arguments has persuaded large numbers of people that devaluations are inflationary, reduce living standards, upset business plans, discourage investment, and ought to be avoided if at all possible. This is the standard case for fixed parities. Even a brief look at economic history, however, shows that these views are almost entirely unfounded. There have been large numbers of exchange rate changes in recent history which can be used to test the validity of the widely believed monetarist case, and several of the most prominent are set out in Table 6.1. Without exception, they show that even large exchange rate changes generally make little or no difference to the rate of inflation, unless the economy concerned was already operating at full stretch, as was the case in France at the end of the 1950s. Even then, however, the sharp increase in prices, to which the double devaluations under Charles de Gaulle undoubtedly contributed, quickly abated.

Table 6.1: The Effects of Exchange Rate Changes on Consumer Prices,
the Real Wage, GDP, Industrial Output and Employment[*]

	Year	Con- sumer Prices	Wage Rates	Real Wage	GDP Change	Industrial Output Change	Unem- ployment %
Britain – 31%	1930	–6.0	–0.7	5.3	–0.7	–1.4	11.2
Devaluation	1931	–5.7	–2.1	3.6	–5.1	–3.6	15.1
against the US	1932	–3.3	–1.7	1.6	0.8	0.3	15.6
dollar in 1931	1933	0.0	–0.1	–0.1	2.9	4.0	14.1
	1934	0.0	+1.5	1.5	6.6	5.5	11.9
France – 27%	1956	2.0	9.7	7.7	5.1	9.4	1.1
Devaluation	1957	3.5	8.2	4.7	6.0	8.3	0.8
against all	1958	15.1	12.3	–2.8	2.5	4.5	0.9
currencies in	1959	6.2	6.8	0.6	2.9	3.3	1.3
1957/58	1960	3.5	6.3	2.8	7.0	10.1	1.2
	1961	3.3	9.6	6.3	5.5	4.8	1.1
USA – 28%	1984	4.3	4.0	–0.3	6.2	11.3	7.4
Devaluation	1985	3.6	3.9	0.3	3.2	2.0	7.1
against all	1986	1.9	2.0	0.1	2.9	1.0	6.9
currencies over	1987	3.7	1.8	–1.9	3.1	3.7	6.1
1985/87	1988	4.0	2.8	–1.2	3.9	5.3	5.4
	1989	5.0	2.9	–2.1	2.5	2.6	5.2
Japan – 47%	1989	2.3	3.1	0.8	4.8	5.8	2.3
Revaluation	1990	3.1	3.8	0.7	4.8	4.1	2.1
against all	1991	3.3	3.4	0.1	4.3	1.8	2.1
currencies over	1992	1.7	2.1	0.4	1.4	–6.1	2.2
1990/94	1993	1.3	2.1	0.8	0.1	–4.6	2.5
	1994	0.7	2.3	1.6	0.6	0.7	2.9
Italy – 20%	1990	6.4	7.3	–0.9	2.1	–0.6	9.1
Devaluation	1991	6.3	9.8	3.5	1.3	–2.2	8.6
against all	1992	5.2	5.4	0.2	0.9	–0.6	9.0
currencies over	1993	4.5	3.8	–0.7	–1.2	–2.9	10.3
1990/93	1994	4.0	3.5	–0.5	2.2	5.6	11.4
	1995	5.4	3.1	–2.3	2.9	5.4	11.9
Finland – 24%	1990	6.1	9.4	3.3	0.0	–0.1	3.5
Devaluation	1991	4.1	6.4	2.3	–7.1	–9.7	7.6
against all	1992	2.6	3.8	1.2	–3.6	2.2	13.0
currencies over	1993	2.1	3.7	1.6	–1.6	5.5	17.5
1991/93	1994	1.1	7.4	6.3	3.9	10.5	17.9
Spain – 18%	1991	5.9	8.2	2.3	2.2	–0.7	16.3
Devaluation	1992	5.9	7.7	1.8	0.7	–3.2	18.5
against all	1993	4.6	6.8	2.2	–1.1	–4.4	22.8
currencies over	1994	4.7	4.5	–0.2	2.0	7.5	24.1
1992/94	1995	4.7	4.8	0.1	2.8	4.7	22.9

[*] All figures are year on year percentage changes.
Sources: OECD, *Economic Outlook* June 1997, IMF, *International Financial Statistics*, July 1997, supplemented by a variety of earlier OECD, IMF and British official statistics.

Furthermore, far from the average standard of living falling after a devaluation, it almost invariably rises, because the GDP of all devaluing countries tends to increase significantly shortly after the currency has depreciated. There is also a marked tendency for industrial output to rise sharply soon after a devaluation, triggering increased investment, while the experience of Japan, after the yen's strong revaluation in the early 1990s, shows the opposite outcome equally strongly. In most cases the real wage tends to rise as well, shortly after the exchange rate falls, this being calculated in Table 6.1 as being the difference between the change in average wage rates and the change in the consumer price level. This tendency is not so pronounced as the increase in GDP, because devaluations tend to increase employment, thus reducing the numbers out of work, but also diluting down average earnings. This bias can be seen in the United States experience after the dollar fell in the second half of the 1980s as the GDP rose, but the number of people in work increased very rapidly. Table 6.1 also shows the opposite results occurring in the major case of Japan's revaluation of the yen during the early 1990s. There the growth rate went down, the real wage stayed static, and unemployment began to creep up.

These may well be unexpected results to many people who have been led to expect a very different outcome. In particular, the figures in Table 6.1 provide no justification at all for the widely believed monetarist view that it is impossible to secure a permanent advantage in terms of competitiveness and growth by exchange rate adjustments. Perhaps the widespread conviction that devaluation will have the damaging results so frequently anticipated stems from the fact that many people might like these predictions to be true. Everyone who has a stake in seeing interest rates kept high and money tight might be inclined to share such a view. This tends inevitably to include a large proportion of the banking and financial community. Those doing well out of importing goods into economies with overvalued exchange rates, because the costs of production are so much cheaper elsewhere than in the home market, may also tend to find the same opinions particularly acceptable. Undoubtedly the monetarists have helped support the case, with appropriately impressive theorising, which no doubt neatly underpinned what many people, from simple motives of self-interest, were only too pleased to hear. All the same, it is extraordinary that so many people believe these propositions to be true when there is so much simple and incontrovertible evidence easily to hand to show that the assumed relationships between depreciation, inflation and the standard of living are wrong.

On the contrary, if, as Table 6.1 shows, it is possible for any industrial economy to devalue, especially when the economy concerned has substantial unused resources, without any significant inflationary penalty being paid, this is a very important policy matter. It means that long-lasting adjustments, which are highly beneficial in terms of growth and reducing unemployment, are in fact entirely feasible, even though their possibility is denied by monetarist theory. It can then no longer be claimed that any economy stuck in the doldrums has no practical way out of its predicament. On the contrary, the way is open for any country which is having difficulty competing and keeping all its resources employed, especially its labour force, to remedy the position by making appropriate exchange rate adjustments. Indeed, far from the results of devaluations being only temporary, shortly to be eroded away by extra inflation, they tend to be self-reinforcing, as arguments in previous chapters have shown. This why any country's ability to change its exchange rate to suit its circumstances is such an exceedingly valuable policy weapon that it should not be given up unless there is certainty that alternative ways of coping with economic imbalances equally effectively are available. The crucial problem about the Single Currency is that no such remedy is possible for participating economies once they have joined – unless they leave.

This is not to say that inflationary problems can be ignored if parity changes continue to take place. Good management of the economy is required in all circumstances. The evidence in Table 6.1 makes it clear, however, that many of the widely held opinions about the relationship between devaluation, price rises and the real wage are at variance with the facts, and therefore cannot be well founded in theory. There is much evidence that the problems with inflation are more diverse and more manageable than is often recognised. We turn now to see what these may be.

DEVALUATION AND THE PRICE LEVEL

Those who believe that exchange rate changes will affect prices are right in at least one sense. Any parity reduction is bound to exert upward pressure on the prices of all imported goods and services in the devaluing country. While the prices of both imports and exports will almost certainly rise measured in the domestic currency, there may also be a tendency for import prices to increase faster than export prices, worsening the terms of trade. In this sense too there is a direct cost to the economy. Furthermore, there is no value in a policy of depreciation unless it makes imports more expensive relative to home market production. A major objective has to be to price some imports out of the home market by making it relatively cheaper than it was previously to produce locally rather than in other countries. It follows that there will have to be price increases for imported goods and services, otherwise there will be no new bias towards production from domestic output.

The evidence presented in Table 6.1, however, clearly indicates that other factors have to be taken into account. If, as is commonly supposed, it is only import prices which are significant, the figures in Table 6.1 would show increasing inflation and declining living standards after a depreciation, and not, generally speaking, the opposite. How are the figures in the table to be explained? The answer is that the impact of a devaluation on the price level is more complicated than is often recognised. Many of the effects are disinflationary rather than the reverse, and tend to increase the national income rather than reduce it.

First, one of the immediate impacts of a devaluation is to make all domestic production more competitive in both home and export markets than it was before. Within a very short period of time, this leads to increased output. Of course there are time lags and not all the potential increases in sales will be realised immediately, but almost any increase in production will help to reduce average costs. Increased capacity working spreads overhead charges across more output. We have seen that production and service industries involved in international trade typically have falling cost curves, a reflection of the fact that the marginal cost of production is well below the average cost. Enterprises of these sorts cannot fail to benefit from a depreciating currency. Obviously some of their input costs, if they include either imported goods and services, or a switch to a domestic producer who has now become competitive, will rise. This is part of the price that has to be paid for devaluing. The increased volume of output which can now be obtained, however, is clearly a substantial factor weighing in the balance on the other side.

Second, some of the policies which have to be associated with bringing the parity of the currency down also directly affect both production costs and the cost of living generally. One of the most important of these is the rate of interest, which must come down with the exchange rate. Borrowing costs at high real rates of interest are a heavy and expensive burden on most firms which produce goods and services. A lower rate of interest lowers production costs. Interest rates are also an important component of the retail price index, particularly in countries where a large proportion of personal outgoings are on variable rate loans, such as mortgage payments. A substantial reduction in interest rates, designed to bring down the exchange rate to a more competitive level, itself makes an important contribution to holding down the rate of inflation.

Third, rising productivity, which flows from increased output, not only has the immediate effect of reducing costs. It also makes it possible to meet wage claims of any given size with less impact on selling costs. Whatever the going rate for wage increases may be, the less the inflationary impact as output increases. Nor is this just a factor which applies for a short period until those responsible for formulating wage claims adjust to a new situation and then increase their claims. The international evidence strongly suggests that economies with rapidly expanding output have a better wage negotiation climate generally, and thus achieve wage increases more realistically attuned to whatever productivity increases are actually being secured.

Fourth, one of the major objectives of reducing the parity is to switch demand from overseas sources to home production. While the price of imports is bound to rise to some extent, there is strong evidence that the increase in costs from exchange rate changes are seldom passed on in full. Foreign suppliers are inclined to absorb some of the costs themselves, calculating that what they lose on margin they may make up by holding on to market share. Furthermore, if demand is switched from imported goods and services to home production, this purchasing power will not be affected, at least not directly and in full, by the increase in import prices. It will benefit in cost terms from the fact that home production is now relatively cheaper than imports.

Fifth, it is possible to employ the much improved fiscal position which higher growth produces to have a directly disinflationary impact, using the tax system. It is often argued that if there is a depreciation, the government of the devaluing country necessarily has to deflate the economy to make more room for exports. This argument cannot hold water, however, if there are large numbers of unemployed people, and considerable slack in the economy. In these circumstances, it is not difficult to combine increasing output, stimulated by a lower exchange rate, with an expansionary monetary and fiscal policy. It is then possible to structure tax changes so that they have a positive disinflationary impact. Reducing taxes on wage earners, in particular, both directly reduces costs and encourages more employment. There are other similar candidates, such as reducing VAT rates. Lowering VAT rates is not as effective as bringing down taxes on employment, however, because VAT is levied both on home produced and imported goods and services, and because bringing down VAT does not help so directly with the unemployment problem as reducing taxes on labour.

If there is a devaluation, taxation policy may help to secure a further crucially important objective to avoid price increases not only immediately after the parity has come down, but subsequently as well. If the first-round effects of higher import prices can be neutralised by higher output, rising productivity and tax changes, then there will be no second and subsequent rounds of price rises flowing from the change in parity. This is clearly an extremely desirable state of affairs to achieve, making it much easier to manage the economy in a way which protects the increased competitiveness flowing from devaluation from erosion.

When each of these disinflationary factors is taken into account, all of which apply in varying degrees whenever the parity comes down, the figures in Table 6.1 become very much easier to understand. It is evidently not true that devaluation necessarily increases the rate of inflation. Still less is it true that it must always do so to such a degree that any extra competitive advantage is automatically eroded away.

At the risk of some calculations, which are important but which do not make particularly easy reading, and which can be skipped by those who will take them on trust, it is possible to set out in quantified form why this should be the case. Suppose that the currency is depreciated by 25%, and that on average import prices rise by two-thirds this amount, while foreign suppliers absorb the rest. Assume that imports of goods and services make up around 30% of gross domestic product – a fairly typical ratio in the EU – so the impact on the price level from increased import prices in these circumstances is likely to be about two-thirds of 25% times 30%, which comes to 5%.

On the other side, consider all the factors which work to reduce the price level when the external value of the currency falls by 25%. First, the output of all enterprises in the domestic economy is likely to rise substantially on average. Suppose that the growth rate rises by 3% per annum. If two-thirds of this increase in output could be achieved in the period immediately following the devaluation by using the existing capital stock and labour force more intensively and efficiently, the benefits from economies of scale of this type would amount to around a 2% contribution to reduced prices in year one.

Second, the total money supply currently represents about 85% of GNP across the EU. All of the money supply is essentially debt of one kind or another, and nearly all of it is interest bearing. If interest charges were reduced from their current levels by an average of 4% not all interest charges would be affected, but a significant proportion would be. If half were, the average interest charged on the whole of the money supply would fall by about 2%. This would produce a reduction of around another 2% × 85%, or 1.7% in the retail price index.

Third, one of the most important reasons for a depreciation is to switch demand from imports to home production. Suppose this happens to 10% of all demand. Allowing for an import content of one-third, the remaining two-thirds of this new output would, broadly speaking, not be affected by increased costs as a result of the exchange rate changes. Perhaps half of it, however, would only become economical to produce at rather higher world prices than applied previously. These ratios multiply up as $10\% \times 25\% \times \frac{2}{3} \times \frac{2}{3} \times \frac{1}{2}$. This factor reduces the inflationary impact by a little more than another 0.5%.

Fourth, another major impact on the economy from reducing the parity would be vastly to improve the public sector's finances, as tax receipts rose and calls on public expenditure for unemployment benefit fell away. If some of this improvement was used to reduce taxes on employment, which would be the most disinflationary way to employ them, it would not be difficult for the EU governments to bring down inflation by a further 1%, by reducing taxes by this amount. The improvement in fiscal balances across the EU achievable by moving unemployment from 12% to 3% of the labour force will easily provide the money for tax reductions on this scale to be achieved.

These calculations are again broad brush, and subject to margins of error. They nevertheless show that the disinflationary impacts that can be garnered from a well managed devaluation are likely to counteract quite possibly in full the impact of higher import costs, even if the devaluation is very substantial. This is why a devaluation is not necessarily inflationary at all, as ample empirical evidence shows is the case, except perhaps when resources were already fully employed, as in the French case at the end of the 1950s. This is clearly an extremely important conclusion, and one with major policy implications.

Nor does depreciation lower the standard of living. In fact it quickly does exactly the opposite in almost all circumstances. It is easy to see why this should be the case. If the domestic economy expands after the exchange rate has gone down, as the figures in Table 6.1 show that it almost invariably does, the standard of living, on average, is bound to go up. So, sometimes after a time lag, does the real wage. The proposition that lowering the exchange rate necessarily impoverishes the devaluing country is the reverse of the truth. Again, this is an outcome of great policy significance, making it politically much easier to implement a reflationary and expansionary policy than is generally supposed.

These conclusions do not mean, of course, that inflation is no longer a problem. A well managed devaluation may not cause inflation to increase, but there are other reasons why the price level may move up. They all need careful management, but with reasonable judgement they are all containable. They are leading sector inflation, external shocks, 'demand pull' inflation caused by bottlenecks and overheating, excessive growth in the money supply which may in particular lead to asset price inflation, and 'cost push' wage and salary increases outstripping productivity gains. Many of these are closely related to other elements of the policies confronting all EU economies, and the following sections of this chapter consider them in turn.

LEADING SECTOR INFLATION

While almost everyone agrees that in general lower rates of inflation are desirable, there is considerable evidence that very low, and especially zero rates of inflation are impossible to combine with any significant rate of economic growth. At some stage a trade-off between inflation and growth has to be faced. The higher the priority given to stabilising prices, the less likely it is that the economy will grow rapidly. Certainly the notion that squeezing inflation out of the economy altogether is the way to economic prosperity flies in the face of universal experience. On the contrary, there is some inflationary price to pay for growth, but it is not likely to be a large or a dangerous one.

Table 6.2 shows the rates of inflation and economic growth in ten OECD countries, and the OECD as a whole, during the fifteen years from 1953 to 1969, a long period of almost continual growth in world output. This table indicates that over this fifteen-year period not one of these countries managed to avoid a steady increase in the price level, albeit a relatively moderate one. It also shows a tendency for those economies growing most rapidly to have rather higher inflation rates than those growing more slowly. Obviously other factors were at work than those solely concerned with the differing growth rates, but the correlation between high inflation and higher growth is clearly there.

At first sight this seems the reverse of what one would expect. How did Japan manage to achieve a cumulative compound growth rate of 10% if the Japanese rate of inflation was above the average for the whole of the OECD, and well above the inflation rate achieved in a number of countries, including the United States and Britain? Why were British exports not becoming more and more competitive with those of Japan? Clearly this cannot have been the case judging by the slow British growth rates over the period, contrasted with the high performance of the Japanese economy.

This paradox is easily resolved. In all the major economies of the developed world, increases in productivity were enabling sustained economic growth to take place, while growth in turn generated increased productivity. These increases, however, were neither spread evenly throughout any of the individual economies concerned nor between them. In all countries there were some parts of the economy where productivity growth was slow, non-existent, or even negative. If the number of children taught by each teacher goes down, each child may be better taught, but the output of teachers measured in economic terms tends to fall. If legal aid is extended to people who could not otherwise afford to obtain justice, society may be fairer, but there is no increase in GDP which corresponds fully to the extra skilled manpower required to make the legal system work. The really high rates of productivity growth were to be found in those parts of manufacturing and the service sectors, especially in fast-growing economies, where mechanisation, falling unit costs with longer production runs, and much more efficient use of labour were possible. The results were costs which dropped rapidly in real terms, and often in money terms too, even though average prices in the economy were rising. These are the sectors of the economy which are the familiar generators of fast rates of economic growth.

Table 6.2: Growth and Inflation Rates in Ten OECD Countries
Between 1953 and 1969

Country	Cumulative Growth Rate	Cumulative Inflation Rate
Japan	10.0%	4.0%
Spain	6.0%	6.3%
Germany	5.8%	2.7%
Italy	5.5%	3.4%
France	5.4%	4.5%
Netherlands	4.9%	4.3%
Switzerland	4.5%	3.3%
Belgium	4.0%	2.5%
United States	3.6%	2.4%
United Kingdom	2.8%	3.4%
OECD Average	4.4%	3.0%

Source: OECD: National Accounts of OECD countries 1953–69.

This phenomenon was seen markedly in Japan, with one of the fastest growth rates, but also an above average rate of inflation. It was caused by leading sector inflation. Those employed in parts of the economy with rapidly rising productivity secured large wage increases, which were offset by increased output. Those working in jobs where such improvement in economic performance were unobtainable also pressed for, and received wage rises. The prices of the goods and services produced by those where no significant increase in output could be achieved therefore had to go up. The faster the economy grew, the more marked these price increases were. The overall inflation rate was a result of the averaging process which took place between the high and low productivity growth parts of the economy. In Japan the results were truly astonishing. Despite the relatively high Japanese overall domestic inflation rate, for many years Japanese export prices barely rose at all. Indeed over the whole of the period from 1952 to 1979, while the general price level in Japan rose by 364%, the average price of Japanese exports rose by only 33%. In Britain, over the same period, the general price level rose by 442%, and export prices by 380%. No wonder Britain kept losing more and more markets to Japanese competition.

The initial competitiveness of Japanese exports, and those of most of the economies of Western Europe after their recovery from World War II, enabled all of them to break into the virtuous circle of rapid growth. Once established, all these countries maintained high growth for years on end, concentrating economic activity in those areas where productivity increases were at their greatest. We see the same process at work today in the Far East, not only in countries such as Taiwan, Hong Kong and Korea, but also, perhaps most conspicuously of all in China. The British experience has been exactly the opposite. Starting from an uncompetitive position after World War II, Britain has allowed the costs of its exports compared to the world average to rise and rise.

Despite all the indications to the contrary, it is still said that price stability is the condition needed to maximise economic growth on a sustainable basis. There is no evidence from round the world that this is true. Nor does economic history provide any support for such a view. During the period when the Gold Standard operated, just as much as subsequently, prices were constantly changing. Only the price of gold remained fixed. It is argued that low inflation allows interest rates to be low too, and in nominal terms this may be correct. Unfortunately, however, it is not only the nominal rate that counts. It is the real rate, when inflation is subtracted from the nominal rate, which is the true cost of borrowing. Squeezing inflation down with monetarist policies has a dismal record of producing much higher real rates of interest than more accommodating strategies, thus pushing up the exchange rate and discouraging investment and growth, by making the real cost of borrowing greater than it would otherwise be.

The lessons from international comparisons and economic history indicate that rapid growth is associated with price changes in all directions, some upward, particularly where productivity increases are hard to achieve, and some downward, especially where there are falling cost curves. Nor has experience shown that nominal interest rates have been particularly low in fast-growing economies, though real rates have often been negative, at least after tax. In very rapidly growing economies – 8–10% per annum or more – rates of inflation tend to be above the world average, mainly because of leading sector inflation, but still relatively stable. In economies growing at 5– 6% per annum, the optimum combination of rapid productivity growth without too much leading sector inflation seems to be achieved. This was the experience of most countries on the continent of Western Europe during the 1950s and 1960s where, over a long period, inflation rates averaged close to 3%, with similar nominal base interest rates. If the objective is to get the economies of the EU to return to the growth rates of the first few decades after World War II, it is likely that we will have to expect the same kind of experience with price rises and interest rates as prevailed then.

SHOCKS TO THE SYSTEM

Seen from the vantage point of the late 1990s, the 1950s and 1960s look like a period of remarkable stability and growing prosperity in Europe. At least until 1968, low and quite stable levels of inflation were combined with rapidly increasing standards of living almost everywhere. After the adjustments of 1949 there were few exchange rate changes, the most significant being the double French devaluations in 1958, the British devaluation in 1967, and the German revaluation in 1968, followed by some consequential parity changes in other countries. By the standards of what was to follow, price increases were low, although they attracted a good deal of concern at the time. All the countries in Western Europe were helped by the falling cost of raw materials, many of which came from the Third World. The biggest shock to the system, albeit a temporary one, was the Korean War at the beginning of the period, which led to a sharp commodity boom. This quickly collapsed, however, as the war ended. Inflation then fell away as the long boom in the 1950s and 1960s got under way. No period of economic history of any length is devoid of inflationary shocks, however, and at the end of the 1960s a much more turbulent period began.

1968 saw a rash of strikes in several countries leading to wage increases considerably in excess of productivity gains, with consequent increases in inflation. The way the United States paid for the Vietnam War, largely by the creation of unfunded debt used to finance a very large balance of payments deficit, destabilised international money markets. In December 1971, the Smithsonian Agreement devalued the dollar, leading a year later to the break-up of the Bretton Woods system. This in turn was a major contributory factor to the quadrupling of OPEC oil prices in 1973/4, following the Yom Kippur War. At the same time, commodity prices doubled as shortages appeared following the boom conditions in most countries in the early 1970s. They fed an inflationary explosion which peaked in most countries in 1974.

The price of oil then declined, only to be doubled again by the oil cartel in 1979.

The rate at which prices increased in the EU during the twenty years from 1975 to 1995 exhibited upsurges when major inflationary shocks materialised, followed by declines back to more usual levels within a year or two, but with some countries much more seriously affected than others. Among the Community countries as a whole, inflation peaked for the first time during this period at 13.3% during 1975 before falling back to 7.2% in 1978. The second oil price crisis pushed it up to another peak of 9.0% in 1981, which was followed by a slow decline to a low of 2.1% in 1986. Thereafter a slow rise took place to a smaller 5.2% peak in 1991, mostly caused by the fall-out from the reunification of Germany, after which it dropped back gradually to 3.1% in 1995. These average figures, however, masked variations over the whole twenty-year period between Britain, where consumer prices rose by a total of 322%, and Germany where they went up by only 84%. In Spain, which did not become a Community member until 1986, the retail price index increased 640% over the same twenty years.

Looking back over the whole period since World War II, the ups and downs which have taken place in inflation both in Europe and in the world as a whole have clearly been caused by a wide variety of different factors. From Europe's point of view, only one of all the major events pushing up inflation was the direct result of changes in the money supply, this being the financing of the Vietnam War by the United States government. With appropriate policies, Europe could have avoided much of the impact of the American inflation, as indeed happened in some countries. Germany's year on year inflation rate in the mid-1970s never rose above about 7%, compared to 24% at peak in Britain. In most EU countries, the real money supply, that is net of inflation, remained remarkably stable, though if fluctuated much more in Britain and the Netherlands. The other causes of rises in prices had little or nothing to do with changes in the credit base. All of them, however, because they caused higher inflation and thus pushed up the requirement for money, had to be accommodated by increasing the money supply if more deflation was to be avoided. When the supply of money fell in real terms, as for example it did during the period of the 1974–9 Labour government in Britain, when it was reduced by 27%, the deflationary effect was very powerful.

The history of the last fifty years also shows a remarkable ability by all the countries in the developed world to absorb inflationary shocks, from wherever they have come, despite the variety of different events which, over the years, have been responsible for initiating rapid increases in the price level. Once the initial cause of the surge in inflation disappeared, however, the rate of price increases soon fell back, given an absence of further shocks and reasonably competent management of the macro-economy. This ought not to cause surprise. Reasonably rapid rates of economic growth are powerfully effective at absorbing inflation.

If this is so, however, it removes the underpinning for a major component of European economic policy employed in varying degrees by all EU Member States' governments since the 1970s. They have all tended to assume that the best way to counteract inflationary shocks was to deflate their economies, rather than to absorb the disturbances by increasing output. The monetarist argument that all increases in inflation are caused by antecedent rises in the money supply, and that only monetary discipline will stop prices rising more and more rapidly, is only a more precise formulation of a view which has underlain conservative economic policy making for a long time before monetarism became fashionable. On the contrary, the international evidence shows that this tendency has been both very damaging and destructive to the economies of the EU, and not particularly effective at keeping inflation rates down to the international average. If most of the events which have generated upsurges in inflation are not caused by anything to do with the money supply, and the international experience is that inflation nearly always recedes once the immediate causes have been removed irrespective of the monetary stance in the economies concerned, what indeed is left of the argument that the money supply is both the cause and the cure for all inflationary ills?

Moreover, the picture is even worse than this if the prospect for the EU is to be a period of continuing slow growth. The historical evidence suggests that economies which have used growth to dampen down inflation have done at least as well at restraining price increases as those which have used deflation, and perhaps better. Table 6.3 shows the record for the major Western economies for the period 1973 to 1978, when all of them were suffering in various degrees from the upsets of the 1970s, and for the following five years from 1978 to 1983. Japan, with much the highest growth rate, was far the most successful in bringing down inflation. All the remaining countries, whose growth rates fell between the first and second periods, had similar or higher rates of inflation in the later period compared to the earlier one. This evidence reinforces the view that economies which have reasonably strong growth rates are better at absorbing external shocks than those which are growing more slowly.

Without doubt, there will be more random shocks and policy changes in the future which will cause upsurges in inflation. The issue is whether, when they come, the best policy to pursue is one of cautious deflation, or whether the safest solution is to keep economies growing to absorb pressures for rising prices with increased output. The evidence from international experience shows that in both the short and the longer term a reasonable measure of boldness pays. Restricting the money supply and deflating the economy is not the most efficient way to contain inflation. Rising output is the most efficacious agent for slowing down increases in the price level. If this is so, the high unemployment, the lost output and the social strains caused by the deflation which so much of Europe has been through during the last two decades, primarily to fight inflation, have been unnecessary, and could have been avoided.

Table 6.3: Economic Growth and Inflation Rates in
Selected Countries Between 1973 and 1978, 1978 and 1983

Country	1973–8		1978–83	
	Average Growth Rate	*Average Inflation Rate*	*Average Growth Rate*	*Average Inflation Rate*
Japan	3.7%	12.8%	4.1%	4.2%
France	3.1%	10.8%	1.4%	11.8%
United States	2.8%	8.0%	1.3%	8.8%
Italy	2.1%	16.6%	1.5%	17.3%
Germany	2.1%	4.7%	1.2%	4.7%
United Kingdom	1.7%	12.4%	0.7%	11.2%

Source: *The Economist*: *Economic Statistics* 1900–83.

TOO MUCH DEMAND

If a much more expansionist policy was adopted in the EU, it would necessitate significant exchange rate changes between Member States initially, with further parity changes almost certainly being required in future. It is not likely that the exchange rate adjustments required, of themselves, would necessarily lead to any significant inflationary problems during the early or later stages. The causes of inflation, however, are not only those already discussed. There is a further potentially substantial generator of prices increases of a different sort. This is to over-expand demand, so that economies become overheated. Once demand on any economy outstrips its capacity to supply, prices will start to rise. This is a prospect which must be taken seriously, and avoided.

'Too much money chasing too few goods' is the classic definition of inflation. While one of the central propositions in this book is that the solution to this problem should, wherever possible, be found by expanding the supply of goods rather than restricting demand, there must inevitably be a point where too many local shortages and bottlenecks have an increasingly serious effect on the price level. This problem has not been significant in Europe for almost all the period since the Korean War, but it could become one in the future.

There are, however, good reasons for believing that these difficulties are likely to be relatively easy to contain during the early phases of economic recovery. The EU economies at the moment are so depressed that there are very large unused resources especially of labour. Years of low demand have taken their toll on EU manufacturing capacity, but plant utilisation of what remains leaves room for significant increases in output before capacity constraints start to bite hard. Some labour will have rusty skills. Much of the plant and machinery may not be as modern or efficient as it should be, as a result of relatively low levels of investment over the last quarter of a century. All these resources, however, are better than nothing, and there is no doubt that substantial extra output could be obtained from them.

While there is a significant reserve of unused or underused resources to draw on, these will not last for ever, and the problems of sustaining economic growth without over-stretching the EU economies will then become more acute. One of the major disadvantages which two and a half decades of deflation have inflicted upon Europe is not just the closed factories and the steep rise in unemployment, but the break-up of teams of people with design and production experience. In the newer industries, such as the advanced use of electronics and bio-technology, there is considerable evidence that European companies are lagging behind in developing new products. It takes time to become familiar with the complicated techniques to be used, the plant that has to be operated, the markets which need to be served, and the right places to purchase raw materials and services. Building up successful manufacturing or commercial operations is not achieved in a day. The damage done by the weakening of Europe's manufacturing base is not going to be put right in a few months. These problems can, however, be solved over a reasonably short period, and meanwhile they can be contained or minimised.

First, we have seen that the more the resources of the economy are deployed into those sectors concerned with falling cost curves and foreign trade, the easier it is for self-sustaining growth to be achieved. The faster we want the EU economy to grow, the more vital it is that wages and salaries in the import saving and exporting sectors of the economy should rise relative to those everywhere else. There will be a pressing need to attract the most talented people, capable of making good quickly the management deficiencies that are bound to exist after years of stagnation. The large returns on investment which are obtainable in these sectors should be able in turn to provide enough new output to finance all the additional investment required, without calling on the resources of the rest of the economy. There is thus an extremely strong case for fostering this kind of self-sustaining growth, and avoiding unnecessary obstructions to its taking place. There will also inevitably be pressure to expand expenditure in other directions. To avoid overheating, however, it is important not to siphon too many resources away from those parts of the economy which are achieving large increases in output towards those which cannot do so, by poorly judged taxation or public expenditure policies. The ways to fast growth are to let wealth be created before it is taxed too heavily, and to concentrate as much investment as possible into projects which have short pay-off periods and high returns.

Second, for at least some shortages, there is considerable scope for importing what is not available from home production. One of the strongest arguments against the strategy of reflating the economy behind the shield of import tariffs or quotas, and protectionist policies generally, is that they would reduce or preclude the availability of alternative sources of supply at competitive prices to cope with domestic shortages. This is not an advantage which the EU can afford to throw away. Not all materials, however, can be imported in practice. Nor, in particular, is there an inexhaustible supply of skilled labour, much of which has been drained away from manufacturing industry, especially in some countries, by relatively poor wages, bad working conditions and uncertain prospects. Far too many skilled engineers have now turned their hands to other ways of earning a living outside the industrial sector. They need to be attracted back with greatly improved wages and conditions.

Third, any serious attempt to reflate the economies of the EU which is designed to bring them back to anywhere near full employment again faces a major training, retraining and educational task, particularly for all forms of engineering and technical work. Some EU countries still do well. In Germany around 50 000 students begin university level engineering courses every year, representing over 20% of all students. This is a similar ratio to Japan where around 100 000 engineering graduates are produced per annum, forming more than 20% of all graduates. In other countries in Europe with a longer history of manufacturing decline, the position is much worse. In Britain only a little over 20 000 students graduate in engineering annually. Over the last two decades the numbers of apprentices starting in British industry has declined drastically, from 120 000 in 1979 to less than 30 000 per annum in the late 1990s, compared to Germany where about 500 000 young people begin high-quality apprenticeships every year. The length of the depression through which the EU economy has gone has left nearly 9m registered unemployed out of work for periods of more than one year. Training courses may have little value if there is insufficient demand available to provide work for those who have been trained. They are a vitally important component of success once new opportunities for employment come on stream. Undoubtedly, they will be supplemented by large amounts of 'on the job' training as employers need to upgrade the skills of their workforces.

The unemployment figures would clearly be much higher if they were to include those not registered as unemployed such as housewives who would like to work but have given up the prospect of finding a job as hopeless. The problem with the type of jobs which modern employment offers is that almost none of them are completely unskilled. Nearly all require at least basic skills such as the ability to drive a motor vehicle or to use a keyboard, and the scope for employment for those who cannot read or write properly is extremely limited. Long years of high youth unemployment have sapped the motivation of a generation of children especially in deprived areas, and in many cases the educational attainments are poor, and considerably worse than they were a few years ago. Similar problems of outdated or rusty skills apply to those who are older. Europe cannot afford either for social or economic reasons to fail to get a high proportion of the unemployed back into the working labour force. We owe it to them and ourselves to get them trained for the jobs which could be created in the future. The experience of the 1930s, in Britain and Germany and even more of the post-World War II period, shows that none of these problems is insoluble.

Fourth, the EU economies should be wary of trying to contain problems of shortages of either raw materials or labour, especially skilled labour, by government action to implement wages and price freezes. The fact that prices and labour costs rise when shortages occur are signals that more resources in these areas are particularly needed. The changes in the economy which are required would involve considerable shifts in relative wage and salary levels, to attract high quality labour into the those parts of the economy concerned with international trading, and away from other sectors. In particular, there would have to be substantial increases in remuneration for those involved in manufacturing industry. Suppressing the necessary price and wage rate signals will only aggravate shortages, leading quickly to even more pressure on prices and wages to rise.

There are better ways of dealing with profiteering and excessive wage increases than centrally imposed freezes. They have never worked for any length of time in the past in any country, and are unlikely to do so in future. Far the best alternative is not to expose the economy to strains which cause excessive bottlenecks and shortages in the first place by a two-pronged approach. The first is to create conditions where output can expand quickly in those sectors of the economy which are capable of achieving fast self-sustaining growth. The second is to refuse to allow overall demand to increase more rapidly than the rate at which even rejuvenated economies are capable of responding. Achieving this balance is not an impossible task.

LABOUR COSTS

In the end the most important determinant of inflation trends is the rate of increase in wages and salaries. Payments to labour represent an average of some 60% of total costs in the economies of the EU. If the wage and salary bill rises faster than output, the extra costs are bound to be reflected in higher prices. If economies are run with a much higher level of demand which is intended, among other things, to produce a very substantial reduction in the level of unemployment, is it inevitable that we shall have high levels of wage inflation?

Before attempting to answer this question, it is worth looking again at the historical record and current experience in comparable countries outside the EU. A glance at the unemployment percentages in other parts of the world and at other periods, and the rates of inflation which go with them, must surely cause some concern even to those who are most convinced that wage inflation is inevitable. Table 6.4 provides some of the relevant figures. Those for the earlier period, before the general increase in inflation in the mid-1970s, show a wide range of countries combining low rates of unemployment with moderate rates of inflation. At the beginning of the 1990s, countries as varied as the United States, Japan, Austria, Norway and Switzerland all had much lower rates of unemployment than those in the EU. The figures for the EU countries are marginally worse for inflation, and much worse for unemployment, the Spanish record being by far the worst of all.

How can it be that so many other countries manage to operate their economies with so much lower rates of unemployment than those in the EU, and with faster rates of growth but lower inflation rates? It is extremely difficult to believe that all these countries have conditions so different that the rates of unemployment in the EU have to be maintained because there is no alternative. It is not inevitable that joblessness should be so much higher in the EU than in other parts of the developed world. The adverse trade-offs between unemployment and wage inflation in EU countries are not unavoidable. They have been caused by the governments responsible for them, and by the economic policies they have pursued. This is much more plausible than putting the blame on any latent characteristics in the labour force, or, for that matter, those who represent them in the trade unions.

Nor is it true that labour oncosts in the EU are completely out of line with those in the rest of the world. For many years, Japan combined exceptionally high rates of economic growth and almost no unemployment with heavy wage oncosts. Of course the more inflexible the labour force is, and the higher the social costs it has to bear, the more expensive it will be, other things being equal, to produce in economies with these conditions than those with high levels of deregulation. These costs, however, can be offset through the exchange rate, and do not necessarily therefore make the whole economy uncompetitive. If this is done, their effect then becomes redistributive within the economy – benefiting labour conditions at the expense of the rest of the community – rather than causing output costs to become overpriced in world terms.

Table 6.4: Unemployment and Inflation in Ten OECD Countries
at Selected Periods Between 1963 and 1993

Country	1963–73 Unemployment Rate	1963–73 Inflation Rate	1974–9 Unemployment Rate	1974–9 Inflation Rate	1980–9 Unemployment Rate	1980–9 Inflation Rate	1990–3 Unemployment Rate	1990–3 Inflation Rate
United States	4.8%	3.2%	6.7%	8.5%	7.2%	5.5%	6.5%	3.9%
Japan	1.3%	6.2%	1.9%	9.9%	2.5%	2.5%	2.2%	2.5%
Austria	1.7%	4.2%	1.7%	6.3%	3.3%	3.8%	3.6%	3.6%
Norway	1.3%	5.1%	1.8%	8.7%	2.8%	8.3%	5.6%	3.0%
Switzerland	0.5%	4.2%	0.5%	4.0%	0.6%	3.3%	2.2%	4.6%
France	2.0%	4.6%	4.5%	10.7%	9.0%	7.3%	10.0%	2.8%
Germany	0.8%	3.4%	3.4%	4.7%	6.8%	2.9%	7.3%	3.6%
Italy	5.3%	3.9%	6.6%	16.7%	9.9%	11.2%	11.0%	5.5%
Spain	2.5%	4.7%	5.3%	18.3%	17.5%	10.2%	18.1%	5.8%
United Kingdom	1.9%	5.1%	4.2%	15.6%	9.5%	7.4%	8.3%	5.1%
OECD Average	3.2%	4.1%	5.0%	10.8%	7.2%	8.9%	7.2%	5.5%

Source: OECD *Historical Statistics* 1995 Edition.

Much of the argument about the level of unemployment in Europe, and elsewhere, has centred round the concept of the non-accelerating inflation rate of unemployment, or its acronym, the NAIRU. It is argued that, unless there are sufficiently large numbers of unemployed people, the pressure for wage increases will tend to outstrip the growth in output which the economy can provide, necessarily leading to increased inflation. The NAIRU, it is said, is exceptionally high in Europe compared to other countries because there are many more rigidities in Europe in the form of restrictive practices both in the way labour is deployed and in wage bargaining. While training and improved economic performance clearly have a role to play, the only fundamental solutions to the problem of unemployment, it is argued, are to reduce supply side rigidities by making wage rates and the labour market more flexible, to reduce job security, and to weaken the power of trade unions to fix wages which are unrelated to productivity gains. There is no doubt that at some point there is a trade-off between fuller and fuller employment and rising inflation. Nor are the prospects for economic regeneration helped by supply-side rigidities or excessive wage increases unrelated to productivity growth. To argue, however, that the NAIRU requires a level of registered unemployment in the EU of 18m people, or anything approaching this figure, appears to be completely incompatible with all the international and historical evidence. It was possible to combine relatively high rates of growth and low levels of unemployment with moderate inflation for twenty-five years after World War II, when supply-side restrictions of all kinds were at least as prevalent as they are now, and in many cases much more so. Why should it therefore not be possible to achieve low levels of unemployment now? It might take some time to get there, but arguments about the NAIRU provide no convincing reason nowadays to believe that it would not be possible to achieve an unemployment rate across the EU of no more than 3% within perhaps four to five years if appropriate policies were implemented.

To start with, there is no evidence that the EU's present unemployment levels have any relationship at all with NAIRU. The NAIRU relates not to the total number of people who are out of work, but to the total who are actively seeking employment and who are therefore competing at least to this extent with those who are in employment. Since there are now nearly 9m registered unemployed in the EU who have been out of work for more than a year, and a much larger number who for the time being have given up hope of finding a job and who are no longer registered, a large proportion of those presently unemployed, probably more than half, are having no influence on the NAIRU. Their unemployment is pure waste in terms of keeping inflation down, as well as in every other way. If these people are taken out of the total, we are then left with a much smaller figure, where there is some evidence that increasing employment will push up inflation. What can be done to bring the NAIRU down to 2% or 3%, as it used to be? There is a great deal that can be done to achieve this objective.

First, wage determination is in the end as much a political as an economic process. The wage increases for which people are prepared to settle are not decided by a totally mechanistic process. Persuasion also counts. What may make even more difference is the prospect of a rational economic policy which is capable of delivering results, and which is therefore seen to be one where some sacrifice of current wage and salary increases is worthwhile to obtain more in the future. Certainly one major objective must be to create a climate for wage negotiation which is conducive to average money wage increases at as low a level as possible, hopefully with the support of trade union leaders, to secure larger real wage increases as soon as practical in the future.

A complicating factor in wage determination, if the EU economies are going to make a transition towards much faster rates of economic growth, is that it will not be possible to have the same wage or salary increases for everyone. There needs to be a substantial relative adjustment. If talent at every level is going to have to be switched to those parts of the economy capable of producing high productivity increases, and rapid investment pay-off periods, rises in pay will have to be considerably higher in these areas of economic activity than elsewhere. This suggests that aiming for relatively low general wage increases, but with substantial wage drift at the level of individual enterprises, is the most realistic policy.

Another problem is that there are going to be shortages of certain types of skilled labour, and also a pressing need for a considerable amount of retraining to enable the labour force across Europe to be adequately prepared for the new types of jobs which will become available. Government programmes have a major role in providing training and retraining to enable there to be an adequate response to this challenge, supplementing training carried out on the job. If bottlenecks in the form of skilled labour shortages are to be avoided, the places where these are likely to occur need to be identified as far in advance as possible, and training put in hand as early as it can be to provide the manpower needed at adequate skill levels. The type of training needed is likely to be fairly precisely orientated towards specific job opportunities. Improving general standards of education and motivation in schools is another vital component, but takes much longer to pay off. Preparing those already of working age will almost certainly have to be given even higher immediate priority.

There clearly is potential for wage pressure if these changes are taking place, and all the dampening effect of increasing output in absorbing whatever wage increases there are will be needed. There is no reason, however, why the major disinflationary influence of increasing production should not be supplemented where possible by government actions on the price level. There is much to be said against prices and incomes policies if they can be avoided, but there are other steps which the state can take apart from freezing or limiting increases in prices, wages and incomes. Lowering interest rates, which has many other advantages, reduces the cost of living. If the economy needs reflating, there are several ways which have already been mentioned in which this can be done which actually reduce costs, such as lowering taxes on employment whether paid by the employer or the employee. The first reduces the cost of labour in production and the second increases real take home pay. Especially if tax thresholds can be lifted, perhaps back to where they were a decade or two ago, there is the potential for a considerable rise in real wages for the worse off as well as for those on higher incomes. All this should help to produce a more helpful wage climate in addition to acting directly on the cost of living and the cost of producing output of all kinds in Europe.

When all these factors are put together, it becomes clear how other countries manage with a NAIRU much below the current EU rate of unemployment, as of course the economies making up the present Union did for many years after World War II. Faster growth makes larger money wage claims possible without inflationary consequences. Rising output in an economy run in a way which appears rational and sustainable makes a degree of wage restraint seem a sensible policy. Flowing from this comes something closer to a consensus, which again prevailed over much of Europe, particularly Germany, during the high growth period in the 1950s and 1960s. This makes economically unjustified wage claims look irrational and greedy, instead of being the only way available to buck trends which never seem to end, as has been the experience too often in the past in countries with a longer record of slow growth such as Britain. If other countries can operate with 3% or 4% rates of unemployment, and the economies making up the EU have done so in the past for many years, there is no reason why they cannot do so again.

SUMMARY

The Single Currency project's primary objective is to promote integration in the EU, binding all the constituent member states more closely together. This is a political objective. There is little doubt, however, that a major reason why many people who might otherwise oppose the Single Currency feel resigned to it is because they believe that there is no realistic alternative. In particular, they think that using exchange rate changes to improve economic performance in the EU would generate inflationary pressures which would spread throughout the Union. They treat it as axiomatic that inflation would rise in devaluing countries, and that their standards of living would fall. It therefore seems worth summarising at the end of this chapter the reasons for believing that these fears are misplaced. On the contrary, the evidence shows that even major devaluations do not lead to any significant rise in inflation, while almost invariably increasing the standard of living quickly in the depreciating economies. If this is true, it then becomes far more feasible and attractive than is generally assumed to use exchange rate changes to provide both the stimulus and the flexibility to allow the economy of the EU as a whole to grow faster, and to reduce unemployment quickly without taking undue risks with inflation.

The proposition that increasing the money supply within reasonable bounds, lowering interest rates, and allowing – or even encouraging – exchange rate changes to take place within the EU will necessarily lead to an immediate increase in inflation, especially in devaluing countries, may be widely believed. There is, however, very little empirical evidence from Europe's economic history, or that of countries in other parts of the world, to support it. On the contrary, the record of all the devaluations over the nearly seventy years since the break-up of the Gold Standard system in 1931 shows the opposite tendencies manifesting themselves to a greater or lesser extent on almost every occasion. The expected impact of a depreciation on the price level does not materialise because lowering the exchange rate involves disinflationary factors which are as powerful, and sometimes even more so, than those tending to push prices up. Furthermore, if policies are implemented which assist these tendencies, such as reducing taxes on employment which are not only possible but desirable on other grounds if there is high unemployment, then the influences working against inflation become even more pronounced. In the medium term, with a much higher growth rate, the prospect would be for fairly low but sustainable levels of inflation, the main generator of price increases being leading sector inflation if the rate of growth is very high. There should be no reductions in living standards at any stage.

The evidence from across the world shows that many of the causes of price rises have had little directly to do with the money supply, though some important inflationary upsurges have been caused by monetary mismanagement and excessive credit creation. Most of the increase in the money supply in all countries has been the result of the need to accommodate economic growth. Inflation has then occurred for non-monetary reasons. Recent developments, particularly deregulation and the growth of new forms of money, have tended to increase the requirement for credit. This makes monetary ratios even more unreliable than they were before. Especially in conditions like the present, therefore, where inflationary pressures requiring any kind of deflationary solution are not a problem, the risk of price rises from excessive money supply is low. The problem across the whole of the EU at present is not too much credit creation, but too little.

There are bound to be more random inflationary shocks both to the world and to the economies of the EU, and governments have to be prepared to deal with them. They ought, however, not to cause undue difficulty. The international evidence strongly indicates that there is a universal tendency for inflation to die back in advanced economies which are reasonably competently run, once the causes of individual upsurges have been removed. This is largely a function of increasing productivity and output acting as a sponge to soak up inflationary pressures, and, in particular, accommodating wage and salary increases which might otherwise push up the price level. There is no evidence for the view that all increases in prices are ultimately due to one sole cause, and therefore only amenable to one solution. On the contrary, the causes of inflation are varied. The way to deal with any particular inflationary problem depends on careful diagnosis of the specifics rather than the application of general monetary theories which may not be relevant, and which may indeed be counterproductive. Different causes of inflation require different policies to deal with them.

Overall, however, the problems associated with ensuring that price rises stay at relatively low levels, at least for most of the time, even if the economy is growing very quickly, do not look particularly daunting. With a sustained growth rate of around 5% to 6%, it ought to be possible to keep inflation at or below 4%, perhaps even around 3% per annum, as it was for years on end in the fast-growing economies of Europe in the 1950s and 1960s. Between 1954 and 1969 the French economy grew cumulatively at 5.4% per annum, with an average annual inflation rate of 4.5%. Over the same period, the German economy grew at 5.8% per annum, with average per annum inflation of 2.7%. Even Japan, which grew at 10.0% per annum over this period had an annual inflation rate of only 4.0%.

If mistakes are made, or external shocks are experienced, either of which push the inflation rate up, it is not usually very difficult to get it down again without plunging the economy into deflation. In the European context, in particular, the main causes of inflation which are subject to policy control appear to be far from unmanageable, though all require self-discipline and good government. Allowing the economy to become overheated, tolerating the creation of an excessive money supply, mishandling the wage bargaining process and using the tax system to pay for wasteful public expenditure are all avoidable provided that relevant policies are implemented reasonably efficiently. Whatever the institutional background, whether nationally or internationally, if mistakes or misjudgements are made in these areas, rising inflation and falling living standards will be the consequences. There are no short cuts to responsible behaviour and political maturity. The cushion of increased output and productivity provided by a fast rate of economic growth, however, ought to make all these policy issues easier, and not more difficult to handle.

Even if events were to prove this thesis wrong, however, which the evidence does not suggest they would, and there was some significant extra inflation if more exchange rate flexibility were allowed, there is still a strong case for believing that it would be worth it. The standard of living is, in the end, far more important than the cost of living. It would be worth paying a modest inflationary price to enable the EU to raise its growth rate from its current level to the world average or beyond, and to reduce unemployment to a much lower figure. In any event, such an inflationary surge would almost certainly be temporary, and quickly absorbed. This does not, however, appear to be the real choice. It is not necessary to choose between more growth with significantly more inflation or less growth and much less inflation. In the short, as well as the medium and long term, high rates of growth and manageably low rates of inflation can and should be made to go hand in hand.

7　The Choices to be Made

'Let us not go over old ground, let us rather prepare for what is to come.'

Cicero

As the twentieth century moves to its close, the choices confronting Europe are as important as any which its leaders have ever had to make. It is still quite possible that decisions will be taken during the first half of 1998, which will establish the first stage of the Single Currency on 1 January 1999, leading to the phasing out of national currencies and their substitution by the euro from the beginning of 2002. Many politicians in Europe, not least Helmut Kohl, have invested vast amounts of political capital in the project. Some countries, especially France, have gone through years of economic trauma to keep the parity of their currencies in line with the Deutsche Mark. Their leaders also are not going to give up lightly a venture to which so much has already been committed. As the date when the Single Currency is due to start approaches, banks and other commercial organisations have had to spend increasingly large sums of money preparing for an eventuality which they certainly cannot afford to ignore. The EU institutions – the Commission, the Parliament, the European Court of Justice, even the Council of Ministers – each has a major immediate interest in the success of integrationist policies, leading to a federal goal. They are all in a powerful position to push the Single Currency project ahead.

Ranged against those favouring the Single Currency are a comparatively small number of members of the élite groups in the EU, although some major politicians in Germany and France have exhibited a much greater degree of scepticism than their countries' leaders. Opposition is much more widespread in Britain and Denmark. Other cracks are appearing. The Bundesbank clearly has serious reservations not so much about the principle of EMU, but about the way in which matters are proceeding in practice. An increasingly large number of those in positions of power and influence, particularly among the banking and financial community, are concerned that a Single Currency, dominated in voting terms not by Germany and France, but dependent potentially on a Mediterranean coalition, may not reflect their original intentions. The electorates in Europe have tended to be much more sceptical than their leaders about the Single Currency, as shown by the referendums in Denmark and France, the results of recent elections, particularly in France, and by many opinion polls, not least in Germany.

Much of the controversy about the advantages and disadvantages of the Single Currency has turned on technicalities and details. Other arguments have concerned the pros and cons of EMU for individual countries, particularly Germany, *vis à vis* other potential members, as the euro takes over from the Deutsche Mark. Not much of this debate has dealt with the central issue, which is whether the Single Currency project has a realistic prospect of lifting Europe out of the economic doldrums. Is it the way to put the EU on to a growth trajectory which will both solve the problems of unemployment and restore Europe to the forefront of rising living standards and technical advance? If not, what are the consequences going to be, as Europe slips further and further behind in the world economic performance league? If the Single Currency has a low chance of promoting high growth rates in Europe, as all previous attempts to lock the currencies of EU members together suggest will be the case, what are the implications for the future?

There is an inexorable quality about the projections which can be made. If the growth rate in the EU maintains the trend established since the mid-1970s, the EU economies will do no better than to grow at about 2% per annum for the foreseeable future. If the deflationary impact of the Single Currency is at the more pessimistic end of the spectrum, the growth trend may be even worse than this. Even at 2%, however, the EU economies will only be achieving little more than half the world's current average increase in output, and much less than that of many countries, particularly a significant number in the Far East. There is no question that the results of this differential in economic performance, over a generation or two, are going to make an enormous difference to Europe's position in the world. The standard of living will drop relative to elsewhere, even if it rises slowly in absolute terms. At the moment, most countries in the EU still see themselves, rightly, as enjoying a share of the world's material comforts which is well above the average. This could change radically over only one or two decades if the EU economies grow at 2%, and others grow at 8% per annum. A difference of 6% per annum entails the fast growers doubling their standard of living *vis à vis* the slow growers in just twelve years. What impact is this going to have when the realisation that it has occurred sinks into Europe's consciousness?

If the future develops along these lines, the impact on Europe's position in the world is bound to be to reduce its influence very substantially. Europe will sink slowly into being less and less important on the world's diplomatic stage, as its relative economic strength diminishes. Nobody knows exactly what problems are going to be facing the world in twenty-five or fifty years' time, although it is not difficult to guess what some of them might be. They will almost certainly include rising sea levels as the earth warms; increasing pressures for migration because of high birth rates in some large but poor countries; water shortages as the world's population expands; pressure on the environment; and, inevitably, outbreaks of civil unrest and local and perhaps regional wars. It is certain that the countries likely to have the most influence on the resolution of these pressing problems are going to be those with the most powerful economies. Part of the reason for this is that, in the past, there has been a high correlation between economic and military power. Even if military capabilities become less important in future – and there is no guarantee that this will happen – the ability to deploy large economic resources in other ways will almost certainly be a close substitute.

As the economies in Europe fail to grow as fast as the world average, an inevitable concomitant will be the weakening of Europe's industrial structure, reflecting its lack of competitiveness. More of the labour force will move from manufacturing to services, where growth and productivity increases are harder to achieve. The proportion of the GDP going into investment will be lower than elsewhere in the world. Much of the missing capital expenditure will be in the internationally tradable goods and services which generate the fastest growth, but which tend to locate and expand, with one wave of investment following another, where costs are lowest. This will not be in Europe. As the competitiveness of Europe's exports weakens, there will be increasing pressure on the currency, which will become more and more overvalued, unless it is allowed to depreciate. If the policies we have seen recently in too many countries in Europe then prevail, more deflation, exacerbating all the problems, will be the recourse chosen to combat increasing balance of payments problems, rather than allowing exchange rate adjustments to take place.

In these conditions, Europe is not likely to be a particularly confident and contented place. As has occurred many times in the past, when countries have allowed themselves, through economic mismanagement, to slip down the economic league, they become unsure of themselves, and doubtful about their culture and traditions. Confidence in their political leaders inevitably wanes. As examples, referred to previously, consider Spain in the eighteenth century, the Ottoman Empire towards the end of its existence and Britain in the twentieth century. On a wider canvas, look at China before the last emperor was dispossessed, and much of South America, at least until comparatively recently.

The cynosure of all the problems of slow growth, if it is allowed to occur, is going to be unemployment. Without more rapid expansion, the problem of lack of jobs, which racks the EU, is insoluble. Rising productivity among the employed labour force means that a growth rate of about 2.5% is needed just to stabilise the present joblessness. With output rising at about 2% per annum, the simplest of calculations shows that there is no alternative but for unemployment to increase and increase. This is an appalling prospect, wasting lives, foregoing output, generating unmanageable fiscal problems, and generating social discontent.

If Europe is to build a good future for itself, it cannot do so on the back of a huge and increasing army of unemployed people. If Europe's leaders do not solve the problem of the lack of work, and particularly if they allow the position to deteriorate still further, they will be in real danger of fomenting the disintegration of social cohesion which is much the greatest civil threat to Europe today. The risks then rise that the way ahead is waning confidence in democracy, an increasingly out of touch corporatism, extremist political parties, racism and xenophobia, and rising crime. This would be a sad reversion away from the civilised life which in many ways Europe has been so good at building.

Perhaps this is too alarmist. It is possible that none of these tendencies will materialise to any significant extent, even if the number out of work continues to rise. Europe has reacted up to now comparatively calmly to the very large increases in unemployment that have been seen over the last twenty years. It would be unwise, however, to take it for granted that still more people out of work will not trigger off new waves of discontent. We need to look back no further than the 1930s to see how much damage was done then by mass unemployment in the heart of Europe. Unemployment in Germany peaked at 6m in 1932. It is 4.7m now. In percentage terms it is higher in France and much higher still in Spain. The darker side of humanity is not so far below the surface that Europe can afford lightly to take the risk with the possible outcomes of another decade or two during which unemployment rises to completely unacceptable levels.

THE PROBLEMS WITH EUROPEAN MONETARY UNION

The major reason why the EU economies' growth rate over the last two and a half decades has been so slow is that all the various attempts which have been made to reduce exchange rate movements between Member States have caused almost all the EU economies to run into balance of payments problems. Because of the power and competitiveness of the German economy, and its low rate of inflation, no other country has been able to compete with it for any length of time without devaluing. The effect of the Snake and the ERM was therefore to force all the countries whose currency parities were linked to the Deutsche Mark to deflate their economies to maintain their trade balances within manageable bounds. In the end, in every case, the dam broke. The strains involved for all participating members in keeping parities in line with the Deutsche Mark proved too great. Some countries have persevered longer than others. France, in particular, has invested enormous resources of national pride into maintaining the link between the franc and the Deutsche Mark, notwithstanding the huge price which France has paid in lost output and lost jobs.

Some relief to the EU currency system, it is true, has recently been provided at least temporarily by German reunification. This greatly increased Germany's imports in relation to its exports, wiping out the German balance of payments surplus which had been the bane of Europe for so long, and pushing up the German inflation rate. This is why, during the last four years, there have not been many parity adjustments. German competitiveness has been reduced. This development, combined with monetary expansion in Europe, has led to the recent fall of the Deutsche Mark against other major world currencies such as the dollar and the yen, and indeed the pound sterling, bringing relief to all the currencies still tied to the Deutsche Mark. As a result, over the next year or two, there may well be some increase in growth rates in the EU. This trend may be fortified by strong expansion of the world economy generally, which is, however, benefiting the fast-growing economies in absolute terms more than those in Europe which are still expanding relatively slowly.

It would be a snare and a delusion, however, for EU leaders to believe that the relatively favourable conjunction of economic circumstances which Europe is currently enjoying will remove the long-term dangers of implementing the Single Currency. Any developments which bring the performance and competitiveness of countries in the Single Currency closer together, however, will reduce the immediate risk of speculative attack on the system, and will increase the chances of it lasting for a longer period before the strains start to build up. In particular, if the Single Currency goes ahead, a honeymoon period for the participating economies between 1999 and 2002 may see the project through the critical period while national currencies are phased out and the euro takes their place. The real test, however, is not whether the Single Currency system will work well enough to survive when events are proceeding favourably. The criterion by which it ought to be judged is whether it has a good chance of producing a much higher growth rate in Europe on a sustainable basis, maintaining this performance in turbulent as well as smooth conditions. Only then will living standards rise at least as fast in Europe as elsewhere in the world, and unemployment cease to be the curse it currently is. Judged in this way, it is impossible to avoid the conclusion that implementing the Single Currency is a strategy with a very high risk of failure.

In the first place, as we have seen, there are major parity adjustments within the EU which urgently need to be made to reduce unemployment to about the same low percentage everywhere in the EU, and to enable all Member States to compete with each other on level terms. Since it is a requirement of the Maastricht convergence criteria that no such parity changes take place, implementation of the Single Currency, if it happens, is bound to occur against a background of existing imbalances. How is Spain, with the highest level of unemployment in the EU, a weak trade balance, a relatively high level of inflation, and a below average growth rate, going to catch up with the performance of other EU countries? How is Italy, with a chronic tendency to have higher levels of inflation than the mean as a result of widely recognised government mismanagement, going to maintain the competitiveness of its exports, if domestic costs keep rising faster than the elsewhere? A major problem for the Single Currency is that, even if it comes into being at a relatively favourable economic period, it will be imposed on disparate economies which are not in any fundamental equilibrium with each other.

Nor is it at all likely, even if there were equilibrium to start off with, that it would last. Economic history is full of unexpected events and changes which have differing impacts on different economies. Variations in technology, fashion, ideas, the competence of governments, and relative prices, are all bound to occur in future, as they have in the past. The discovery of new products and sources of supply, while others dry up or become too expensive, always tends to change relative competitiveness, and hence trading patterns, dependent on continually altering supply and demand. It is inconceivable that the future will not see radical alterations in the economic environment, some of which may occur entirely unexpectedly, as, for example, the oil price hikes did in the 1970s. If the economies of the EU are going to be able to weather these events successfully, and to take full advantage of the opportunities which some of them will open up, they need a flexible environment in which to do so. In particular, these events are bound to affect some countries more favourably than others, and some way of compensating the losers at the expense of the winners will have to be found, if all are to grow together at about the same rate.

Within a unitary state with large-scale taxing and spending capacities, the process of evening up the advantages and disadvantages of economic changes to different parts of the country can be accomplished, at least in part, by fiscal transfers, with migration from less favoured to more favoured areas as a second safety valve. The EU is not, however, a unitary state of this nature, and it is extremely unlikely that it will be in the foreseeable future. There is therefore no scope for compensating transfers on anything like the scale which might be required. Nor, with all the linguistic and cultural barriers that are in the way, is migration remotely likely to be able to take the strain. Surveys have shown that, even within EU countries, the propensity to migrate from high to low unemployment areas is much less pronounced than in the US. The prospects for mass migration from one country to another, in response to differing job opportunities, are still less favourable. Furthermore, differences in language and culture, as well as administrative procedures, between countries of the EU would almost certainly make them politically unacceptable as well. This is why the Snake and the ERM both came to grief. In the end, the tensions they generated became intolerable. The immediate cause of their demise, as is always likely to be the case, was market pressure from foreign exchange traders. Once they begin to realise that the position of weaker currencies is steadily deteriorating, with their exchange rates held up only by central bank intervention, speculators are presented with an increasingly profitable one-way option, as the odds against the parities being held shorten. Foreign exchange traders are not the fundamental cause of arrangements such as the Snake and the ERM breaking up, however, even if they are blamed at the time. The root causes are unsustainable trade and payment imbalances. If the Snake and the ERM really were the solutions they were supposed to be, their influence would have been more positive and their impact more secure and long-lasting in times of turbulence than when conditions were easier. The fact that they failed to meet these tests underlines their weakness and artificiality. The Snake did not collapse because of the demise of Bretton Woods, the devaluation of the dollar, the boom of the early 1970s, and the great increases in the prices of commodities, and especially oil. It was abandoned because it was the wrong structure to contain the pressures which built up as a result of all these events. It made the position worse and not better. The ERM lasted longer than the Snake mainly because the 1980s were less turbulent than the 1990s, but in the end it too was seen to be exacerbating rather than ameliorating the problems which it was designed to address.

One of the major arguments put forward by the proponents of the Single Currency is that it would not be liable to attack from the markets, as were the Snake and the ERM. Once the seamless euro exists, there will be no place to put in speculative wedges. Just as no-one gambles against the dollars circulating in California *vis à vis* those financing transactions on the east coast of the US, so the euro will have the same homogeneity and inviolability in the EU. It is no doubt true that once the euro starts to circulate within all the participating countries, there will be no scope for speculating on Italian or Spanish euros being weaker than German ones, for the currency will be the same everywhere. This will not, however, guarantee that the euro will remain the currency of every participating country for ever. If any of the countries involved reach a point where it believes that being part of the Single Currency is doing it far more harm than good, sooner or later it would be impossible to stop it going back again to having its own currency once more. There are plenty of examples in history of single currency areas breaking up. If the strains get too great, this is likely to be the outcome within the EU. Almost certainly, however, such a break-up would only occur after a long and painful deflationary period while the authorities who had invested so much in trying to make the Single Currency a reality fought a bitter rearguard action to keep it in place.

The likelihood of the Single Currency breaking up relatively soon after its establishment may also be enhanced rather than diminished by some of the arrangements designed to increase its stability. The powerful role given to the new European Central Bank, charged with keeping inflation low as its overriding priority, is bound to add to pressure for the further implementation of the deflationary policies beloved of central bankers almost everywhere. Indeed, the ECB may sit hard on one of the safety valves which might keep the Single Currency running for longer than it otherwise would. It is no coincidence that, over the last year or two, there has been a relaxation in monetary policy in Europe. As the need to tighten the fiscal balance to meet the Maastricht criteria has become an imperative for all Treaty signatories, but especially for those intending to be in the Single Currency first tier in January 1999, monetary policy has been loosened to take some of the strain.

Whether such laxity will be allowed once the ECB is in full operation seems much less likely. This could lead to even worse strains, creating the monetary and fiscal stance which the EU needs least. An important feature of the Single Currency proposals is that nearly all the monetary control will rest with the European Central Bank, leaving the governments of the Member States with most of the powers of taxation and expenditure, although there will be constraints from the EU centre. This is bound to lead to democratic pressures to increase expenditure at national level, which are likely to be countered by monetary tightening by the ECB.

Fiscal laxity and tight money, however, are entirely the wrong combination of policies, leading as they generally do to deflation and rising cost pressures. Unfortunately, the divisions of responsibility in the Single Currency proposals are all too likely to produce this outcome. On the contrary, the policy mix which produces the best results, generating rapid growth, full employment and manageable inflation, is an accommodating monetary strategy combined with fiscal balance. These are the conditions which keep the economy competitive, investment high, output expanding, and inflation at bay. Buoyant tax revenues and low welfare costs on unemployment make it relatively easy to keep taxes and expenditure in balance. Inflation can then be kept in check by using rapid productivity increases to soak up pressure for wage increases. The danger for the EU, if the Single Currency proceeds even against a relatively favourable economic background in the world at large, is that fiscal deficits all over Europe become difficult to avoid as all the constituent countries try to meet and then to maintain compliance with the Maastricht criteria. It may in these circumstances begin to look probable that inflation, the primary enemy of the ECB, is about to start to rise again. The ECB will probably then tighten monetary policy in response, this being the major economic weapon at its disposal. The result would then be a yet more difficult fiscal position for most countries to contain, as growth in Europe is further restrained, and all the consequential problems of falling tax revenues and rising expenditures ensue. This is the recipe for the combination of rising inflation and stagnant output that, rightly, is most to be feared. This is the heavy downside risk from implementation of the Single Currency with the arrangements for operating it currently in prospect, even if it is successful at least in the sense that monetary union is not broken up by deflationary strains. Is this really a risk that Europe can afford to take?

ALTERNATIVE POLICY ANCHORS

Proposals that the EU should not proceed with the Single Currency are on their own, however, inadequate. All countries need to have a framework within which to fit their economic objectives. If the Single Currency is not going to be the main way of providing it, other policy anchors are going to be required. Furthermore, there needs to be a method of co-ordinating economic policies together within the EU, and for Europe as a whole, in ways which do not involve some countries gaining undue advantages at the expense of others. In the longer term, there may be a case for more substantial transfers to help those countries with lower standards of living in Europe to rise closer to those at the top end of the spectrum. The immediate requirement, however, is for all the countries in the area to grow faster, to conquer unemployment, and to enable each of them to compete more successfully in the world.

The primary requirement is not to find some other way of locking European currencies together, but to establish a framework which enables exchange rate changes which are necessary to take place in a generally acceptable way. Parity changes are much too important to be left to the markets, and there is no evidence at all that the markets, on their own, will produce an optimum outcome. The reason for this is that there is a wide band of parities for all countries which are sustainable within parameters which the markets will accept, depending on the fiscal and monetary stances taken up by their governments. If these are tight and restrictive, the markets will accept an overvalued exchange rate for a long period, as they have in France. Similarly, if they are relaxed and accommodating, as they were for a long time in Germany, there will be no great commercial pressure for a revaluation. Of course, if any country allows conditions to arise where the stance of the government in relation to its currency is clearly unsustainable, the markets will intervene, forcing up parities as in the case of the Japanese yen in the early 1990s, or driving the exchange rate down, as they did to sterling in 1992. Within wide limits, however, governments can control their countries' exchange rates.

A co-ordinated process is therefore required to manage exchange rates to produce more or less equal opportunities for all countries to compete, with adjustments allowed to cater for changing circumstances and unexpected events. For the reasons set out earlier in this book, the most appropriate target initially might be to engineer sufficient exchange rate adjustments to enable all countries to bring their unemployment rates down to around 3%. This should be done primarily by changes in the money supply and interest rates, supported by central bank intervention, based on a clear statement of objectives to which the market can relate, to minimise the risk of destabilising speculation. There is no evidence that the impact of exchange rate changes based on these criteria would automatically be followed by excess inflation in the devaluing countries, or more generally. On the contrary, higher growth rates and a more favourable wages climate should ensure that price rises stay at manageable levels, although it is an illusion to believe that it is possible to combine high rates of growth with very low levels of inflation. All the evidence from everywhere in the world is that even well managed growth rates of 5% or 6% per annum will be accompanied by rises in consumer prices of around 3% to 4% per annum, mainly because of the impact of leading sector inflation. This appears to be a fact of life for democratically run countries, operating reasonably free wage bargaining systems, with which everyone will have to live. Such price inflation will not, however, be apparent in the tradable goods sector, where productivity growth is likely to be much higher than the average, and price increases therefore much lower.

At the national level, good government and responsible policies will still be required as they always have been. Inflation will occur if, beyond a fairly low threshold, tax revenues are insufficient to pay for public expenditure, wage increases outstrip productivity gains, governments spend large sums of money on programmes or subsidies which bring little or no economic benefit, or credit booms are allowed to take place which generate asset inflation and excess demand. One of the great illusions in the Community has been that there is a way of bypassing the need for good government at every level by locking the EU economies together in a way which would impose fiscal and monetary discipline from outside. Such abnegation of responsibility is neither realistic nor credible. The discipline of being attached to the low inflation tradition of the Deutsche Mark is not sufficient. It is for government administrations at every level to tackle inefficient and subsidy ridden national airlines, to curb corruption, to grapple with wasteful public expenditure where it occurs, and to hold the line against unjustified wage and salary increases from its own employees. It is also for the EU authorities to get to grips with the inefficiency, corruption and extravagance of the Common Agricultural Policy, to produce a tougher and more effective auditing system for EU expenditures, and to curb the unnecessary costs of some of its operations.

While there is room for scepticism about some of the claims made for the benefits of the Single Market, there is an overwhelmingly strong case for maintaining free trade in Europe over as wide an area as possible, and including within the free trade ambit as large a range of products and services as can be achieved. Europe's food supplies are likely to be made more and not less secure if the countries of Eastern Europe could supply the West more readily. It may be unrealistic to talk of wholesale reform of the CAP in the immediate future, but over a period of time it must make sense to reduce food costs within the EU, and to open up the EU market to outside suppliers, while still ensuring that some arrangements are kept in place to deal with the peculiarities of the market for agricultural products. There may be a case for treating agriculture rather differently from other economic activities, but there are few people who would defend the CAP as it operates at present as being the best way of doing this.

If all these changes in policies were pursued, there would be some important alterations to the way in which the EU operates, but they would not be unduly difficult to accommodate. The powers of national governments would be increased relative to the role they would play with the Single Currency, since they would comprise the basic building blocks of a European system of monetary and financial co-operation. The EU would develop more into a *Europe des Patries*, along the lines envisaged thirty years ago by Charles de Gaulle, than the federalist structure which was the goal of Jean Monnet and the many enthusiasts for European integration who have followed in his steps. There would still, however, be plenty of scope for co-operation and working together in a much looser EU than the one to which the Single Currency is designed to lead. There is a large list of subjects where, in almost anyone's judgement, a joint approach by all the EU countries must make sense. All the nations of Europe occupy the same environment, have similar problems with drugs and crime, share the same transport and telecommunications systems, and have a wide range of common interests *vis à vis* the rest of the world. They also enjoy visiting each other's countries, buying each other's goods, and experiencing a common culture. These are the solid foundations on which international co-operation needs to be built.

A change of course on the Single Currency does not therefore involve a massive upheaval away from present or planned arrangements and institutions. There may be a case for reform of the EU institutions, but this is not a pressing requirement for the immediate future. The role of the proposed European Central Bank would clearly have to be scaled down, but this does not yet exist except in the planning stages. The most important change would be one of direction. Those responsible for the moves towards a federal Europe, which have triggered such expensive efforts to link the EU's currencies together, would have to realise that these ambitions were now off the agenda. They would have to accept a more flexible and less centralist approach.

Other important changes in social and political attitudes would be necessary, not least to ensure that talent is concentrated in those parts of the economy where the scope for growth and increases in productivity is highest. One of the major problems with long periods of slow growth is that these conditions are invariably reflected in falling profitability in those sectors of the economy most exposed to international competition. This leads in turn to worsening conditions for those working in these parts of the economy, a relative decline in their incomes at every level, and a corresponding reduction in their status, power and influence. The pace then tends to be set by sections of the population which know less and less about production and international sales. The most able individuals choose careers in the civil service, the media, academic life and the professions. In the commercial environment, bankers and those employed in providing financial services gain in prestige *vis à vis* those working in manufacturing, as do large scale retailers and distributors, importing a higher and higher proportion of the goods they sell from abroad. Nearly all these increasingly powerful groups of people have no particular reasons instinctively to favour the kinds of monetary and economic conditions which generate fast economic growth. On the contrary, across the developed world there has been a marked tendency for the established classes to favour old money as against new, to prefer high interest rates on their accumulated assets, to look askance at the *nouveaux riches,* and to despise trade and industry.

Changes in the economic environment will soon provide strong enough price signals to overcome these social pressures. All the evidence shows that once production for the international market becomes profitable enough, talent

The Choices to be Made 167

will find its way to take advantage of the opportunities which open up. The problem is the attitudes of those who do not understand the changes which need to be made, and the social and economic pressures which lead them to oppose the alterations in policies which are really needed. Perhaps the single worst legacy of a quarter of a century of slow growth in the EU has been the accumulation of power among those least likely to respond positively to the prospect of the kinds of shifts in policy which are most needed.

This may pose problems for the élites in the EU, but at a popular level, opposition to changes in policy on the Single Currency and other integrationist issues seems to be much less likely. The evidence of elections, referendums and polls everywhere suggest strong support for peace, friendship and co-operation across Europe, but much more scepticism about monetary union, with all its deflationary consequences, and the relegation of the nation state to the role previously carried out by regional and district councils. It seems more than probable that if the Single Currency project died, a majority of people in Europe would breathe a sigh of relief.

A BETTER FUTURE FOR EUROPE

The vision which created the European Union we now have began with the European Coal and Steel Community, leading to the Common Market, the European Community and the European Union, as more and more countries came together. No-one can deny that there was merit in attempting to build some kind of system of co-operation among the nations of Europe that would serve them better than the arrangements during the first half of the twentieth century, with its two devastatingly destructive wars. It is not that the basic vision of better co-operation has ever had anything wrong with it. The problems have been partly with the institutional structures which have been created, which have developed a centralising tendency more powerful than was needed to secure the required level of co-operation across the Union. More fundamental, however, have been flaws in the ideology which has lain behind so much of what has been done, which have allowed too many of Europe's political leaders to gloss over increasingly serious deficiencies in the EU's performance for much too long.

The major problem, at least since the 1970s, has been the preoccupation with integration, and perhaps even the creation of a United States of Europe, at the expense of dealing effectively with the real requirements of Europe's disparate economies. The result has been the development of policies which have dramatically slowed down the Community's growth rate, and generated levels of unemployment which only a quarter of a century ago would have been regarded as inconceivable. In practice, the drive for integration has meant the establishment of Community institutions, some of them very powerful, with functions which inevitably developed a centralising role. Since any policy changes which increased the scope and competence of the Community institutions at the expense of the nation states increased their power and influence, it was inevitable that they would become strong advocates of a centralised EU system of government. Unfortunately, the policies which were then initiated to create an increasingly federalist structure were directly responsible for the Community failing to deliver anything approaching an acceptable level of economic achievement.

Power politics being what it is, more of a counter-reaction might have been expected from the national legislatures than has actually been seen. They have lost out heavily as influence has moved to Brussels. Jacques Delors may have been exaggerating when he claimed in 1988, as President of the Commission, that within ten years 80% of the economic and social legislation governing member countries would be formulated at Community rather than national level. Nevertheless, the Single European Act, to which Delors was referring, and all the other amendments to the Treaty of Rome which have taken place before and since, have greatly strengthened the EU centre against the national periphery. National governments have not objected as strongly as they might have done, perhaps because so many of their leaders have enjoyed treading on the European stage, a much bigger and more significant platform than has been available to many of them at home. For whatever reason, it is clear that the vast majority of European leaders have gone along, if with varying degrees of enthusiasm, with the development of strong and self-confident Euro-governmental structures. At the very least, they have acquiesced in the development of the EU institutions' powers and influence.

The combination of the enthusiasm and idealism of the proponents of European unity, and the understandable self-interest and access to money and power of those charged with putting their ideas into practice, has produced a self-confident and well financed bureaucratic and institutional structure. It is hardly surprising that, to support its intentions, it has helped to develop and support the ideology of a uniting Europe which has swept away much potential opposition. Armed with large sums of money, it has been able to put forward its views with great aplomb and sophistication to wider and wider audiences.

The momentum thus generated has created the centralised EU which we now know, but it has always had a fatal flaw. The drive for federalism was continually too inclined to brush economic realities on one side. From the early days of the ECSC through to the Maastricht plans for the Single

Currency, politics has taken precedence over economics. Policies have been pursued which produced the appearance of unity and purpose, in their drive towards the goal of a United States of Europe, while their core was hollowed out by the economic deficiencies endemic to them. By its political lights, the European Movement's successes have been dramatic. Measured in economic terms, the history of the EU for the last twenty-five years has been disastrous compared to that of most of the rest of the world. The major threat to the states of Europe nowadays is not large-scale wars like World Wars I and II. It is crime, alienation, racism and social disintegration, as the gap widens between the rich and the poor, the employed and the unemployed, the favoured regions and those which are apparently irredeemably depressed. Other dangers are the gradual marginalisation of Europe as its economic power declines *vis à vis* the rest of the world, its industries become increasingly outdated, and its most talented people turn their backs on the commercial world. If Europe's liberal élites manage the EU's affairs as badly as this over the coming decades, it could yet lead to nationalist and extremist parties gaining support, with platforms much less orientated to international co-operation and goodwill than those with which most of Europe is currently familiar. The biggest risk to the EU at the moment may be that the Single Currency project goes ahead, but that within a comparatively short period of time, it breaks up in recrimination and disillusionment, after a long and damaging deflationary battle to keep it in place. If this happens, it could sweep away a dangerously large proportion of Europe's liberal and democratic traditions in the process.

Signs of the dangers and divisiveness of monetary union lie in the reluctance of Britain and Denmark to go ahead with the Single Currency, at least in the initial stages. Even if their economies fulfil the Maastricht criteria at the time when decisions about the countries to be in the first tier are taken during the first half of 1998, they will probably not want to participate. If they are not tied to the birth of the euro, they would still have the capability to embark on expansionist policies independently of the rest of the EU. They may take advantage of this opportunity. If they did so, and they were successful in growing faster than the EU average, reducing unemployment and increasing living standards in the process, their example, so close to home, may well encourage others to lose confidence in the Single Currency. Other Member States might then well be more willing to strike out towards policies with, on the evidence which would then be in front of them, a greater chance of producing a better future for their peoples than Single Currency deflation. There is little doubt, however, that this would be a deeply divisive way for European politics to develop, and one which it would be better to avoid.

Much the best solution would be for Europe as a whole to have a change of heart, and for everyone to adopt expansionist policies in unison. Then there need be no recrimination. Everyone could then enjoy the benefits of higher living standards and rising prosperity together. This might not be the way the European Movement thought it would happen, but it would almost certainly be more likely to create long-lasting political solidarity in Europe than the Single Currency. The risks of chronic depression in the European Union from EMU are much too high to be worth taking. A less centralised, more flexible Union provides a much better hope for the future. This is the future that the people of Europe should choose, including not only the existing EU members, but those outside who would like to join. If there is truly going to be a brotherhood of nations in Europe, it needs to be as inclusive as possible, based on prosperity and full employment. A *Europe des Patries* is much more likely to produce this outcome, on acceptable terms to everyone, than the centralised but exclusive alternative now in prospect, heavily constrained by self-inflicted but avoidable economic problems.

Bibliography

Aldcroft, Derek H. *The European Economy 1914–90*, London: Routledge, 1993.
Aldcroft, Derek H. and Ville, Simon P. *The European Economy 1750–1914*, Manchester: Manchester University Press, 1994.
Bainbridge, Timothy and Teasdale, Anthony *The Penguin Companion to European Union*, London: Penguin, 1996.
Beckerman, Wilfrid *In Defence of Economic Growth*, London, Jonathan Cape, 1974.
Beckerman, Wilfrid *Small is Stupid: Blowing the Whistle on the Greens*, London: Duckworth, 1995.
Beloff, Lord *Britain and European Union: Dialogue of the Deaf*, London: Macmillan, 1996.
Blinder, Alan S. *Hard Hearts Soft Heads*, Reading, Mass: Addison-Wesley, 1987.
Booker, Christopher and North, Richard *The Castle of Lies* London: Duckworth 1996.
Bootle, Roger *The Death of Inflation*, London: Nicholas Brealey, 1996.
Brittan, Samuel *The Price of Economic Freedom*, London: Macmillan, 1970.
Brittan, Samuel *Is there an Economic Consensus*, London: Macmillan, 1973.
Brittan, Samuel *A Restatement of Economic Liberalism*, London: Macmillan, 1988.
Burkitt Brian, Baimbridge, Mark and Whyman, Philip *There is an Alternative*, Campaign for an Independent Britain, *London: 1996*.
Burkitt, Brian and Baimbridge, Mark *What 1992 Really Means* London: British Anti-Market Campaign, 1989.
Caves, Richard E. *Britain's Economic Prospects*, Washington: The Brookings Institution, 1968.
Coates, Ken and Santer, Jacques *Dear Commissioner – An Exchange of Letters*, Nottingham: Spokesman Books, 1996.
Connolly, Bernard *The Rotten Heart of Europe*, London: Faber and Faber, 1995.
Denison, Edward E. *Why Growth Rates Differ*, Washington: The Brookings Institution, 1969.
Denman, Roy *Missed Chances: Britain and Europe in the Twentieth Century*, London: Cassell. 1996.
Einzig, Paul *The Case Against Joining the Common Market*, London: Macmillan, 1971.
Eltis, Walter *Growth and Distribution*, London: Macmillan, 1973.
Ferris, Paul *Men and Money: Financial Europe Today*, London: Hutchinson, 1968.
Friedman, Irving S. *Inflation: A World-wide Disaster*, London: Hamish Hamilton, 1973.
Galbraith, J.K. *The Affluent Society*, London: Hamish Hamilton, 1960.
Galbraith, J.K. *Economics and the Public Purpose*, London: Andre Deutsche, 1974.
Goldsmith, James *The Trap*, London: Macmillan, 1994.
Grieve Smith, John *Full Employment: A Pledge Betrayed*, London: Macmillan, 1997.
Gunther, John *Inside Europe Today*, London: Hamish Hamilton, 1961.
Guttmann, William and Meehan, Patricia *The Great Inflation*, Farnborough: Saxon House, 1975.
Hallett, Graham *The Social Economy of West Germany*, London: Macmillan, 1973.

Hama, Noriko *Disintegrating Europe,* London: Adamantine Press, 1996.
Henig, Stanley *Political Parties in the European Community,* London: George Allen & Unwin, 1979.
Herman, Valentine and Lodge, Juliet *The European Parliament and the European Community,* London, Macmillan, 1978.
Hicks, John *Capital and Growth,* Oxford: Clarendon Press, 1965.
Hirsch, Fred *Money International,* London: Allen Lane, 1967.
Hirsch, Fred *Social Limits to Growth,* Cambridge, Mass: Harvard University Press, 1976.
Holt, Stephen *Six European States,* London: Hamish Hamilton, 1970.
Holland, Stuart *Out of Crisis: A Project for European Recovery,* Nottingham: Spokesman Books, 1983.
Johnson, Christopher *In with the Euro, Out with the Pound,* London: Penguin, 1996.
Jamieson, Bill *Britain beyond Europe,* London: Duckworth, 1994.
Jay, Douglas *Sterling: A Plea for Moderation,* London: Sidgwick & Jackson, 1985.
Jay, Peter *Employment, Regions and Currencies,* London: Eurofacts 1996.
Jones, E.L. *The European Miracle,* Cambridge: Cambridge University Press, 1993.
Kemp, Tom *Industrialization in Nineteenth-Century Europe,* London: Longman, 1994.
Krugman, Paul *Peddling Prosperity,* New York and London: Norton, 1994.
Kuznets, Simon *Modern Economic Growth* London: Yale University Press, 1965.
Lamont, Norman *Sovereign Britain,* London: Duckworth, 1995.
Lang, Tim and Hines, Colin *The New Protectionism,* London: Earthscan, 1993,
Layard, Richard *How to Beat Unemployment,* Oxford: Oxford University Press, 1986.
Leach, Rodney *Monetary Union – A Perilous Gamble,* London: Eurofacts, 1996.
Lipton, Michael *Assessing Economic Performance,* London: Staples Press, 1968.
Maynard, Geoffrey and van Ryckeghem, W. *A World of Inflation,* London: Batsford, 1976.
Michie, Jonathan & Grieve Smith, John *Unemployment in Europe,* London: Harcourt Brace, 1994.
Maddison, Angus *Economic Growth in the West,* London: George Allen & Unwin, 1964.
Maddison, Angus *Dynamic Forces in Capitalist Development,* Oxford: Oxford University Press, 1991.
Marsh, David *Reculer pour mieux sauter,* London: Prospect, 1997.
Mayne, Richard *The Recovery of Europe,* London: Weidenfeld & Nicolson, 1970.
Mishan, E.J. *21 Popular Economic Fallacies,* London: Allen Lane, 1969.
Monti, Mario *The Single Market and Tomorrow's Europe,* London: Kogan Page, 1996.
Nevin, Edward *The Economics of Europe,* London: Macmillan, 1994.
Ormerod, Paul *The Death of Economics,* London: Faber and Faber, 1995.
Okita, Saburo *The Developing Economies and Japan,* Tokyo: Tokyo University Press, 1980.
P.E.P. *Economic Planning and Policies in Britain, France and Germany,* London: George Allen & Unwin, 1968.
Pilbeam, Keith *International Finance,* London: Macmillan, 1994.
Pinder, John *The Economics of Europe,* London: Charles Knight, 1971.
Postan, M.M. *An Economic History of Western Europe 1945–1964,* London: Methuen, 1967.

Robbins, Lord *Money, Trade and International Relations*, London: Macmillan, 1971.

Roberts, J.M. *A History of Europe*, Oxford: Helicon, 1996.

Rome, Club of *The Limits to Growth*, London: Potomac Associates, 1972.

Roney, Alex *EC/EU Fact Book,* London: Chamber of Commerce and Industry/Kogan Page, 1995.

Rostow, W.W. *The Stages of Economic Growth*, Cambridge: Cambridge University Press, 1960.

Schonfield, Andrew *In Defence of the Mixed Economy*, Oxford: Oxford University Press, 1984.

Sampson, Anthony *The New Europeans*, London: Hodder and Stoughton, 1968.

Stewart, Michael *Keynes in the 1990s: A Return to Economic Sanity*, London: Penguin, 1993.

Thurow, Lester C. *The Zero-Sum Society*, New York: Basic Books, 1980.

Tsoukalis, Loukas *The New European Economy*, Oxford: Oxford University Press, 1993.

Index

The subjects listed in the index do not include references to Britain, Germany, France, the European Union, and World Wars I and II, nor to concepts such as monetarism, unemployment, growth and inflation, because references to them occur so frequently in the text.

Index 177